GAZA in the SINAI

The Only Viable Two-State Solution

Second Edition

RUTH MOSS

ISBN: 1719370877
ISBN 13: 978-1719370875
Library of Congress Control Number: 2017902712
LCCN Imprint Name: City and State (If applicable)

"I enter negotiations with Chairman Arafat, the leader of the PLO, the representative of the Palestinian people, with the purpose to have coexistence between our two entities, Israel as a Jewish state and a Palestinian state entity, next to us, living in peace."

"Give peace a chance."

Yitzhak Rabin

"We will win because they love life and we love death."

Hasan Nasrallah, *leader of Hezbollah*

Also by Ruth Moss

Gift of the USA

Poison of Love

For Jasiu: the other side of the story.

Table of Contents

CHAPTER 10

CHAPTER 11

CHAPTER 12

CHAPTER 13

CHAPTER 14

CHAPTER 15

CHAPTER 16

If tomorrow, Israel laid down its arms and announced, "We will fight no more," what would happen? And if the Arab countries around Israel laid down their arms and announced, "We will fight no more," what would happen?

In the first case, there would be an immediate destruction of the State of Israel and the mass murder of its Jewish population. In the second case, there would be peace the next day.

from *"The Middle East Problem: One Side Wants the Other Side Dead"*

By *Dennis Prager*

Preface to the Second Edition

On Sep 28, 2017, Mosab Hassan Yousef, the son of a Hamas founder and leader, shocked his fellow delegates to the United Nations, who, as shown on You Tube, were visibly writhing in astonishment and disbelief that one of their own would "out" them by openly attacking the Palestinian Authority for its blatant abuse of its own people. Yousef, who grew up in Ramallah in a leading Hamas family, in this address to the UN asked of Hamas, "Where does your legitimacy come from? The Palestinian people did not elect you and they did not appoint you to represent them." Yousef told the UN that the PA routinely kidnaps and tortures Palestinians, students and political rivals, and is the primary cause of the Palestinian people's suffering stating that if Israel didn't exist, Hamas would have no one to blame.

Mosab Yousef's expose` supports the premise of *Gaza in the Sinai,* that it is not Israel but the leaders of the Palestinian people who, for their own selfish profit, have been exploiting their own people for close to three quarters of a century, conveniently having Israel as a scapegoat, and that there is a solution to the Israel/Palestinian problem, a totally new and different approach which will give the destitute, manipulated Palestinian people a flourishing lifestyle in a thriving, bourgeoning economy with Israel as its benevolent ally in a new home in the current Gaza contiguous to a portion of the Sinai Desert.

The road to peace runs through the Sinai.

Introduction

In the summer of 2014, Israel launched "Protective Edge," the invasion of Gaza to halt the constant rockets fired from Gaza into Israel, rockets which could come at any time but most usually around 8: in the morning and 3: in the afternoon when children are in the streets going to and from school. World opinion turned against Israel as Israel was forced to bomb civilian enclaves where Hamas headquarters were deliberately placed as well as UN schools and hospitals where caches of armaments to be used against Israel were calculatingly stored to elicit sympathy for the poor Palestinians against the brutal Israelis in this war that was fought by six year old Palestinian girls? No? It wasn't fought by six year old Palestinian girls? Then why did we not see either on television or in the newspapers even one photo of a camouflage-clad, masked, machine gun-wielding militant, only six year old girls in the arms of their wailing, sixty-year-old fathers accompanied by, perhaps, the nine year old brother?

Newer problems have arisen. The handclapping over the recurring triumphs of getting the opposing sides to resume the continually re-started, continuously stopped Middle East peace negotiations is as thin as former Secretary of State John Kerry's verbal add-on to any reference to the Israelis and Palestinians "...living together in peace and security." *Alice in Wonderland!* Will stubborn repetition devoid of any basis make this a reality? A two-state solution may be attainable, but not the overworked one that has been deliberated relentlessly.

There is a resolution to the Israel/Palestinian problem. The diplomacy that has been going on for decades has not been effective, nor will it be because copious modifications to the same rudimentary, unfeasible design do not fulfill the needs, or the desires, of either the Israelis or the Palestinians. *Gaza in the Sinai* presents a realistic, sensible alternative that will profit both sides giving the Palestinians the thriving economy they so desperately need and have been denied, not by the Israelis but by their own leadership, and giving Israel what she seeks, peace.

What has been done to the Palestinian people causing the dismal situation they find themselves in is constantly blamed on Israel. Israel did not create the Palestinians' situation; their own leadership did, and this leadership has continued to repress its people for close to three quarter of a century. Today, under Hamas's governance, the subrogation continues. Until the true reasons for their condition are recognized and dealt with, as long as these people are subjected to the same abuse and the wrong people, those who are not afflicting the harm on them are blamed, nothing will change, neither for the destitute Palestinians nor for the peace and security seeking Israelis.

"Destitute Palestinians" begs the question, "What would be the situation of the Palestinian people if they had won what they call the *Nakba,* the "catastrophe," and the Israelis call the War of Independence in 1948? Would they be better off, today, or worse off? A look at the Arab Spring which started in Oman, Tunisia, Yemen, Egypt, Syria, and Morocco in January 2011 when the government in Tunisia was overthrown, protests erupted in Syria, and thousands of protesters in Egypt demanded the resignation of Pres. Hosni Mubarad answers this question. No!

Let's look at Gaza in the Sinai: The Only Viable Two State Solution to the Israel/Palestine problem.

CHAPTER 1

GAZA in the Sinai:

The Palestinian Homeland in the Sinai

How can a region with seven universities and a ninety-two percent literacy rate "boast" the highest unemployment rate *in the world,* forty-three percent unemployment with sixty percent youth unemployment? What can be done about this bizarre situation? A solution can be negotiated quickly resulting in not only solving the problem of the Palestinians of Gaza but, also, those in the West Bank if the West Bank Palestinians choose the better life that will be available to them; will get the three million Palestinian refugees out of the squalid, wretched refugee camps they have been held in for close to seventy years in various Arab countries as well as in their own West Bank, in Jenin and in East Jerusalem; create a greatly improved Egyptian economy; and give the Israelis what they so direly crave, peace.

Praise, *again*, for all the successful ingenuity in getting the two sides, the Palestinians and the Israelis to, *again*, come to the negotiating table. After weeks or months of more angry discussions during which each side will, *again*, blame the other with accusations of narrow-minded stubbornness, the negotiations will, *again*, fail. At what point will the determined gurus of, *again,* fine-tuning the same, unfeasible two-state stratagem wake up to the reality that more and more alterations to the same well-worn, flawed stratagem, two states living side by side, in as former U S Secretary of State John Kerry always adds with no basis for his wishful thinking, "in peace and security," will not succeed for a basic, simple reason: it meets the needs and desires of neither the Israelis nor the Palestinians? A solution is achievable, but not the well-worn, unattainable West Bank/Gaza Palestinian State next to Israel. Won't work, which is the reason that it hasn't worked.

A new element has appeared that was not evident in the huge number of prior endeavors to resolve the Israeli/Palestinian conundrum. Today, many of the Arab States have *the same strategic* concerns as Israel: dismantle Iran's nuclear capabilities and stop ISIS. Since the enemy of my enemy is my friend, Jordan, Egypt, Saudi Arabia, the United Arab Emirates, Bahrain, Kuwait, Sudan, and other Arab States might, for the first time, be willing to join together to pressure the Palestinian leadership into accepting a mutually beneficial agreement giving each what it needs, security and economic advantage. Instead of looking for an Israeli/Palestinian Agreement, perhaps it is time, now, to look at an Israeli/Arab Agreement.

There are common interests between countries like Saudi Arabia and Israel. They share opposition towards Iran. Saudi Arabia has, recently, severed relations with Iran in reaction to the assault and firebombing of Saudi Arabia's embassy in Tehran in early January 2016. Bahrain and Sudan rapidly followed suit in empathy with Saudi Arabia. The United Arab Emirates (UAE) and Kuwait have both reduced diplomatic relations with Iran. Habitually, Israel has been the catalytic agent in the Middle East that united the Arabs; today Iran is the catalyst.

Saudi Arabia's Foreign Minister, Adel Al-Jubeir stated that Iran has been unashamedly intruding in the internal affairs of several Arab countries, particularly in the affairs of Iraq, Syria, Lebanon, and Yemen. Even with the Iran Nuclear Deal that was signed by the six world powers, China, France, Russia, United Kingdom, United States, and Germany in July 2016, Saudi Arabia's Foreign Minister Al-Jubeir, stated in the *Saudi Gazette* that Iran will persist in manufacturing nuclear weapons. The Foreign Minister said he based his certainty on the fact that Tehran has over and over declined to permit nuclear inspectors to see a number of its military installations.

This same newspaper, the *Saudi Gazette,* also reported that Prince Bandar Bin Sultan, a former head of Saudi Arabia's intelligence services stressed that the Iran nuclear deal would allow it to "wreak havoc in the region."

German foreign minister, Frank-Walter Steinmeier, said that he understood the concerns of Saudi Arabia and other Gulf countries regarding the Iranian nuclear deal.

Although Saudi Arabia and the other Arab States may be uniting against Iran, this has not directed the Ayatollah Khomeini's vitriol away from the US stating, "Despite the negotiations and the agreement that was achieved, our policy towards the American regime of arrogance has in no way changed," said the Ayatollah. The thousands present during the Ayatollah's address responded with "Death to the USA, Death to the Britain," and "Death to Israel."

His state must think about establishing a "defense pact" with Tel Aviv with the purpose of stopping Iran from becoming embroiled in the evolving Middle East crisis, Saudi Arabian prince al-Waleed bin Talal has said, according to Kuwaiti's *Al Qabas Daily*. He went on to say that in the case of another Palestinian uprising, he would side with Israel in order to stop Iran. "I will side with the Jewish nation and its democratic aspirations in case of outbreak of a Palestinian Intifada…because I deem the Arab-Israeli entente and future friendship necessary to impede the Iranian dangerous encroachment."

As of July 2017, Israel was considering direct flights to Mecca to facilitate those six thousand pilgrims who, annually, make the tedious journey for the Hajj. Currently, the Israeli Arabs travel by bus close to a thousand miles through Jordan and much of Saudi Arabia to reach Mecca. In May, the Wall Street Journal reported that some Arab nations are prepared to improve ties with Israel and would be willing to establish cross-border telecommunications networks, some trade, and flight paths from Israel over Arab States' airspace.

Al Monitor: The Pulse of the Middle East reported that Jordan's turn towards Saudi Arabia, explicitly over Saudi Arabia's forceful attitude on Iran and its apparent meddling in Arab countries' affairs, took a major leap forward. *The National World* on July 6, 2016, quoted United Arab Emirates' Dr. Anwar Gargash, Minister of State, referring to Iranian intervention in UAR affairs, "Equal relations should be based on respect of sovereignty and non-interference."

Bahrain's parliamentary outcry against Iran comes amid severe sectarian, diplomatic clashes that have been taking place between the two states since October when Bahrain recalled its ambassador to Iran after discovering a bomb-making factory (on its soil) which it said was established by the Iranian Revolutionary Guards.

Is history standing on its head? The various Middle East Arab States have declared their rejection of a fellow Arab State, Iran, referring to Iran's nuclear objectives and its strategy of meddling in the region which provokes sectarian sedition and stimulates terrorism. The Arab countries have routinely joined together against Israel; in their cause against a common enemy, is there the likelihood of improved cooperation between Israel and states such as Saudi Arabia, Egypt, Jordan, and other Arab countries which had believed their common enemy to be Israel now that Iran has turned out to be the common enemy to all of them? How could all these States profit by allying themselves with Israel not only to oppose the danger presented to them by the Iran-backed terrorist groups, Hezbollah and Hamas, but to stop Iran, even with the newly signed nuclear agreement which none of them have faith in, from attaining nuclear capability, and to stop ISIS?

An alliance of these Arab states could side with Israel to lean on the Palestinian leadership to agree to a plan to bring to an end what has been, up till now, only an Israel/Palestinian problem. Stability in the area with a nuclear-free Iran is what they are searching for. A flourishing, thriving Gaza which is achievable with force on the present Palestinian leadership from a unified Arab alliance would relieve the financial weight on the UN to which they all underwrite, the United States contributing disproportionately at approximately twenty-two percent of all United Nations funding.

If the intransigence, the narrow-minded stubbornness of the Palestinian leadership can be surmounted, Egypt will gain financially and emerge from its persistent economic torpor; Gaza will be a blossoming, middle class society, homeland to the Palestinians of Gaza and of the West Bank if the West Bank Palestinians elect to move out of their poverty, enticed into a Gaza that would extend to them jobs and a good quality life for themselves and their children; and the Palestinian refugees would, at long last, be able to go back "home" to a prospering, self-supporting Palestinian State, Gaza in the existing Gaza which would be linked to a portion of the Sinai Peninsula.

Egypt, Egypt, which has unendingly been in economic stagnation has only one profitable enterprise, the Suez Canal which Egypt has been, for many years, endeavoring to develop by expanding the volume of traffic in the Canal with the construction of an added lane and neighboring industrial resources. According to *Doing Business in the Arab World*, Egypt still has difficulties to overcome for its Suez Canal development. Egypt, actually, launched its newly-expanded Suez Canal to two-way traffic in August 2016, but there is still no assurance vis-à-vis the financial viability of the development. The Suez Canal Project is part of a broader multibillion-dollar proposal to shape an industry and transport hub concentrated in the neighborhood of the canal and including the development of six current Mediterranean and Red Sea ports in its surrounding area. This should bring about one million new jobs. The realization of the more comprehensive project will hinge on Egypt's competence to entice elevated amounts of investment.

"The doubling of the lanes in the canal will make the region more attractive to shipping" says Yehia Zaki, director of the Cairo office of Dar Al-Handasah, the engineering company that developed the master plan for the Suez Canal Zone. He says the infrastructure requirements for the first phase until the year 2030 should cost $15 billion to cover energy, sewage, and water desalination and another $20b-$25 billion will be needed to develop the ports, and some $15 billion for industries.

Here rests the core: there is an answer to Egypt's search for the essential moneys to perfect its project and put Egypt on positive financial stability while simultaneously resolving the Palestinian problem as it relates to Israel, the Palestinian refugee problem, and create a coalition of nations, both Arab and Israeli, to battle Iran's designs for a nuclear facility and its meddling in nearby countries' internal affairs.

It has been believed for quite a few years that Egypt's president, Abdel Fattah al-Sisi, had tendered the Palestinian leadership the opportunity to annex to Gaza an area of sixteen hundred square kilometers in the Sinai Peninsula which would enlarge Gaza fivefold. This has been scorned as "fabricated and baseless" by Egyptian and Palestinian officials. Not only does Egyptian law (laws can be changed) prohibit foreign nationals from possessing land in Egypt, the rapport between Egypt and the Palestinians in Gaza is hostile, to say the least.

Even though Gaza was occupied by Egypt between 1948 and 1956 and again from 1957 till 1967, when Israel endeavored to give Gaza back to Egypt, Egypt, prudently, refused the offer. Associations between Egypt and Gaza have been severely sprained with Egypt persistently attempting to fend Gaza off. The border between Egypt and Gaza is continuously closed, Gazan-dug tunnels are continuously being demolished, and a buffer zone between Egypt and Gaza has been projected. Allowing potentially antagonistic Gaza to be located nearer to Egypt is considered by many to be a risky, irresponsible move. Consequently, the proposal of a deal for a sizeable portion of the Sinai Peninsula to be developed into a new Gaza has been written off as, merely, propaganda.

Nevertheless, Egypt must have funds to finish its Suez Canal Project with all the financial advantages to the Egyptian economy this will produce. *AWD News* reported that on 24 Apr. 2016, speaking at the Egyptian police academy cadet graduation ceremony in the resort town of Sharm el-Sheikh, President el-Sisi said in his address, "We are ready to sell (a part of the) Sinai Peninsula to our Saudi brothers where an independent Palestinian nation can come into existence." Egypt would collect $84 billion for the property in the Sinai. Whether Saudi Arabia would be the only buyer could be worked out, but the hypothesis is well-founded. Egypt is inclined to sell a large section of the Sinai Peninsula which would develop into the substitute homeland for the Palestinians.

According to *International Business Times*, the price tag of the Suez Canal Corridor Area Project made up of the building of the new lane of the Canal, improving six ports, establishing an international free trade zone, industries, and mining will be about $55 billion. An infusion of $84 billion, what Egypt will obtain for selling the sixteen hundred square kilometers of the Sinai, will generate a bonanza of about $30 billion to this cash- bound, impoverished country. Egypt has been exploring any avenue to secure a $12 billion loan from the International Monetary Fund to alleviate its ominous fiscal situation. Currently, with prices escalating the way they are, a civil service salary in Egypt does not last out the month. Electricity is up 20 to 40%. Food is up. Workers' pay is not up and the government is deliberating about cutting subsidies. Inflation is at 14%. The government is recommending a 14% VAT. There is a scarcity of foreign currency and businesses are not capable of getting enough foreign currency to pay for imports.

According to Reuters, Oct. 17, 2017, in Egypt, corruption is raising bread prices. (The poor of Gaza are not the only desperate people to pay more for the basic, bread.) Egyptian wheat inspectors who travel to foreign ports to inspect the wheat countries ship to Egypt have, traditionally, enjoyed expensive perks raising, of course, the cost of the wheat to Egyptian bakeries. The Egyptian government inspectors enjoyed not only the expense-covered trip but, also, expensive dinners, shopping, hotel upgrades, and, often, $3,500 in pocket money, *per inspector.* The amount spent for an inspection for a shipment is, typically, around $30,000, a cost passed on to the consumer, even with the bread subsidy.

Nevertheless, the infusion of the $30 billion extra over the cost of the Suez Canal Project together with the creation of the jobs required to develop the different stages of the project should put Egypt on a healthy financial structure. Subsequent to completion, with the delaying period of ships reduced thanks to the amplified volume of the Canal, passage time is projected to be decreased from eighteen hours to eleven hours. The Suez Canal Authority believes that daily traffic will double by 2023 expanding from forty-nine to ninety-seven ships daily permitting the canal to more than double its yearly revenue from $5.3 billion to over $13 billion. By selling a piece of the Sinai Peninsula to establish a Gaza enlarged into the Sinai, Egypt will be on the road to economic strength.

The road to peace between the Israelis and the Palestinians can run through the Sinai Peninsula.

So, what would the new Gaza in the Sinai be like? How would it differ from the decrepit, crumbling, poverty-stricken Gaza of today? Stephen Gabriel Rosenberg portrayed the new Gaza, which he dubbed Gaza City West, in his article "West Gaza: The Palestinian State." After a comprehensive review of all the reasons--and they are many--that the current proposed Two State Solution will not work concluding that it is not a solution for either the Israelis or the Palestinians, Mr. Rosenberg advocates the premise of Gaza in the Sinai contiguous to the present-day Gaza, sets out his view of what he calls "Greater Gaza in the Sinai," and poses three well-defined economic explanations why this design is practical and doable. The first reason is that the proposal will significantly advantage the Palestinians, placing them on sound financial stability and benefiting from a warm, cordial relationship with their neighbors, the Israelis.

Here is the foundation for non-belligerency, for two states, side by side in peace and security, what the whole world has been craving.

After a large expanse of the Sinai Peninsula is obtained from an Egypt now agreeable to put on sale for Gaza to grow into, tourism which is Israel's main domestic industry, could, clearly, become the backbone of the newborn Gazan economy. The Sinai seaside has delightful, tepid water to lure tourists to attractive, fine-sand beaches to savor the pleasingly warm water and the twelve month long, plentiful sunshine. Restaurants and cafes abundant with scrumptious Arabic foods and thimbles-full of thick, sweet Arab coffee along with those luscious Arabic pastries that look like shredded wheat and taste like pistachio heaven and hotels to lodge the tourists would mushroom by the coast as they have along Israel's Mediterranean coast giving jobs to the, now, work-shy, discontented workforce. And what about casinos in the new hotels to lure the Monte Carlo crowd? The men could gamble while their wives sunbathe and go for camel rides.

The Sinai has picturesque mountains offering hikers and nature lovers the prospect of discovering and investigating their beauty and, perhaps, to enjoy the hospitality of the Bedouin villages where they would stop for lunch or a Dunkin Donuts alternative; and it offers the hospitality of the Greek monastery, Santa Caterina, where those wishing to climb Mt. Sinai would overnight. The mountain climbers would be awakened at 3: am to enjoy a breakfast prepared by the monks after which those wishing not to hike the whole way would start up the mountain by camel, each led by an Arab boy who would, no doubt, be asking for cigarettes as he held onto the camel's rein. Camels can only go up two thirds of the way, the ascent to the summit becoming too steep for them, so the Mt. Sinai climbers will have to scale the remaining ascent on foot, arriving there in time to see the sun as it comes up over the mountain range. There is a chapel at the summit for those so inclined. But going down is difficult. The climbers would have to be warned of the difficulties of the descent and asked to sign waivers of liability. In years gone by when Israel had mandate over the Sinai before she gave it back to Egypt, where the terrain became too steep for the camels, the camel tenders would leave with their camels leaving only one young boy to continue along with the tourists. He was the "telephone." In the event help was needed, he would run, quickly, down the mountain to summon help.

An additional bastion of the new Gazan economy would be agriculture as it was in contemporary Gaza when the Israelis were there. Flowers, fruits, and vegetables were grown in the high tech, computer-run hothouses the Israelis had installed and which were looted and destroyed by the Palestinians within days of the Israelis leaving Gaza just over a decade ago. Those hothouses had employed thousands of the, now, unemployed Gazan workers. These experienced workers could, again, work not only in hothouses, but with the expanded territory, in fields producing various agricultural products including those developed in Israel for dry climates, products for their own consumption, to feed the demands of the country teeming with tourists, and for export bringing foreign currency into Gaza in the Sinai. The Sinai has underground water and with the enhanced affiliation with Israel, Gaza would be able to acquire the technology to extract this underground water and for the water desalination processes that Israel employs so fruitfully, assuaging her own, previous water deficiency.

The third area of economic development is a natural offspring of the tourism and the agricultural progress. There must be a system of transportation in and out of the new, prospering Gaza. There are flat lands just right for constructing an international airport or enlarging the present El-Arish airport; and the seaboard presents a number of sites fit for developing an active seaport both to convey in the tourists and the imports the Palestinian people would, by means of their industriousness, have the income to buy and to take out not only the tourists but, also, the products grown in Gaza in the Sinai and, perhaps, handicrafts or whatever else presents itself as an exportable product.

Not only tourism may overflow from neighboring Israel, but Israel has a flourishing high tech industry. Almost all the American computer industry has facilities in Israel. Would not Gaza in the

Sinai with its ninety-two percent literacy rate be ripe for the computer industry, also, to spill into?

Was there ever a more win-win situation, the Palestinians from Gaza and those who wish to relocate from the West Bank would have a thriving, middle class society, a near wonderland for themselves and their children; Egypt would have the funds for her expanded Suez Canal project and to build her economy; and the United Nations, which means to a large extent the United States, could decrease or wholly do away with the financial assistance disbursed annually to sustain the Palestinians?

As Stephen Gabriel Rosenberg predicted in his "West Gaza: The Palestinian State," Gaza in the Sinai "will be the new Palestine, a country in one piece, in one area, with one economy and one bright Islamic future," a mother country not only for the Gazan and West Bank Palestinians but, also, a homeland to receive back the three million Palestinian refugees who even now, after almost three quarters of a century, are existing in refugee camps in neighboring Arab states, states which have declined to permit these refugees to assimilate into their societies. As the Palestinian generation to come grows up in a robust middle class culture with minimal unemployment, with money in their pockets, unlike the present generation, to buy what they need and to enjoy themselves, it will be more and more difficult for their elders to indoctrinate them into blind hatred of the Israelis, Israelis who would, no doubt, be Gaza's largest market and who would, also, be a major segment of Gaza's flourishing tourist trade.

The road to peace runs through the Sinai.

CHAPTER 2

Why Isn't Gaza the Monaco of the Middle East?

Why isn't tourism Gaza's major industry boasting gorgeous hotels and gambling casinos? When Israel pulled out of Gaza in 2005, what prevented the major American and European hotel chains from viewing this potential paradise as a lucrative source of income?

Along the Israeli shore line right down to the Gaza border, one views beautiful, white, sandy beaches studded with hotels of the major American and European hotel chains, a mainstay of Israel's biggest industry, tourism, which provides thousands of jobs for Israeli hotel workers and workers in the industries that supply and maintain these beautiful hotels. Hugging the beautiful beach in Tel Aviv, one finds every hotel chain from the Hilton and Sheraton to the Holiday Inn and Ramada Inn all the way south along the beach to the splendid Intercontinental Hotel. In recent years, Hilton sold its beachfront Tel Aviv hotel to the European Leonardo chain which has hotels all over Israel and built a bigger hotel. The Waldorf Astoria has just opened its magnificent hotel/residential complex in Jerusalem. Tourism, along with one of Israel's largest exports, medical technology, account for much of Israel's strong economy. What prevented Gaza from piggy backing on Israel's affluence?

Continue along the shoreline of the blue Mediterranean with its white, sandy beaches across the border into Gaza to find only a couple of small, modest, locally-owned hotels. Where are the big American and European hotel chains attracting vacationers from all over the world, creating jobs, and infusing huge amounts of money into the Gazan economy?

On Israel's departure in 2005, it dismantled what it had built and left Gaza as it had been, a barren desert. Israel had built hundreds of hothouses employing four thousand Palestinian workers growing vegetables and flowers for domestic consumption and for export. The International Finance Corporation purchased these hothouses from the Israeli government for $14,000,000 so the four thousand Palestinians employed in them could keep their jobs. *James Wolfensohn, President of the IFC and of the World Bank, contributed $500,000 of his own money to the project.* Within days of Israel's withdrawal, the Palestinians looted the greenhouses taking the plastic sheeting, the agricultural pumps and the piping, and then burned the eight hundred greenhouses to the ground! What was their purpose? Was this destruction the means to build a flourishing society?

Had the Palestinians, at the point of Israel's withdrawal, stopped its ongoing attacks on Israel, the essence of the "Land for Peace Agreement," had they not destroyed the source of employment for thousands of their population bought for them by the IFC and Mr. Wolfensohn but, instead, worked in those hothouses amassing the income from this work so desperately needed by the workers' families and this fledgling society and, also, approached the Hilton and Sheraton, the Leonardo and other hotel chains with an invitation to come to Gaza to build a Monaco on the eastern shores of the beautiful Mediterranean Sea, what would Gaza be today? A virtual paradise, a Shangri-La, the beautiful, affluent seaside resort it could have and should have become.

The Israeli border was open, then. Israel needed the Gazan workers, especially in construction and agriculture. With Hamas elected to replace the Palestinian Authority within two years of Israel's withdrawal and the concurrent increased terrorism, Israel was forced to close its border and, instead, import the workers it needs from Romania, Thailand, and the Philippians, and elsewhere, workers now doing the jobs the Palestinians of Gaza used to do. The UN isn't building schools in US cities. An affluent Gaza, the Monaco of the Middle East, with its workers, also, manning the Israeli construction and agricultural industries could afford to build its own schools and not depend on the US taxpayer, the largest financial supporter of the UN, to pay for its schools. Americans can use a tax break instead of building schools for those who looted and burned their places of employment and, subsequently, used the cement and funds given them to build schools, hospitals, and roads for terror tunnels. It costs approx. $200,000 to build one kilometer of an attack tunnel, money that could go to building hospitals and improving living conditions in Gaza. Make hospitals, not terror tunnels!

On Mar. 22, 2018, the New York Times ran an op-ed article by a University instructor, Atef Abu Saif, a fourth generation Gazan born in the Gazan Jabaliya Refugee Camp, "Why I Stay in Gaza." Mr. Abu Saif says, "Life in Gaza is hard. Then it gets worse. Then it gets even worse." In this op-ed article, he states the current fifty-eight percent youth unemployment and tells of the tensions between Hamas and the Palestinian Authority and the problems this friction causes for the people of Gaza. Abu Saif laments the isolation of Gaza, borders both with Egypt and Israel closed; but he does not mention the reason for these closures, that Gazans worked in Israel in construction, farming, and as household workers until their, constantly, killing of Israelis forced Israel to close its border and to employ, instead, agricultural workers from Thailand and Sri Lanka, construction workers from Romania, and household workers from the Philippians (a foreign worker program that the United States might be wise to emulate).

Abu Saif speaks of his younger brother who graduated from university nine years ago and has not found a job and of his students at Al Azhar University who tell him that after graduation they will do "nothing," and of former students that he meets years after their graduations who tell him they have been doing "nothing." Mr. Abu Saif says he is the fourth generation of his family to grow up in the refugee camp, one of ten children. At forty-five years old, he has five children. At least he is working.

CHAPTER 3

The "Final Solution"

to

European Culture

In 2004, an article purportedly written by a Spanish writer named Sebastian Vivar Rodriguez and published in a Spanish newspaper was widely disseminated. No record of a writer by this name could be found nor the article's publication in any Spanish newspaper, or in any other periodical. The name was likely fictitious to disguise the true author's identity. The following commentary incorporates a number of "Mr. Rodrigeuz's" concepts.

In Hitler's death camps throughout Eastern Europe in World War 11, the Nazis exterminated much of Europe's culture. Creativeness, initiative, and skill were murdered. The chosen people, indeed chosen because they brought forth a remarkable and exceptional populace which added enormously to humanity, were painstakingly obliterated and in their place, Europe received and greeted twenty million Muslims.

The influence of the people who were eradicated is evident in all be significant themes of life: science, art, international trade, and in particular, the conscience of the world. This is the sector of European society, of the world's civilization, that was obliterated, snuffed out.

Years later when Europe decided to demonstrate that it had turned into an upholder of open-mindedness, no longer hideously racist, it embraced into its environs twenty million Muslims, the majority of whom were quiet and peaceful but there were amongst the new refugees those who carried in with them their lack of knowledge, religious intolerance, crime, and the poverty caused by their reluctance to get jobs and work to provide for their families. These new refugees tended to not integrate into European society. They did not take on the language and customs of their host countries. The children of this disgruntled segment of the refugees, the second generation, made up the Paris terrorists of 2016, French and Belgium nationals, born in the host countries that had welcomed their parents, terrorist whose coordinated attacks killed one hundred and thirty and woulnded hundres more in one evening.. Instead of taking their places in their benevolent host countries and contributing to the society, they twisted Europe's ancient and lovely cities into the third-world cities from which their parents had come, immersed in grime and crime.

In the public housing apartments their parents were provided, free, by the European governments that had welcomed them, the children of these refugees strategize the murder and devastation of their munificent hosts. They bomb Europe's trains and magnificent buildings, delighting in the murder of the harmless civilians they were effective in murdering in appalling, brutal actions.

Europe replaced culture with fanatical animosity, ingenious skill for injurious skill, intellect for backwardness, wisdom for superstition. It swapped the quest for knowledge of the Jews of Europe and their mission to bestow on their children a better future, their unswerving cleaving to life because life is holy for those who pursue death, for people who crave death for themselves and for those they hate, and for their own children as well as for ours. The quiet majority of the, now, European Muslims is helpless against the more aggressive minority.

What a frightful mistake pathetic Europe crafted!

To a great extent, America has become so withdrawn from reality that it cannot envisage that America could, conceivably, experience defeat at the hands of like people. Not too long ago in the United Kingdom, there was debate about removing The Holocaust from its history classes because it offends the Muslim population which disavows that the holocaust ever happened. At present, it is still in the curriculum. But, isn't this is a terrifying premonition of the terror that is clasping the world and how ungrudgingly each country is surrendering to it?

It is now almost three quarters of a century since the end of the Second World War. Six million Jews, twenty million Russians, up to a half a million gypsies, ten million Christians, and nineteen-hundred Catholic priests were humiliated, raped, starved, beaten, experimented on, and murdered and burnt to ashes. Now more than ever, with Iran and others consisting of the vast majority of Islamic extremists maintaining that the Holocaust never occurred, that this is a "myth," it is critical that this stain on human history be recorded, verified, and safeguarded so the world will never forget. "Never again!" or as Franklin Roosevelt said, "A day (time) that will live in infamy."

How much time will pass before the attack on the World Trade Centre in New York "never happened" because it offends some Muslims in the U S? If our Judeo-Christian culture is so abhorrent to some Muslims, they can, simply, collect their families and move to Iran, Iraq, Syria, or some other Muslim country.

CHAPTER 4

Letter From Boaz to Kh'alil

By *Boaz Kantor*

To Kh'alil in Gaza,

Do you know how much we're alike? We're both thirty, and we both have seven-year-old daughters. We both go to sleep at night in bed with the women we love, not before tucking our daughters in under comforters because it's starting to get chilly, eh? We both kiss our girls on the forehead, go to bed and hug our wives, you in Gaza and I in Tel Aviv. Before we fall asleep, we both think of the next week at work and the heavy responsibility of providing for our families, feeding our children, and more importantly, making sure our wives know that we are real men, eh Khalil? ;-) We both, probably, think about sex and fall asleep once again only with this one thought in mind.

We are just alike, Kh'alil, but there is something different.

Your child will die tonight.

You will not find out in the morning. You'll wake up in the night to the sound of an explosion. Your whole house will tremble. Parts of the ceiling will fall on you. You'll run to the girl's room and find the northern wall is gone, and she is lying on the floor, completely burnt. Do not worry, Kh'alil; she wasn't burned alive. She died quickly from the explosion, and then burned. Does that make it easier on you? No? And suddenly a guy will show up and introduce himself as Jamil and will start photographing her.

But now, before you get angry at the Zionist pigs who murder your children, let's talk about Imad, your neighbor.

You remember, he came to ask you for a loan a year ago? Yes, I know you'd have given him one if you had more money. But do not worry. He managed. Someone offered him 2,000 shekels a month to rent one of the rooms in his house. So last year, without you knowing, one room in Imad's apartment was filled with Qassam rockets. Qassam rockets, you know?

Two meter long tubes containing about ten kilograms of explosives. So, in this room were fifty rockets. And this room, Kh'alil, shared a wall with your daughter's room. That means she rested her head on a pillow right next to half a ton of explosives. How did you sleep quietly at night? Imad didn't tell you?

But wait, don't get upset at Imad. He's in financial difficulties, and all he can think of is providing food for his children. He was desperate. Jamil, the guy who pays him the rent, convinced him that the room is just a warehouse, and no one will use these rockets.

So forget Imad. Let's talk a second about the rockets, and understand why they are bad.

What are rockets, Kh'alil? A rocket is like a bullet. Wherever you aim it, that's where it'll hit. Only unlike a rifle, it has an engine that burns all the way and extends its range. The Qassam, for example, goes up to about ten kilometers.

And how can you aim gunshot ten kilometers away? You can't. You hit approximately. And to make sure you hit your target, you fire ten rockets together. We call it a "volley." Rockets are used when you don't care what you hit. Fire a bunch towards a city and hope that something will hit a kindergarten.

The world calls this "terrorism."

And Israelis do not like terrorism. Call us crazy, but we want to keep our civilians safe.

So we spend millions of dollars and buy missiles, which are kind of like rockets, but accurate, which allow us to hit the warehouses full of rockets and launchers. We could have fired rockets and shells in the general direction of these targets, but then we'd risk hitting many of your citizens. And we do not want that. So we fire very costly and very accurate missiles at your rocket warehouses. And unfortunately, sometimes little girls sleep with their heads against these warehouses.

But wait, before you get angry at the missiles the Zionist pigs used to kill your daughter, Jamil is a Hamas activist, and his role is to locate "warehouses" such as Imad's and see to it that a little girl sleeps with her head against the wall of the “warehouse” and that rockets are stored in it. Let's talk for a moment about Jamil. We call him a "quartermaster," but it's bit different. Jamil received some instructions:

First, that warehouses mustn't be close to each other. Second, that they be in residential neighborhoods, at kindergartens, at hospitals and the homes of the elderly. Close to your daughter's wall. And you know why? Because Jamil doesn't really care if your daughter dies. In fact, he will come with his iPhone and photograph her burnt body and upload it to YouTube, as they did on the first day of the "pillar of cloud."

Now you can get annoyed. Yes, at Jamil.

But Kh'alil, my friend. It's not enough to worry about Jamil. You need to get upset at Hamas. It is your sovereign government, and they decided on this strategy. Hamas invests the majority of itself in militarization next to your house, building launchers next to hospitals, and doing all that it can so that civilians will die, ours, as well as yours. Hamas must fall.

And how does one get angry at Hamas? Think Internet. Think friends. Think demonstrations. Think revolt. Think criticism. Think organization. Think blog. Think interviews with the media. Think that Hamas must fall and you should get a government that sees you, your job, your future and your daughter as a top priority. Think of your daughter. Think peace.

I assure you, that when you stop aiming weapons at us and reach out to us with a hand of cooperation, that is the day when you can be sure your daughter will wake up in the morning to another day that will build her future.

And it starts with you, Kh'alil.

Good night.

CHAPTER 5

Repeat the Lie Often Enough and It's Accepted as Truth

An introduction to the Miko Peled Talk

On November 5, 2015, an Israeli Jew, Miko Peled, who had emigrated from Israel when he was thirty-nine years old spoke at the Unitarian Universalist Church in Santa Fe, NM, a speech full of far-reaching perversions and distortions that are easily disproved by multiple, authoritative sources like the Associated Press, United Press, Reuters, and additional sources such as Encyclopedia Britannica and the Oxford Encyclopedia of the Modern World.

Santa Fe is a rather upscale, relatively expensive community in which to live with various cultural offerings including a Center for Visual Artists and Performing Arts, Native American History and Art Museum, the summer Opera Festival, and more. The population tends to be well educated. Many professional people live in Santa Fe, and many retire there to be able to enjoy the numerous cultural offerings. Santa Fe boasts a university, the Santa Fe University of Art and Design; St. John's College, a world-renowned liberal arts college with programs based on the study of the world's most important books; and a community college where retirees can enjoy continuing education courses. An audience comprised of Santa Fe residents could, possibly, not be too aware of much of what goes on in Israel or any other foreign country but would be expected to be at least a little skeptical when presented with details that appear to be outlandish. Not so! The audience in this enlightened community responded to this eloquent and manipulative speaker as he maneuvered it to.

Possibly, this audience was as unwitting as its reactions made it appear to be or, maybe, having been continuously fed deceptions such as those detailed that evening, the audience actually believed what it heard. A theme throughout the evening was the statement, "There never was a Gaza. That's just an imaginary line drawn by the Israelis." In fact, Gaza has a history four thousand years old dating from the Philistines, from which the term Palestine is derived and played a crucial part in World War 1. Just as there are the Timothy McVeys who hate America, Mr. Peled, the son of a former Israeli general, appears to hate Israel. Could it be that it's difficult being the son of a general?

The woman who introduced Mr. Peled told of various other pro-Palestinian/anti-Israeli organizations which, she maintained, the audience should support. Miko Peled is only one of the many anti-Israel speakers disseminating easily disproved "facts" (alternative truths?) sponsored by these anti-Israel associations; however, Peled's speech is a good example of the type of disinformation constantly disbursed by these groups. The following excerpts from the Miko Peled speech is an example of what the American public is exposed to by speakers from these Anti-Israel organizations.

CHAPTER 6

Miko Peled Talk, Universalist Unitarian Church, Santa Fe, NM November 5, 2015

Miko Peled, an Israeli Jew who grew up in Jerusalem and moved to the US when he was thirty-nine years old, was introduced by a woman who named various pro-Palestinian, anti-Israel organizations and stressed the need to support these groups. She told the audience that she had been in Israel when Israeli police beat Peled and asked if him if he wanted to be brought to a Jewish town or dumped on the side of the road. "You know which he chose!" The audience reacted as though it was well aware which option Peled would choose, the first of almost constant audience reactions throughout the speech stimulated by the main speaker.

Why had the audience reacted as it did? One of Israel's main exports is medical technology, and its main domestic industry is tourism. Is tourism the main domestic money maker in Syria, Libya, Tunisia, Yemen, Lebanon, Iraq or Iran, or even in Egypt? Hardly! People come to Israel to vacation, including a preponderance of Christian tours that come to visit the many holy sites in Jerusalem, in the Galilee, and throughout the country, to luxuriate in the beautiful American and European-style hotels, and to enjoy the beautiful white, sandy beaches on the shores of the blue Mediterranean and the Dead Sea, and the many cultural events.

But Peled would, instinctively, choose to be dumped on the side of the road rather than be taken to an Israeli town where he would, no doubt, be transported, immediately, to a hospital for treatment? The woman introducing Peled said she was called and went to pick him up, beaten, on the side of the road. Peled's first words, when he spoke, were to thank her for coming to pick him up.

No authentication to allow for verification of this beating was given, such as where and when it happened, or the reason for the alleged beating. Peled hadn't called the local media or the international press so they could see how brutally he had been beaten by the Israeli police nor had he gone to the American Embassy as soon as was physically able to report and document this beating of an American citizen by the Israeli police. All the major American newspapers and broadcasting networks as well as magazines such as *Time* have a presence in Israel and, certainly, would have reported this alleged brutality.

Before Mr. Peled spoke, a Hispanic PhD was introduced. His forbears had come to Santa Fe four hundred and fifty year ago. He spoke only briefly, just to state that the Israelis had to be stopped.

Mr. Peled opened his talk by announcing, "Netanyahu is coming (to the US) next week to receive a humanitarian award" which elicited the second audience reaction, contemptuous laughter. In fact, Netanyahu was *en route* to the US to meet with Pres. Obama in an attempt to mend fences after their rift over the newly signed Iran Nuclear Agreement. If one were to scour the major American newspapers for the month of November, 2105, he would not find a single word about Netanyahu coming to receive a humanitarian award. A fabrication designed to elicit negative audience reaction. And successful!

Two days after this talk, the *New York Times* had both an article and editorial about Netanyahu's upcoming visit, and no mention in either of a humanitarian award. Again, on November 11th and 12th in the *Times* articles about Netanyahu's visit, no mention of his coming for a humanitarian award, just talk of the Iran deal and its effect on the Obama/Netanyahu relationship. The audience was, also, told that there would be a march against Netanyahu's coming in neighboring Albuquerque. Several in the audience asked when and where this would take place, and were told. A search of the Albuquerque, NM, newspapers for several days before and after the supposedly scheduled march showed no mention of this march.

Peled crammed copious denunciations of Israel into his talk. He spoke of the Balfour Declaration which stated, "His Majesty's government views with favour the establishment in Palestine of a national home for the Jewish people." According to Peled, "Balfour, the British Foreign Secretary, was paid by Rothschild for the Balfour Declaration."

Was Balfour a king or an emperor who could do what he might want? Even if he had been King of England, not merely its Foreign Secretary, in England the Prime Minster is the head of government, not the King (or Queen). Peled did not state that the Declaration was accepted by the League of Nations, which it was. In Peled's fantasy, were the British Prime Minister, the British Parliament, and the League of Nations, also, supposed to have been secretly bought off by Rothschild?

Peled made no mention of the very strong reason England was in favor of the Balfour Declaration: her determination to protect the Mosel-Haifa pipeline, a crude oil pipeline from the oil fields in the former Ottoman valley of Mosul in northern Iraq, through Jordan, to the Haifa oil refineries, both the pipeline and the refineries having been built by Britain. The area through which the pipeline passed was within the British mandate, approved by the League of Nations. The pipeline had been the target of numerous attacks by Arab gangs in Palestine.

It was in the British interest to have this strategic pipeline and the refineries protected within a Jewish State. Starting more than a decade before Word War 1, the conversion of the Royal Navy from coal to oil was encouraged and started by First Lord of the Admiralty Sir Winston Churchill and Admiral Sir John (Jacky) Fisher, an advisor to Churchill for the duration of his term as First Lord of the Admiralty.

This conversion embodied a serious supply risk to a nation which had large coal reserves, but no oil. Uncovering and acquiring supplies of oil portended to be the most challenging part of the conversion endeavor. To begin the process, Britain converted her smaller ships to oil but hesitated to convert the larger battle ships as the former First Lord of the Admiralty, Lord Selborne, had held the position that "the substitution of oil for coal is impossible because oil does not exist in this world in sufficient quantities. It must be reckoned only as a most valuable adjunct [to coal]." Lord Shelborne, also, recognized that the switch would be difficult to implement; to change the foundation of the British navy from British coal to foreign oil was a formidable decision in itself. Also, opposing the transition was the weight of naval tradition, magnified by loss of the strategic advantage of large coal supplies in Britain. (from "Naval Innovation: From Coal to Oil" by Erik J. Dahn, *JFQ* Winter 2000-01)

However, oil proffered many advantages: it had twice the thermal content of coal so that boilers could be smaller and ships could travel twice as far. Greater speed was possible, and oil burned with less smoke so the fleet would not disclose its presence as promptly.

Oil had other advantages over coal. Shifting coal from shore to ship, and aboard ship, was filthy, exhausting labor that entailed extensive manpower. In the same article, Churchill is quoted as saying, "The ordeal exhausted the whole ship's company. In wartime, it robbed the seamen of their brief periods of rest; it subjected everyone to extreme discomfort.

Also, it was almost unmanageable to refuel at sea. A quarter of the fleet might be compelled to put in to harbor for coaling at any one time. Supplying the fleet with coal was the biggest logistical difficulty. On the other hand, oil could be stowed in tanks anyplace, permitting more effectual design of ships, and it could be conveyed through pipes without reliance on stokers, lessening manning. Refueling at sea was possible, which afforded better flexibility.

Dahn states that in 1912, Fisher wrote to Churchill, "What you do want is the super-swift all oil…There is only one defense, and that is speed!" The war college was asked how much speed a fast division would require to outmaneuver the German fleet. The response was twenty-five knots, or a minimum of four knots quicker than achievable at the time using coal. Churchill deduced, "We could not get the power required to drive these ships at twenty-five knots except by the use of oil fuel."

A British company, the Anglo-Persian Oil Company (APOC), was founded following the discovery of a large oil field in Masjed Soleiman, Iran. Britain had a compelling reason to seek out oil resources, and to protect these resources.

The pipeline and the Haifa refineries remained strategically important to the British Government as they provided much of the fuel needs of the British and American forces in the Mediterranean Sea during the Second World War. According to *Al-Monitor: The Pulse of the Middle East*, during WW2, the oil arriving in Haifa through the Mosel-Haifa pipeline was distilled in the Haifa refineries and put into tankers for shipment to Europe.

Mr. Peled grew up in Jerusalem. History is a required course in Israeli schools. Is it even possible that he didn't know of the Mosel-Haifa pipeline? Hardly. That's like saying that one who went through an American high school had never heard of the Civil War.

But according to Peled, "Balfour, the British Foreign Secretary, was paid by Rothschild for the Balfour Declaration." It is understandable that the audience that evening at the Universalist Unitarian Church in Santa Fe, NM, might not know of the British navy's conversion from coal to oil or of the Mosel-Haifa pipeline that had supplied desperately needed fuel not only for the conversion but, also, for British and American fleets during World War 11 and had been, for many decades, so strategic to Britain. However, many of the outright falsehoods later in Mr. Peled's talk were not so alien to the American mind.

"Zionists sabotaged efforts to place Jews in western countries but led them to Israel. The Jews had considered other places, including in the Americas."

In what western countries were the Jews considering establishing a Jewish homeland, Mexico, the US, or perhaps in a European country such as France or Germany? Were they considering establishing the State of Israel in Santa Fe, New Mexico, or New York City rather than in their ancestral home in the Land of Canaan where they'd had a presence for more than three thousand years, for over a thousand years before the birth of Christ, a land where there never has been a time without a Jewish population speaking the same language then as today in this Holy Land? Idi Amin invited the Jews to Ethiopia, an offer which was refused. What attachment did the Jews have to Ethiopia, never mind to a western country? Foolishness, but accepted by an uninformed audience which was relying on the speaker they had come to hear.

Peled spoke about the Arab/Israeli War of 1948, the war the Israelis call the War of Independence and the Arabs call the *Nakba,* the "catastrophe." It is hard to duplicate in writing the way in which Peled sneered, "Five Arab nations didn't attack *until six months after the partition!*" he stated with a wave of the hand as though even mentioning this attack is ridiculous, simply pointless. *Hello!* Who were the Arabs going to attack six months before on Nov. 29, 1947, the date the Partition Plan was approved while the land was still under the British Mandate? Were they going to attack the British army with its superior force and armaments?

The United Nations announced the Partition Plan on Nov. 29, 1947, with caveat that the British end its Mandate and leave six months later on May 14, 1948.

Actually, there were some incursions by the Iraqi, Syrian, and Lebanese armies in the sparsely populated north before the British left. Mr. Peled had studied in an Israeli high school. He would have studied that Jamal Husseini, the Arab High Committee's spokesman, had told the United Nations prior to the partition vote that the Arabs would "drench the soil to the last drop of blood" to prevent the partition taking place. But when Peled was asked the reason for the war, his reply was that it was because the Jews wanted the entire land, not just what was allocated to them by the UN, and that they were perpetrating "ethnic cleansing"!

"*Ethnic cleansing!*" a phrase that is, perhaps, the most abhorrent possible to Jews, a phrase that makes Jews shudder in remembrance of the Holocaust was a theme repeated continuously throughout the talk. Does this even make sense? Five Arab nations attacked eight hours after the British left what had been the British Mandate and the State of Israel was proclaimed on May 14, 1948, after the Arab High Committee had declared it would "drench the soil with blood" if the UN voted to partition the land and the reason Mr. Peled gives for the War of Independence, the *Nakba,* which, according to the Arabs even today was the "catastrophe" was because the Jews wanted it all, that they were "ethnic cleansing"!

The Arabs attached within eight hours of the British departing, not six months later as Peled said, but eight hours later. He stated, "Only Egypt had an army; the rest, *negligible*!" again with sneer and a wave of his hand as if to wash the whole thing away.

Negligible? *Negligible!* The fledgling nation, eight hours old, was invaded by not only the Egyptian army from the south, which Peled acknowledged was strong, but simultaneously across the Jordan River from the east by Lieutenant-General Sir John Bagot Glubb, a British-trained general who had trained and who led the Arab Legion, and by Syria, Iraq, and Lebanon in the north.

During the Arab/Israeli War, Gen. Glubb's Arab Legion was considered the strongest Arab army. Glubb led the Arab Legion across the River Jordan to occupy the West Bank in May of 1948.

The Iraqi, Lebanese, and Syrian armies, also, along with the Egyptian army, attacked at this same time. In its March 8, 1986 obituary on the death of Gen. Glubb, the *New York Times* states that Gen. Glubb in his 1958 memoir, "A Soldier With the Arabs," describes his battles with his Arab Legion in the 1948 war against the newly-formed Israel.

But according to Peled, "By the time Arab nations got involved six months later, it was all over." It was, in fact, very far from over. The war lasted for over another year, until April 3, 1949.

"The Jews massacred, including in East Jerusalem," Peled stated. There were massacres, all right. The ill-equipped and outnumbered Jewish settlers were overwhelmed. Many Jewish defenders were massacred *after* they had surrendered. The Arabs did not deny responsibility. They were blunt in taking responsibility for starting the war. Jamal Husseini, member of the Arab Higher Committee in Palestine and its representative to the UN, 1947-48, told the Security Council that the Arabs had begun the fighting. "We did not deny this. We told the whole world that we were going to fight."

In *1948: A History of the First Arab-Israeli War* by Benny Morris, Yale University Press 2008, pages: 34, 59, 82, 89 "One Foreign Office cable, in the wake of the report, spoke of Arab hatred of the Jews as being greater than that of the Nazis." In a letter from Jamal Husseini to Clement Attlee, Prime Minister of England, Husseini issued an "ultimatum" and threatened "jihad." In a follow-up interview with British High Commissioner Sir Alan Cunningham, Husseini declared his willingness "to die for the cause." When Cunningham replied that this didn't really bother him and that what concerned him was the well-being of "the common Arab population," Husseini retorted that "they were willing to die, too."

Really? Had Husseini checked with the ordinary Arab population?

The publication of the story generated vehement protests in Baghdad and Palestine. In Beirut, the US Information Center was set on fire. At least one Baghdad newspaper denounced "[the] western gang which, it wrote, comprehends only the language of power." A different newspaper urged the Arabs to "annihilate all European Jews in Palestine." Azzam Pasha, Secretary-General of the Arab League proclaimed in a cablegram to the Secretary-General of the United Nation on May 15, 1948, "It will be a war of extermination. It will be a war of annihilation. It will be a momentous massacre in history that will be talked about like the massacres of the Mongols or the Crusades." This threat was, also, made in a meeting with the Egyptian media on the same day soon after the Arab nations' incursion into the newly-proclaimed State of Israel. The quotation is regularly represented as evidence that the Arab states were intending genocide when they attacked in 1948.

So much, again, for Miko Peled's, "The Jews wanted it all. They were 'ethnic cleansing.'" Murder by the Israeli army and the reason for the war being that Jews wanted all the land to form an apartheid state was stressed throughout the talk with constant, positive responses to the speaker by the ill-informed audience.

Did Israel even have an army at the time of the partition when the Arabs invaded? No. Israel had the *Hagana,* a militia such as the colonies had at the beginning of the American Revolutionary War. This is what faced the armies of Iraq, Iran, Lebanon, and Syria in the north, Egypt in the south, and the well-trained and equipped Arab Legion from Jordan under the leadership of British schooled and trained Gen. John Glubb.

"...and the *looting!!!"* Peled exclaimed.

The embattled Jews were trying, desperately, to survive. Peled's description of Arab East Jerusalem would lead one to believe that it was an area like a present day American suburb. That didn't exist in those days. (It hardly existed even in America in those days, the days of the start of Levittown.)

The Lemon Tree by Sandy Tolan, p. 52, "Arab forces had cut off Jewish supply lines...and the hunger was growing among the Jewish population of Jerusalem."

Herman Wouk's *The Hope*, p. 3 "The Arabs have closed the highway…The Jews in the Holy City are besieged. The hilltop outpost has been taken, lost, and retaken by the *Hagana* in a desperate effort to reopen the road."

There was hunger and, more important, a lack of water in Jerusalem. If there had been any looting, it would have been water that was looted, or food. The Jews in Jerusalem were under attack, they hardly had food and they didn't have water, and one was to believe they were scrounging around looking for non-existent Arab treasures? They were under attack, they didn't have water or food and they ignored these basics for themselves and their families and were, instead, looking for a rug or a coffee pot?

The Hope by Herman Wouk p. 46, describes the suffering of the besieged Jews in Jerusalem. "Rations had been cut, and cut again. Electric power had been cut to several hours a day." Although many shortages were becoming serious, flour for the daily loaf was the worst. Only an eleven-day supply was left; after that, the Jews would begin to starve.

The road to Jerusalem having been cut off, an alternate route had to be enabled; however, this was no more than a path that a jeep could traverse but not a convoy carrying the two hundred tons of food, fuel, ammunition, medical supplies, and other essentials that the Jerusalemites needed daily, nor the groaning tank truck filled with drinking water. Trucks would come from Tel Aviv for as far as they could go then their cargo off-loaded onto mules which would carry the precious life-saving goods to where they would be met by other trucks for the final lap of the journey into Jerusalem. Women, many with children in their arms and carrying buckets, jars, and all sorts of containers, came for the water, first. The men, mostly, were in fighting units.

Each Jew was allotted one liter of water a day, a liter being a little less than a quart. And this water was used six times: first, the vegetables were washed; then the dishes; then they, themselves; their clothing; the floors; and, lastly, what was left of the one liter of water was poured down the toilet in an attempt to flush it. A woman who, after the siege, managed to get to Tel Aviv was greeted by her relatives in their apartment with the sound of Brahms on the Victrola. She went into the bathroom and flushed the toilet. Ahhh! That was the music she wanted to hear.

Peled said that the Arabs were outnumbered by the Jews at all times. Really, even when the five Arab armies were on Israeli soil? (Don't forget, the State of Israel had been established.) But Peled had come to this speech with assorted handouts which spouted many of his outlandish and easily disproved "facts." Alternative facts? Taken directly from his handout, "A Synopsis of the Israeli-Palestinian Conflict" is the following under the paragraph headed, "UN Partition Plan."

The Jews "represented only about thirty percent of the total population." In the next paragraph headed, "1947-49 War" he states, "While it is reported that the resulting war eventually included five Arab armies, less well known is the fact that throughout this war, Zionist forces outnumbered all Arab and Palestinian combatants combined—often by a factor of two to three."

What! Seventy percent of the population which amounted to two and a third times the number of Jews, plus five Arab armies were outnumbered "by a factor of two to three" by thirty percent of the population! Dear reader, get out your calculator! In the same paragraph, Peled states, "Moreover, Arab armies did not invade Israel—virtually all battles were fought on land that was to have been the Palestinian state." A view of the maps from various sources show that the Arab armies penetrated deep into the new State of Israel and the battles fought on designated Palestinian land were the counterattacks when the Israeli militia, the *Hagana,* pushed the Arab armies back.

A little further on in the same article in a paragraph titled, "Current Conflict," Peled states, "The original population of what is now Israel was ninety-eight percent Muslim and Christian." So, according to Peled's handout, the Jews weren't thirty percent of the population but really less than two percent, but they outnumbered the Palestinian Arabs plus all the invading Arab armies by a factor of two to three!

Perhaps, you, dear reader, can understand Mr. Peled's numbers, but this arithmetic is too difficult for this writer. The audience he was speaking to was, obviously, more intelligent than I as it didn't seem to have any difficulty with this arithmetic, or with anything else Mr. Peled told it.

According to Peled, the Arabs just left. One might wonder how they did that. Did they go on airplanes that they didn't have and take off from an airport that they, also, didn't have? Did they board cruise ships that sailed right up into the desert to get them? He made no mention of Haj Amin al-Husseni, the Grand Mufti of Jerusalem who had been an adviser to Hitler and Himmler during World War 11 and was a leading architect of the "Final Solution," the extermination of the Jews of Europe during the Second World War; and according to *The Holocaust Encyclopedia* published by the United States Holocaust Museum in Washington, DC, active in recruiting young men of Islamic faith for service in the German military's Waffen SS. The Grand Mufti al-Husseni made the radio broadcasts telling the Arabs to leave so the armies could push the Jews into the sea and then they could return *in fifteen days* to claim all that the Jews had left behind. He declared "a holy war and ordered his 'Muslim brothers' to 'murder the Jews. Murder them all. There are to be no survivors or refugees.'" Larry Collins and Dominique Lapierre, *O Jerusalem* p.400

Was the Grand Mufti even concerned about what might happen to those who obeyed him and left their homes if the Jews were successful in fending off the attacks, if they did not, simply, take their children and their old folks and walk right into the sea to drown leaving their homes, their possessions, leaving everything for the invading armies and the returning Arabs? No mention of Palestinian refugee camps, not in Lebanon, not in Jordan, and certainly not in the West Bank where they still exist, today, in the city of Jenin and in East Jerusalem, the Shuafat camp, and in the Jabaliya refugee camp in

Gaza which is, today, home to eighty thousand refugees and their descendants, according to the February 29, 2019 *The Electronic Intifada.*

The Shuafat Refugee camp is in the heart of East Jerusalem. A narrow corridor leads to a revolving metal door like one sees in railroad stations, entrance to a concrete jungle of massive buildings, dirt roads with no sidewalks, and the odor of burnt garbage. Walls are lined with portraits of martyrs and prisoners. No one knows how many pitiable Palestinians are living in this hellhole; estimates range from thirty thousand to eighty thousand. Although residents complain of the lack of city services in the camp, the main problem is the high level of crime and the murder rate. At one point, a murder a night was reported. The unreported?

Peled's inference was that the Palestinians could not have left, that they were murdered by the Jews. (Strong, horrific, reaction from the audience!) Israel, on the other hand, at that time, was prepared to extend full citizenship to whatever Arabs remained in the Jewish State...although Israeli military commanders did order the evacuation of several hostile towns that had served as bases for Arab units which were preventing access to the main road to Jerusalem. Martin Gilbert, *Israel, a History,* p.216.

The Arabs still exist, today, in refugee camps in Arab lands, but where are the Jewish refugee camps? Are they in the Negev Desert where there is plenty of room for camps, or anyplace else in Israel? No, the Jews of Israel integrated the devastated refugees who poured in from devastated Europe into their society. In the late 40s, the refugees were put to work building the roads. There was a cliché at the time: when a pick ax was needed, what was heard was, *"Bitte shoen, Herr Doctor. Danka shoen, Herr Doctor."* Former professionals, medical doctors and university professors, not only built the roads but were taught to be farmers in Herzilia, north of Tel Aviv, and elsewhere throughout the country. Talk about apartheid: who is it that has kept refugees segregated in dismal refugee camps all these many years supported by the United Nations, actually, by our US tax dollars? It's not the Jews who were unwilling to share the land with them. It's their own Arab brethren.

Peled spoke of more than the 1948 war. He spoke of Jaffa and the "non-existent" Gaza. Jaffa, or Yaffa, "The Jews call it Tel Aviv-Yaffa. Palestinians live there under persecution." (Strong, negative reaction from the audience.) The following is from Wikipedia, "Today, Arabs of various denominations constitute about twenty-five thousand inhabitants out of a total of thirty-five thousand people. Jaffa has an old fishing harbor, modern boat docks, and a tourism center. Jaffa is a major tourist attraction with a combination of old, new, and restored buildings. Its visitor attractions include art galleries, souvenir shops, restaurants, sidewalk cafes, boardwalks, and shopping. It offers a variety of culture, entertainment, and food (fish restaurants). Noted for its export of Jaffa oranges. Currently home of Asma Agbarieh, Israeli Arab journalist and political activist; Rifaat Turk, Arab-Israeli football player and manager and deputy mayor of Tel Aviv; and until his death in 2008, Raja El-Issa, Palestinian journalist."

Today, Jaffa is a delightful place to visit where one can eat the excellent foods in Arabic restaurants, including the wonderful *shashuka,* eggs cooked in tomato sauce (delicious); shop for souvenirs in charming Arab shops; and enjoy the flea market. Jaffa is Israel's ultimate model of coexistence. Arabs, Jews and Christians live, socialize, and work together peacefully, eating in the same restaurants, drinking in the same bars, and working in the same stores. An Arab native of Jaffa, Naell Hamid, said that his neighbor is Jewish and his brother is married to a Jew. Another Jaffa Arab, Samia Chamy said that his grandchildren attend the Hand in Hand bilingual school with Jewish classmates. Coexistence appears to be primarily reinforced by economic necessity as they live in an interconnected economic environment. An elderly Christian Jafffa resident said, "When Muslims threw stones at busses, here…when there was a lot of tension in Gaza, {we} told them to stop because it was driving away business."

"The Palestinians live there under persecution." Really! And, the Arabs of Jaffa are far from stupid. They see how their Arab brothers live in PLO and Hamas-dominated areas. (See "Hell of Israel Better than Paradise of Arafat"). Does anyone think they don't know they're so much better off being Israeli citizens and having their children go through the Israeli school system? The Arabs of Jaffa have the same problem many American families have: their children become professionals and don't want to take over the family business. A man builds a business for his sons and then his sons want to become doctors or computer scientists or go into medical research, not stuff pita bread with falafel or sell cheap souvenirs.

And Gaza, according to Jerusalem school system-educated Miko Peled, "There never was a Gaza. This is an arbitrary line drawn by Israel." This "fact" was repeated by Peled along with his claim that the war was because Israel wanted all the land, not only what was allotted to it by the UN, to conduct "ethnic cleansing" and form an apartheid state. *Wow!*

According to The Columbia Electronic Encyclopedia, 6th ed. copyright 2012, Columbia University Press, the history of Gaza spans four thousand years, just like the history of Jaffa. "Gaza, a settlement in Canaan, came under the control of the ancient Egyptians and was one of the Philistines' main cities." The article goes on to relate how Gaza succumbed to the Israelites and subsequently became a segment of the Assyrian Empire and a seat of Hellenistic education and philosophy. It tells how Gaza was resettled by the Bedouins and then changed hands, frequently, between two Greek kingdoms, the Seleucids of Syria and the Ptolemy of Egypt, until it was seized by the Hashmoneans and explains how Gaza was, in due course, reconstructed by the Romans. It tells of Gaza's varied population of Greeks, Romans, Jews, Egyptians, Persians, and Nabateans and divulges how Gaza was the first city in Palestine to be overcome by the Muslims and that the Crusaders gained jurisdiction over Gaza from the Fatimids but were ejected by the Saladin. Gaza was in the control of the Ottoman-appointed Ridwan Family in the 16th century."

In more recent times, Gaza was a major player in World War One. From *First World War.com*, A Multimedia History of World War One, 22 August, 2009 "The First Battle of Gaza," "On 26 March 1917, during the Sinai Campaign of the First World War, British-led forces, commanded by Sir Archibald Murray defeated the Egyptian Expeditionary Force...The Second Battle of Gaza was fought between 17 and 19 April 1917. Gaza was defended by the strongly entrenched Ottoman Army garrison which had been reinforced after the first battle by substantial forces."

"This Day in History, World War One, Oct. 31, 2009" describes the "Third Battle of Gaza" telling how after the two earlier attacks were unsuccessful, with profound allied fatalities, the British brought in Gen. Edmund Allenby from the Western Front in June 1917 to relieve Sir Archibald Murray as commander of Allied forces in Egypt. Reinforcements were brought in, together with Italian and French troops, to sustain a restarted attack against Gaza which lay imposingly between the Allies and the most important city of Jerusalem.

"Early on the morning of October 31, 1917, Allied forces under Gen. Allenby launched an attack on Turkish positions." The article explains how the Turkish defensive line tumbled on October 31, 1917, permitting the British and her allied forces to outmaneuver the Turkish defensive line. This weakened the security of Gaza which collapsed to the British on November 7, 1917, after little more opposition from Turkish forces.

And Peled told his audience at the Universalist Unitarian Church, "There never was a Gaza. This is an arbitrary line drawn by Israel." (Is it possible that Peled left Israel because he couldn't manage within the Israeli school system, couldn't pass History?)

Even if Miko Peled was not capable of mastering his high school history lessons, that would be no explanation for his, "There never was a Gaza...an arbitrary line drawn by Israel." Does that mean that Gaza was, actually, a part of Israel instead of a part of Egypt? By the time Israeli youngsters graduate from high school, they know their country; they have travelled all over it. Their yearly school field trips start as early as first grade. The little children are taken on a half day field trip, perhaps to the local children's museum. During elementary school, the trips are expanded to full day excursions to various locations of note, both historical and cultural. By the time they are in high school, the yearly field trips are expanded to a full week. By the time they graduate from high school, young Israelis have been all over their country, but they have not been to Gaza. Too dangerous. Miko Peled would have been all over Israel, but he would not have been taken to Gaza, across his imaginary line, on his dozen or more school trips.

Peled, on Nov. 5, 2015, appeared to be a man in his fifties. Therefore, he would have been in high school in the seventies when he was going off on his school trips that lasted for up to five days. What happened to Israeli teenagers on their high school field trips was not history that had to be learned by the teenage Peled. It was current, real life.

BBC News, May 15, 1974 "Arabs attacked and held hostage for two days Israeli high schoolers on a field trip who had made an overnight stop at an elementary school in the town of Ma'alot in the Galilee. One hundred and fifteen pupils and teachers were taken hostage. This ended in the murder of twenty-eight of the hostages before the attackers were killed…"

Actually, what happened was that the Arabs who were going to the school to assail the high schoolers murdered a young couple and their four-year-old son on their way to the school and then went into the elementary school where they took the one hundred and fifteen hostages, the pupils and their teacher chaperons who were on a field trip from the town of Safat in the Galilee and were overnighting in the school. "The students were forced to sit on the floor at gunpoint with explosive charges between them. The Arabs killed the high schoolers with grenades and automatic weapons," the BBC reported. Twenty-eight hostages were killed and sixty-eight more were injured, many with limbs blown off by the grenades. During a burst of fire, two grenades were thrown at a group of girls huddled on the floor. Students jumped from windows to the ground some ten feet below.

On the way to Ma'alot, the Arabs had not only killed the young couple and their small child, they fired on a small truck. The truck was transporting Christian Arab women home from work. "One woman was killed and the driver and the other women were wounded, one of whom later died of her wounds." They, also, stopped a sanitation worker to ask for directions to the school. They beat the sanitation worker and shot him dead after he gave them the directions.

It is not even imaginable that Miko Peled, then a high school pupil going off on field trips throughout this country, this small country, didn't know of this massacre. In the United States, a country of three hundred and forty million people, the emotional reaction is intense when there is a mass shooting of, say, five people; so one can imagine the immense, emotional reaction when twenty-eight school children and their teachers were shot dead and another sixty-eight wounded, with limbs blown off!

Was Peled even attempting to level with his relatively sophisticated Santa Fe audience?

And the massacres were not limited to students' field trips. The following month on April 11, 1974, the World Public Library, sourced from *World Heritage Encyclopedia* "The Kiryat Shmona massacre was an attack by three members of the Popular Front for the Liberation of Palestine General Command on civilians in the Israeli town of Kiryat Shmona. Eighteen people were killed and sixteen more were wounded."

MK Media Watch, February 28, 2013 "A *Palestinian Media Watch* bulletin revealed that a recent Palestinian Authority broadcast paid tribute to the terrorists from the group Democratic Front for the Liberation of Palestine who committed the Ma'alot Massacre in 1974 in which twenty-eight children were brutally murdered inside an elementary school." During the Palestinian Authority broadcast, pictures of the terrorists, labeled as "martyrs" with their weapons were shown.

Palestinian incitement is not unusual. Israeli security forces arrested Muhammad al-Barghouti from the village of Beit Rima, near

Ramallah. Al-Barghouti, a popular Palestinian wedding singer, praised the terrorist who killed Chaya, Elad, and Yosef Salomon on July 21, 2017. He recorded a song that glorifies the stabbing murders of the three members of the Salomom family. Also arrested were the producer and distributor of the music video. The radio station that played the tape was closed as that the station regularly broadcasts content that incites violence and terrorism.

On Sept. 26, 2017, there was an attack in the village of Har Adar. The world can sympathize with the Palestinians of Gaza and the West Bank and deplore the unemployment in those places and the barriers Israel must put up to defend herself, and then a totally unexpected attack occurs. Five days a week, some two hundred Palestinians including Nimr Mohmoud Ahmed al-Jamal, a father of four who possessed a legal work permit, enter from the West Bank to work. On this day, al-Jamal shot and killed three Israelis. Residents were shocked! "I know him!" Orit Fainshtain grasped. Drora Bardizchev, who had employed al-Jamel in her home was stunned. She said she had spent time alone with him in her home, at times talking and drinking coffee together. The killings were likely to cause the Shin Bet, the Israeli Security Agency, to reevaluate its vetting process of Palestinians who apply for work permits and could have serious implications for their employment and would, certainly, not ease their conditions of entry.

The ability to work in Israel provides the Palestinians with a living and a normal life. About thirty thousand Palestinians hold permits to enter and work in Israel and about another twenty thousand enter and work illegally. The average wage they earn is $57 a day, more than twice the average wage paid by Palestinian employers. Although there are spats of violence amongst the workers and, at times, trusted workers like al-Jamal shock their employers, and all of Israel, on the whole there has been co-existence as economics is more powerful than politics.

Many of the permit holders work in the West Bank industrial zones such as Barkan Industrial Park where about half of the seven thousand employed are Palestinians. Esther Allouch, spokeswoman for Barker Industrial Park, said that Palestinian livelihoods would be destroyed if the Boycott, Divestment, and Sanctions movement succeeded in shutting down the site. She said the Palestinians working in the Park enjoy the same labor and health protections as Israeli workers and are paid at least the Israeli minimum wage, NIS 26.88 or $7.62, most considerably above that, and they receive sick days and vacation. She said there has never been an attack in the Park during its thirty-year existence.

Peled didn't mention these things that were not history to him that he could conveniently "forget" but situations he, actually, lived through. Would his jaundiced view be different if it had been his own outing that had been overnighting in that school in Ma'alot and not only had he been terrorized for two days and, perhaps, maimed but those he was close to had been killed or had had arms or legs blown off on that school field trip? In a small country like Israel, the size of New Jersey but with a fraction of its population, it's impossible to be unaware of such tragedies, especially for a high school pupil who was going on school field trips at the time.

"The Jews wanted all the land...murders...ethnic cleansing...an apartheid State!" Peled told the church audience over and over again.

Peled spoke of the last war, Operation Protective Edge in 2014. He showed pictures of Israeli tanks lined up on the border of Gaza. He said, as he had said repeatedly during his talk, "There never was a Gaza. This is an arbitrary line drawn by Israel. Who were the Israelis going to fight? There was no army in Gaza. They had no tanks, no airplanes. This was, simply, ethnic cleansing. The Israeli army murdered thousands of innocent Palestinians. Hamas is the resistance." He showed pictures of the bombed out devastation. (Of course, the audience responded, strongly. He was effective.)

Somehow, Peled forgot to mention the thirteen thousand Iranian rockets, including long range rockets that were, at the time, reaching Tel Aviv and Jerusalem and had come within one mile of Ben Gurion Airport threatening to close the airport, Israel's lifeline to the outside world, that the Gazans had been bombarding Israel with, or the tunnels built with UN funds, funds that had been given to Gaza to build schools, hospitals, roads, etc., from which armed Hamas fighters had started to come up out of the ground to penetrate Israel, one tunnel found to have an exit directly under a preschool. UNWRA sealed a Hamas tunnel it found under two boys' schools in Meghai Refugee camp, placing their own pupils at risk.

Israel vacated Gaza in 2005 in a "Land for Peace" deal and since that time, rockets have been bombarding Israel. (Some peace for the land Israel gave up!) The rockets come at any time, but especially around 8: in the morning and 3: in the afternoon. Commuters would be out on the street at 8: am, but who's on the streets at 3: pm? Children, going home from school!

Netanyahu (of the non-existent humanitarian award) had accepted a cease-fire agreement to end the eight-day war in 2012 instead of infiltrating Gaza with troops to, finally, weed out the Hamas militants as many, especially mothers of school children, were pressing him to do. At the time that Israel accepted that cease-fire agreement signed by both sides in the confrontation, television showed the Gazans dancing and yelling in the streets in celebration of "the defeat of Israel." TV, also, showed Gazans accused of collaborating with Israel being dragged behind speeding cars until their deaths over pot-holed roads that could barely be called roads. (They had, only, been accused of collaborating with Israel, not tried and convicted. Good way to get rid of someone to whom one might owe money, isn't it?)

The *New York Times,* August 22, 2014, reported on extrajudicial killings in Gaza. "As many as eighteen Palestinians *suspected* of collaboration with Israel were summarily executed in public on Friday in what was seen as a warning to the people of the Gaza Strip." The article described how masked gunmen in black T-shirts and pants exhibited seven of the assumed traitors, handcuffed and hooded, hacked to their deaths before an unruly, enthusiastic crowd assembled in the street outside a downtown mosque after the Friday prayer in an extremely histrionic display. Photographs displayed a couple of militants leaning over a doomed man on his knees alongside a wall and lots of men and boys applauding and manipulating for a better viewpoint.

Al Majd, a website run by the Internal Security Service of the Hamas government that governs Gaza, advised that potential collaborators would be dispensed with in the field, not in courthouses, to establish terror among those who might toy with collaborating with Israel.

This time, in 2014, Israel was determined to use ground forces to accomplish what it had to accomplish for the safety of its civilians precisely as the US was being forced to use ground forces in Syria because aerial bombing, simply, cannot do the job. That's who the Israelis were fighting, Mr. Peled, as you very well knew but was not about to tell your audience at the Universalist Unitarian Church! That's why the tanks were lined up, for a ground invasion to, finally, stop the rockets from bombarding Israeli cities when school children were walking to and from school!

Did the audience with its elicited responses really think that Israel with a GDP running habitually at close to five percent compared to America's one and a half to two percent would simply mobilize, take its workers from their jobs in factories, force teachers and other professionals to leave their work and families to man the tanks and ground forces because there was no one to fight?

"Who were the Israelis going to fight? There was no army in Gaza. They had no tanks, no airplanes. This was, simply, ethnic cleansing," said Peled. Mr. Peled lives in California. He doesn't have grandchildren coming from school at 3: in the afternoon and running for cover as the sirens announcing the approaching rockets scream their warning.

Peled showed a chart of how accomplished these Gazans are, and what he proffered, for once, was true and can be verified. Gaza has a forty-three percent unemployment rate, seven universities, and a ninety-two percent literacy rate. On May 11, 2015, the World Bank reported that Gaza has the highest unemployment rate *in the world* at forty-three percent, with youth unemployment at sixty percent. The report was to be presented to the Ad Hoc Liaison Committee (AHLC) at its bi-annual meeting in Brussels on May 27, 2015. Amongst other recommendations, the report recommended the easing of the blockade to allow construction materials to enter in sufficient quantities.

On what planet had the Ad Hoc Liaison Committee been living! Construction materials had been entering Gaza, in large quantities, and were being used instead of to build schools and roads and hospitals to reinforce tunnels in order to infiltrate Israel, even via kindergartens! There were, also, tunnels to Egypt which Egypt discovered and filled in. We hear, constantly, that Israel has closed its border with Gaza. Well, so has Egypt. Egypt occupied the Gaza Strip between 1948 and 1956 and again from 1957 until 1967 but did not allow the refugees to become Egyptian citizens, or to migrate into Egypt.

As far as Gaza's severe unemployment, according to the World Bank report, *"the highest in the world,"* read "Why Isn't Gaza the Monaco of the Middle East?" Why is a locality with ninety-two percent literacy the place with the highest unemployment rate in the world? Why? They must be doing something wrong. Perhaps, using all their resources, both human and material, to build their economy instead of using these to attempt to destroy Israel is where their efforts should be spent so they wouldn't have the highest unemployment rate in the world!

Peled said that Gaza is five minutes from Israeli hospitals, "...but they cannot go there. Once in a while, they take a Palestinian child, and they charge hundreds of thousands of dollars to treat the child." Well, first of all, with seven universities and building materials shipped into Gaza, why aren't there hospitals and excellent doctors, trained at their universities, to treat their children instead of tunnels to kill Israeli children? It's all a matter of prerogatives. And how often is "Once in while"? Let's see, Israel, supposedly, charges the Palestinian family that is living in a society with the highest unemployment rate in the world hundreds of thousands of dollars to treat its child, like Israel believes that the family would have that hundreds of thousands of dollars. Peled didn't say that the child wasn't treated, just that Israel would charge hundreds of thousands of dollars to treat the child like the hospital, stupidly, thought it would be paid.

There are, constantly, stories and pictures in the Israeli newspapers of Palestinian and, also, Lebanese children being treated in Israeli hospitals, but let's ignore this source as unreliable or self-aggrandizing. So, we'll look at the Oct. 20, 2014 article in England's *The Telegraph,* "The daughter of Ismail Haniyeh, Hamas's leader in Gaza, has undergone treatment at an Israeli hospital just weeks after a fifty-day war between Israel and the Palestinian Islamist movement. She was transported to Ichilov hospital in Tel Aviv as an emergency case after suffering complications from a procedure carried out in Gaza."

The daughter, who is one of Mr. Haniyeh's thirteen children, was not named nor were details of her infirmity released by the hospital. Her admission to an Israeli hospital so shortly after the end of the conflict shows that compassionate collaboration between Israel and the Gazan authorities continues despite the bitterness caused by the warfare which concluded on August 26 after both factions consented to the stipulations of an Egyptian-brokered cease-fire.

The article refers to an unnamed Israeli doctor who had advised Reuters that the appeal of a Palestinian physician was normally sufficient to ensure the admission from Gaza of patients believed to be crucial.

Another of Mr. Haniyeh's descendants, a granddaughter, was let into an Israeli hospital last November and his mother-in-law was treated for cancer at a Jerusalem hospital in June.

Israeli imposes firm restrictions on the admittance of Palestinians from Gaza, most cases accepted only for health or humanitarian causes. Doctors at Gaza's under-resourced hospitals protested that the near-closure of the border crossing throughout the July-August war meant they were incapable of transferring sufficient numbers of severely injured patients into Israel for emergency treatment.

Hmmm, Gazan doctors complained that they were "unable to transfer *sufficient numbers* of...patients for treatment!" That doesn't sound like "Once in a while..."

But it was an unnamed Israeli doctor who said that the request of a Palestinian physician was usually sufficient to guarantee the admission from Gaza of patients deemed urgent cases. So let's discount his word and let's look further.

Germany's *The Algemeiner Journal* in an article dated Oct. 2, 2013 "Increase in Palestinians Treated in Israeli Hospitals" stated that "219,464 Palestinian patients received medical treatment in Israeli hospitals during 2012, 21,270 of them children." Those accompanying the patients to Israel were incorporated into these numbers. The article stated that this was a notable upsurge in the number of Palestinians obtaining treatment by Israeli medical professionals. "197,713 Palestinians got medical treatment in Israel in 2011 compared with 144,838 in 2008." So, according to the article in *The Algemeiner Journal*, in the three years from 2008 to 2011, fifty thousand additional Palestinians were treated in Israeli hospitals and that in the one year from 2012 to 2013, the number went up by twenty-two thousand.

(Was Peled mistaken? Did he mean hundreds of thousands of dollars or hundreds of thousands of patients from Gaza treated in Israeli hospitals, as according to Germany's *Algemeiner Jounal*?)

"The Civil Administration, through its health department (HDCA), works closely with the Palestinian Ministry of Health to provide for the medical needs of the Palestinian population throughout Judea and Samaria." Coordination of Military Activities in the Territories (COGAT), a military unit which is responsible for implementation of the Israeli government's method of providing for these needs in Judea and Samaria, the region generally identified as the West Bank, stated that the HDCA manages all matters regarding Israeli-

Palestinian healthcare administration, primarily the transportation of Palestinian patients to hospitals in Israel.

Palestinians are, also, transferred to Israeli hospitals by the Parents Circle-Families Forum, a private citizen group which was begun by a young man called Yuval Roth after his brother, Udi, was murdered by three Hamas militants. Parents Circle transports Palestinian children from borders and checkpoints to hospitals in Israel. (Two different organizations to transport Palestinians to Israeli hospitals!)

And the Wolfson Medical Center in Jerusalem is the base for Israel's "Save a Child's Heart" where needy children from abroad are brought. The Center has been treating Kurdish children, albeit to the disdain of Turkish Pres. Erdogan. Children are, currently, being treated at Wolfson from Afghanistan, Togo, Zanzibar, Iraq, Syria, and Jordan as well as, of course, Palestinian children. Until now, life-saving treatment has been given to about five hundred children with heart diseases.

The HDCA, also, functions to allow professional medical instruction for Palestinians by the State of Israel by means of medical conferences and the training of Palestinian medical professionals in Israeli hospitals. Training conferences take place several times a year, instituted mutually by both the HDCA and the Palestinian Authority. The Israel Civil Administration paid out two million NIS (Israeli shekels, over $500,000) in 2012, alone, to send Palestinian doctors, nurses, and paramedics for training in Israel.

In Dec. 2017, a joint Soroka-Ben Gurion University Medical Center, Harvard University, and Beth Israel Deaconess hospital in Boston consortium hosted Palestinian doctors from the West Bank and Gaza along with Israeli doctors at a special course in advanced ultrasound systems to improve diagnosis and obtain vital findings at the patient's bedside. One participant, Dr. Abu Greis, stated, "I welcome the cooperation between Palestinian doctors and Israeli doctors. I know many Palestinian interns study in Israeli hospitals because there is no doubt that medicine in Israel is strong and we can learn from them."

For Palestinian patients who are not insured through Palestinian or UNRWA health insurance and are unable to pay for these medical procedures, the Civil Administration maintains a budget to finance critical medical procedures.

Tazpit's Anav Silverman reported last year that Suhila Abd el-Salam, the sister of Hamas's Prime Minister in Gaza, Ismail Haniyah, accompanied her husband when he went for treatment in Israel. Ms. Al-Salam was permitted to enter Beilinson Hospital in Petach Tikva for vital medical treatment vis-à-vis a life-threatening heart condition. Since Gazan hospitals were not able to properly deal with the malady, Haniyah's sister and her husband requested permission to travel to Israel to get the critical medical treatment.

A fifteen-year-old Palestinian boy was transported to the Kaplan Medical Center in Rehovot after suffering life-threatening burns and shrapnel wounds from an alleged rocket launching pad that was assembled in Jabalya, a neighborhood in northern Gaza this past March.

An article by Itay Stern in the August 31, 2016, *Haaretz* describes an Israeli documentary by filmmaker, Nili Tal, called "Saving Nur." The film, which had been aired on Israeli television the previous evening, followed a young girl from Gaza who was critically ill and had to undergo a life-saving kidney and liver transplant. Nur had not only been allowed into an Israeli hospital for surgery but was transported from the border to the hospital by the Parents Circle-Families Forum. "Nur's mother, Maha Hajj, said that if her daughter should die after the liver transplant surgery, she would like her daughter's organs offered to Israelis first."

In this documentary, Tal, also, tells of "Salah Abel Rahman Na'im, a tall, handsome man from Gaza with his grandson who was to have open heart surgery at Sheba (Medical Center)."

Israeli surgeons enabled a four-year-old boy to leave his wheelchair after complex surgery. The boy had been operated on several times in Gaza but had not been properly diagnosed or treated. He had no feeling in his lower limbs and had stopped moving his legs. A Red Crescent ambulance brought the boy to Hadassah Hospital where he arrived suffering from pneumonia. When the pneumonia was cleared up, the boy underwent complex surgery and his rapid recovery surprised even the doctors who said to him, "Come on, kid. We start walking." The boy had great determination, put one foot after the other and pushed his wheelchair around. He was being transferred to Alyn Hospital Pediatric and adolescent Rehabilitation Center.

Another four-year-old Gaza Boy underwent complicated surgery at Hadassah University Medical Center to remove a tumor from his chest. Born with a number of birth defects in his spine and chest, the boy was taken to several hospitals in Gaza where unsuccessful attempts were made to diagnose his condition. He underwent several operations in Gaza hospitals but his condition did not improve. After surgery at Hadassah Hospital in Jerusalem, the toddler was able to get up from his wheelchair.

In May 2015, the Palestinian Minister of Health, Dr. Hanni Abadin, visited the Hadassah Ein Kerem Hospital in Jerusalem. This official visit was the first of its kind. Dr. Yuval Weiss, director of the hospital, said at the time of the Minister's visit, that there were about sixty Palestinian medical personnel in training at the hospital. Dr. Abadin voiced his appreciation to Hadassah for the chance to visit and for its help. He later headed to meet Palestinian children hospitalized at Hadassah and presented them with gifts.

The Civil Administration Health Department has stated that it will continue collaborating with its Palestinian counterpart and international organizations in Judea and Samaria to advance healthcare for all populations in the area.

So much for Miko Peled's, "Once in a while, they take a Palestinian child…" (with a disdaining wave of his hand).

Now, the *New York Times,* "Palestinians Stop Paying Israeli Hospitals for Gaza and West Bank Patients" "Scores of Palestinian patients being treated in Israeli hospitals, a rare bright spot of coexistence here, are being sent home because the Palestinian Authority has stopped paying for their treatment." The article said that Hadassah Hospital in Jerusalem stated that no imbursements had been collected for the past week for the treatment of the Palestinian children it was caring for and that Palestinians whose children are being taken care of in the hospital have been commanded by Palestinian health officials to remove them from the hospital and take them to hospitals in the West Bank, Jordan, or Egypt.

"Suddenly, we have had fifty-seven patients dropped from our rolls," said Dr. Michael Weintraub, director of pediatric hematology, oncology, and bone marrow transplantation at Hadassah hospital. "We have been bombarded by frantic parents. This is a political decision taken on the backs of patients."

The Palestinian Health Minister, Fathi Abu Moghli, emphasized that he was assessing the complete referral process because he was disgruntled with augmenting what he called Israel's "oil well," denoting the payments for Palestinian patient care. Especially, he specified, he had no desire to behold the wounded from the Gaza war receiving Israeli treatment.

(Wasn't he concerned for the "wounded from the Gaza War"? Didn't he want them to get the best care available after they had fought for his cause?)

An Israeli clinic opened with unmistakable fanfare on the Israeli-Gaza border the day the war ended, Jan. 18, 2014, closed soon afterward because both Hamas, which governs Gaza, and the Palestinian Authority rebuffed it. Israel has for a long time stressed its medical consideration of Palestinians as an example of its progressive aptitudes and humanitarianism. (What was that about a humanitarian award?)

Palestinians, generally, are happy to get the aid, but are also irate. As relations have waned, each side has accused the other of political misrepresentation, so wounded Palestinians have been banned from getting the medical care Israel was ready to provide them with.

Dr. Abu Moghli, the Palestinian Health Minister, conveyed that with twenty-four hospitals in Gaza and the West Bank, there was no reason for so many Palestinian patients to proceed impulsively to Israeli facilities, which he declared, were much more expensive and promoted a culture of dependence.

Israeli doctors and nonprofit groups advocate having the Palestinians provide more care for their own people; nevertheless, they express that the inequality with Israel in quality is tremendous, and that the Palestinian Authority is generating a blunder that could cost lives.

"Cutting it in one day makes no sense," said Ron Pundak, Director General of the Perez Center for Peace which underwrites treatment for a thousand Palestinian children a year in Israeli hospitals and training for forty Palestinian doctors. "Such a move needs to be coordinated, but dialogue with the Palestinian Authority has been much harder since the war."

Anan Dahmi, a salesman from the West Bank city of Tulkarm, revealed he had been informed by the Palestinian Health Ministry that his four-year-old son, Aous, had to cease going to Hadassah Hospital for further treatments following a bone marrow transplant there a year ago, and should be taken as an alternative to a Palestinian or Jordanian hospital.

Mr. Dahmi stated that his six-year-old daughter had died from the same affliction as he had not brought her to Hadassah quickly enough, and that now he was very worried about his son. "I don't know how I am going to manage," he said by telephone. "I don't want to lose my son the way I lost my daughter."

Hadassah officials say that removing Aous from their nurture could endanger his life because his medical needs are rigid and defined and there is not yet a pediatric oncology facility in the Palestinian areas (one in East Jerusalem is anticipated to become operative, with Israeli assistance, in the next year).

The officials stipulate that although the costs for treatments are considerably higher in Israel than in the West Bank, Palestinians are not charged the higher prices for foreigners but those for Israelis which are significantly lower than prices in the United States or Western Europe. Besides, they say, there are subsidies from foreign governments, charities, and the hospital itself.

"The cure percentage for childhood cancer is about eighty percent, but only in the first world," Dr. Weintraub, of Hadassah, said. "It costs between $50,000 and $100,000 here. It costs four times that in the U.S." He added that the parallel between an Israeli hospital in Jerusalem and patients in the West Bank was like that between a hospital in El Paso and patients on the Mexican side of the border.

"People in the third world crave first-world tending exactly as we do," he said. "If they live in Malawi, they have no hope for it. But if they live ten minutes from Hadassah Hospital, they will do everything they can to get admitted." Dr. Weintraub said that the Israeli hospitals were pleased to allow them in. He said that there are no politics in Israeli hospitals. Twenty percent of the patients at Hadassah are Palestinians, and there is, only, one common enemy: cancer. The rest doesn't matter. The problem, today, he said, is how can we get those patients back into to our care.

And actually, while Palestinian authorities were insisting that Palestinian children be removed from Israeli hospitals and treated in their own hospitals, Hamas was stealing the supplies sent by the UN.

JERUSALEM (Reuters) — The United Nations said Monday that Hamas had returned all of the aid supplies that it had seized from the agency in the Gaza Strip last week. "The United Nations Relief and Works Agency said the return of the supplies cleared the way for it to resume all of its operations in Gaza. The agency had suspended imports of goods on Friday after accusing Hamas of twice seizing aid supplies, which included food and blankets."

Enough! An article from a British newspaper, one from a German Journal, and one from an American newspaper. Obviously, enough articles could be gathered to publish a book on the topic of Palestinians, both adults and children, being treated in Israeli hospitals even though the Palestinian Authority has attempted to stop this. But this should suffice to counter Miko Peled's, "…but they cannot go there. Once in a while, they take a Palestinian child and they charge hundreds of thousands of dollars to treat the child."

The only thing that's hindering Palestinian children being treated in Israeli hospitals is the Palestinian Authority.

Since we're on the subject, here's something Peled didn't touch, and why would he in the grossly deceptive view he was feeding his most receptive audience: Israel's treatment of Syrian children.

The *New York Times* article, Aug. 5, 2013 "Across Forbidden Border, Doctors in Israel Quietly Tend to Syria's Wounded" Nahariya, Israel "The three-year-old girl cried, 'Mama, Mama' over and over as a stranger rocked her and tried to comfort her. She had been brought from Syria to the government hospital in this northern Israeli town five days earlier, her face blackened by what doctors said was probably a firebomb or a homemade bomb." For over a month, a thirteen-year-old girl had been at the hospital convalescing from gashes that required complicated surgery to her face, arm, and leg. She and her nine-year-old brother had gone to the supermarket in their village when an explosive struck the market. Her brother was killed in the attack. Lying in the next bed to her, a twelve-year-old girl was in a deep sleep. The twelve-year-old had been transported to the pediatric intensive care unit with a severe stomach wound that had earlier been operated on in Syria, and a hole in her back.

A two-day-old baby born on Cyprus in a Syrian refugee camp with a severe heart defect was flown on Friday evening before Christmas, 2017, in a special medically-equipped Israeli plane to Israel for a life-saving operation. The newly-born infant was accompanied by his Arabic-speaking father. The hospital Arabic-speaking medical team was able to communicate with the father about the baby's complex congenital heart defect. The baby underwent surgery at three days old and was expected to have a full recovery.

Dozens of Syrian injured individuals were inconspicuously whisked off past the hostile frontier for what was often lifesaving treatment in Israel as fighting between Syrian government forces and rebels burst out in zones in the locale of the Israeli-held Golan Heights. A preponderance were men in their twenties or thirties, lots of them with gunfire wounds who, clearly, were involved in the warfare. Besides for them, there were civilians with blast wounds from explosions, among them women and children who arrived at the hospital alone, and traumatized.

On July 17, 2017, Dr. I. Brook, Prof. of Pediatrics at Georgetown University who had served in the 1973 Yom Kippur War treating captured Jordanian and Egyptian soldiers stated, "The Israel Defense Force has, always, provided medical care for all wounded soldiers, even if they were adversaries. This is one of the core values of the IDF and is being implemented today as the military operates a field hospital near the Syrian border and cares for victims of that county's civil war." He said he had been hopeful that the wounded enemy soldiers cared for in Israel became emissaries for the care Israel gave them on their return to their homes Israel has, over and over again, stated a policy of nonintervention in the Syrian civil war, other than its intention to strike at stores of advanced weapons it deems a threat to its security. Officials have also elucidated that Israel would not open its progressively more fortified border to an inflow of refugees, as Turkey and Jordan have, allowing that Israel and Syria formally continue in a state of war.

This low-profile, humanitarian response to the devastation going on in Syria is endorsed by the Israeli authorities who are weighing decades of antagonism with the requirements of proximity and neighborliness. Encyclopedia Britannica has an article by the Heritage Foundation's *The Daily Signal*, July 15, 2015, "How an Israeli Hospital Builds Bridges with Syria by Caring for the War's Wounded" International News, ZEFAT, Israel "An Israeli hospital near the border with Syria quietly has become a sanctuary for Syrians wounded in their country's bloody civil war."

The articles says that for close to three years, Israel has inconspicuously treated injured or agonizing Syrians, many of whom were brought up to hate all Jews and, especially, to hate the Jewish state. As stated by a hospital official, the Ziv Medical Center in Zefat is at the frontline of this humanitarian medical mission. A foremost reason hurt Syrians prefer to go to an Israeli hospital as an alternative of to a Jordanian hospital is the outstanding treatment that is given to these Syrians with no payment. The Israeli government has approved four hospitals to care for the Syrians, both civilians and wounded soldiers. Only nineteen miles from the Syrian border, Ziv Medical Center admits the most gravely wounded civilians, and, also, fighters.

In *The Daily Signal* article, Dr. Masad Barhoum, the Director General of the Western Galilee Hospital in Nahariya on the Mediterranean coast six miles south of the Lebanese border said, "Most come here unconscious with head injuries." He told of a Syrian soldier that was brought to the hospital subsequent to his having had *seventeen previous operations* in Syria. The soldier was operated on, again, successfully and, characteristically, when patients wake up and become aware of an unintelligible language and suddenly see foreign people, if they can talk, the first question they ask is, "Where am I?" Dr. Barhoum said he was positive there is an initial shock when they comprehend they are in Israel. They are anxious and frightened. They are not interrogated at all, he said. "We just do what we can to make them feel comfortable."

He said that the identity of the patients is judiciously preserved so they will not be in danger when they return to Syria.

In order to protect them from possible threats and prying journalists, soldiers sit outside patients' rooms. Doctors are allowed access to the young people in the secure intensive care unit on the precondition that no particulars that could negatively affect their security are released. The Western Galilee Hospital, like many Israeli hospitals, cares for a diverse population of Jews and Arabs. **B**oth

Jewish and Arabic-speaking doctors, nurses, and social workers comprise the staff of the hospital. "In the lobby, a glass display case contains the remnants of a Katyusha rocket that was fired from Lebanon and hit the hospital's eye department during the 2006 war between Israel and Hezbollah. The rocket penetrated four floors but nobody was injured because all of the north-facing wards had been moved underground."

"A droplet in the ocean" is what Dr. Barhoum, an Arab Christian citizen of Israel, granted that the Israeli medical support comes to with more than a hundred thousand people surmised to have been killed in the Syrian civil war. But he said he was fortunate to be a citizen of a nation that permitted him to care for all human beings equally and that he was elated at the quality of the treatment his units have provided. He said the charges for the treatments up till now had come to hundreds of thousands of dollars and this cost would be absorbed by the Israeli government.

NBC NEWS: Israeli Hospital is "Sanctuary" for Syria War Victims by Oren Kessler 09.06.13 "Since late March, almost one hundred Syrians have arrived at two hospitals in the Galilee. Forty-one severely wounded Syrians have been treated here at Western Galilee Hospital, twenty-eight in the new neurosurgical unit and the pediatric intensive care facilities." The article stated that two of those brought to the hospital have died, thirteen have recuperated and have been transported back to Syria, and eleven continue to be treated at the hospital.

NBC News last week, also, termed Israel a "sanctuary" for injured Syrians with doctors having treated many dozens of patients who have run away from war-torn Syria. "More than one hundred and twenty Syrians have received medical treatment in various Israeli facilities during the two and a half years of the Syrian civil war." The story stated that Israel has, by design, stayed inconspicuous and modest about its humanitarian medial measures. Syrians transported to Israel for treatment, usually by IDF (Israel Defense Force, Israel's army) soldiers at the border with the Golan Heights could, presumably, confront reprisals when they are returned to Syria.

"I brought my girl here because she was hit by a sniper's bullet," said a weeping mother as she gazed at her thirteen year-old. The woman said that the hospital in her town had been demolished. She was grateful that the doctors at the hospital saved her daughter, but now she was frightened to go back. "We will be marked," she said.

NBC News reported that fifty-two more Syrians were transported to the Rebecca Sieff Hospital in town of Safed in the Galilee. A fifty-year-old woman was admitted to the hospital with a piece of shrapnel jammed into her heart and was dispatched, immediately, to the Rambam Hospital in the northern port city of Haifa for surgery. A twenty-one-year-old man arrived at the hospital on Friday with gunfire and shrapnel wounds. Not much is disclosed about by what way they arrive at the hospitals except that the Israeli military runs the technical side of the procedure. All the hospital administrators divulge is that Syrian patients get to their hospitals by military ambulance and that the hospital phones the army to come collect them when they have convalesced sufficiently to go back to Syria.

On Nov. 22, 2017, the *Jerusalem Post* reported, "Syrian Casualties of Chemical Warfare Being Treated in Israel" "Helicopters belonging to the Assad regime threw explosive drums containing toxic gases on a strategic site controlled by the rebels called Bardaya Hill." Those who suffer from the gas, believed to be chlorine as the regime has used this in the past, were brought to Israel for treatment.

Conan O'Brien, visiting Israel for his upcoming documentary, "Conan in Israel," told Safed's Zvi Medical Center, "You deserve a Nobel Peace Prize for your treatment of Syrian wounded." He went on, "I am amazed and excited by what is being done…for the sake of people from a neighboring country, an enemy." Zvi and Western Galilee Medical Centers have been provided life-saving medical care for thousands of civilians whom the IDF has brought from the Syrian border to receive medical treatment.

Jason Greenblatt, US envoy to the Middle East Sp. Rep. for International Negotiations, stated, "The world should hear about

Israel's quality treatment of Syrian patients in its hospitals…to show how peace in the region can be possible."

The Israeli army also administrates a field hospital and mobile medical teams along the Syrian frontier, but it has been disinclined to spread the word about these facilities, partly because the army is apprehensive about being flooded by more wounded Syrians than it could deal with. A military spokesman, Lt. Col. Peter Lerner, said that "a number of Syrians have come to the fence along the border in the Golan Heights with various levels of injuries." He said that the military has "on a purely humanitarian basis," assisted by administrating immediate medical aid on the spot and in some cases has dispatched them for further treatment in Israeli hospitals."

So as to aid in calming youngsters who reach at the hospitals alone, efforts are, presently, under way to bring over relatives of the youngsters. Dr. Ze'ev Zonis, the head of the pediatric intensive care unit at his hospital, said a scared thirteen-year-old arrived at the hospital in complete high anxiety. "A large part of our treatment was to try to embrace her in a kind of virtual hug," Dr. Zonis said. The girl's aunt came from Syria a few days later. The aunt, immediately, began to look after the Syrian children. She stayed with them in the intensive care unit. The hospital staff and their assistants, mostly volunteers, contributed clothing and presents. The aunt, who sported a tight hijab, said a mortar had careered into the supermarket in their village, unexpectedly, after a week with no attacks. She said that a few days later, an Arab man, whom she wasn't acquainted with, came to her village.

"He told us they had the girl," she said. He said he would take me to her. On the road, he told me that my niece was in Israel. The aunt said that she saw soldiers when they arrived at the border. She said she was a little bit scared. But the aunt said, with some relief, that the hospital care had been good and that her nervousness was completely relieved. The aunt said she would not speak of the war when they are back home in Syria, only that she would pray for peace.

Smiling, dressed in a pink Pooh Bear T-shirt and shored up in bed, the niece said that she would like to go home. She and her aunt were slated to go back to Syria, soon. The aunt said that when she would be asked where she and her niece had been when she goes back home, "I won't say that I was in Israel. It is forbidden to be here, and I am afraid of the reactions."

These are examples of Arabs from Gaza, the West Bank, and Syria being cared for in Israeli hospitals. On Dec. 16, 2016 the Jerusalem Post reported, "IDF Births Syrian Maternity Hospital" "Responding to requests from Syrian doctors, the IDF opened a maternity hospital on the Syrian side of the Golan Heights in the village of Bariqa two weeks ago. The IDF feels that by helping the Syrian people and creating good will, the border will remain quiet. The hospital is staffed by Syrian doctors but the incubators, beds, and ultra sound equipment come from Israel.

About Arabs from Lebanon, here is an excerpt from *1001 Facts Everyone Should Know About Israel* by Michael Geoffrey Bard, p.165 "The Good Fence is a border crossing in Northern Israel where some Lebanese are permitted to pass into Israel for work and medical care." Back in 1976 when a Lebanese child was allowed to come to Israel for medical treatment, the fence that she arrived through to gain entry to Israel was branded "The Good Fence." During the following five months, Israeli doctors and hospitals cared for in excess of eleven thousand Lebanese children and adults who passed through the fence to look for medical care in Israel. When Israel departed Lebanon in May 2000, six thousand five hundred Lebanese crossed into and became residents of Israel by passing through The Good Fence.

Perhaps the audience in the Unitarian Universalist Church in Santa Fe, NM, might want to rethink its reaction to, "Netanyahu is coming here to receive a humanitarian award."

More about Netanyahu and, perhaps, the most outlandish item in Mr. Peled's speech: Peled said his sister had lost a child in an intifada attack and that Benjamin Netanyahu had called his sister to make an appointment to come visit "as he does in all such cases."

First, the writer's condolences to Mr. Peled's sister on losing a daughter; however, the Prime Minister of Israel who is the head of the government does not make condolence visits or perform any other procedural services except in the most extraordinary circumstances. The Prime Minister runs the government. Israel has a President who performs such duties, just as in England, the Prime Minister is the head of the government and the Queen is the ceremonial head. The President of Israel would have had his staff make the telephone calls to families and in some specific instances, he might, actually, make a personal visit; and more bizarre is the thought that the head of the government, the Prime Minister, would act as his own secretary and make his own phone calls, as though he doesn't have a staff which can set appointments, official appointments, and not appointments to visit bereaved families, except in a most exceptional case.

Peled described his sister's telephone conversation "with Mr. Netanyahu" when Netanyahu, allegedly, telephoned telling him that he was not welcome to come as it is Israel's fault that her daughter was killed. The audience, actually, believed this! I think the audience would have believed and responded positively to Mr. Peled if he had told them that pickles and doggy biscuits grow on ice cream trees.

Peled spoke of his father, a general during the 1967 War, the war in which Israel devastated the Egyptian Air Force within six hours and won the war in six days. He showed a picture of the Israeli generals at that time and stated that *there had been no reason for that war*, that the generals had gotten together in a secret meeting and conjured up reasons for the war.

What does that mean, that Israel was to start a war for no reason and his father would go home and confide this to his little son who would, probably, have been between the ages of two and seven years old at the time? Oh, maybe his father didn't go home and tell his little boy about this secret meeting; perhaps, this general just made a habit of blabbing to his family and, perhaps, to others so little Miko as he was growing up could overhear talk of such a high level, secret meeting.

Do generals declare war? A group of generals can decide to mobilize troops and go to war, not the government for whom the generals work?

Generals don't make policy. Generals carry out orders, and when they don't, they get fired, like Gen. Douglas McArthur in the Second World War. He did what he wanted, perhaps what he thought was best and, maybe, what was the best option at the time; but he didn't listen to his boss, Pres. Harry Truman, and he got fired! "Old soldiers never die; they just fade away."

Let's see what some reliable sources reported at the time. We'll start with *The Middle East: The Origins of Arab-Israeli Wars* Oxford University Press 1996 pp. 219-40. "The combatants in 1967, Israel, Egypt, Jordan, and Syria as well as Iraq and other Arab states were, on the whole, the same as those who fought in the first Arab-Israeli war of 1948." In the weeks immediately before the Six-Day War, the speeches of the Arabs reverberated that of 1948, such as the speech on May 15, 1948, the day the Arab states began their attack on Israel, when Arab League Secretary General Azzam Pasha declared on the air that "[this] will be a war of extermination and a momentous massacre which will be spoken of like the Mongolian massacres and the Crusades."

(Sounds like Saddam Hussien's 'Mother of all wars' doesn't it?)

Exactly nineteen years later on May 18, 1967, three weeks before the war in 1967 started, Egypt's Voice of the Arabs radio station imitated this broadcasting that "the sole method we shall apply against Israel is total war, which will result in the extermination of Zionist existence." (What was this about 'Ethnic cleansing'?) Two days later, Syrian Defense Minister Hafez Assad asserted, "I, as a military man, believe that the time has come to enter into a battle of annihilation."

(Peled: no reason for the war. The generals held a secret meeting to come up with reasons to attack!)

An additional policy that plummeted the region into war was the state of affairs regarding the international waterways by which to move toward Israel which, too, had its origins in the years before 1967. In the late 1940s and early 1950s, Egypt had blocked the Suez Canal and the Straits of Tiran to ships sailing to Israel. These constraints not only damaged the fledgling Jewish state but were regarded as a mishandling of the 1949 Armistice Resolution approved by both Egypt and Israel and, also, the Constantinople Convention of 1888, the Security Council Resolution 95, and international legal practices for gulfs and bays contiguous to the lands of more than one coastal state.

Israel appealed to United Nations Secretary General U Thant, who stimulated an incomparable UN censure of the Arabs. The Secretary General deprecated the Arab intimidations on May 11, 1967, but a purported Security Council debate on the topic was ousted by Soviet delaying. In mid-May, Soviet intervention scrupulously exaggerated the imminent struggle.

According to *Arab-Israeli War: Origins and Consequences* by William Roger Louis, Cambridge University Press Feb. 13, 2012, "On May 14, Gen. Muhammad Fawzi, the Egyptian chief of the general staff, visited Damascus and toured the Syrian border with Israel where he saw no Israeli troop buildup." Fawzi's pronouncements, authenticated by the chief of Egypt's military intelligence, the U.S. embassy in Cairo, and the CIA were communicated to Nasser. Yet, Nasser elected to proceed with his alarming troop buildups.

Because of three consecutive actions that Nasser embarked on, war became inevitable: he stationed his troops in the Sinai in the proximity of Israel's border; he dismissed the United Nations Emergency Force from the Sinai; and, on 22 May, he barred Israeli shipping in the Straits of Tiran.

The Committee for Accuracy in Middle East Reporting in America (CAMARA) described Egypt's Pres. Nasser's May 23, 1967, speech to his troops in the Sinai in which he proclaimed the new blockade. Nasser told his troops that the preceding day, the armed forces [of Egypt] had occupied Sharm el-Sheik at the tip of the Sinai Desert and that in no way would he permit an Israeli ship to traverse into the Gulf of Aqaba.

CAMARA also related that Prime Minister Eshkol's reaction to the Egyptian troop buildup in the Sinai was to put the Israeli army on a first-level alert and authorized the locating of several tank companies in the south. Not anxious to send a suggestion that Israel was desirous for war, Eshkol did not mobilize the reservists. However, he did reveal Nasser's plan to blockade the international waterway which transcends the Straits of Tiran and joins the Gulf of Eilat to the Red Sea to Israeli flagships and ships of other nations whose cargoes were heading for Israel.

During the progress of the development phase of the emergency, the American attitude was timid, feeble and vague. President Johnson tried to avert the war by restraining Israel and issuing warnings to the Egyptians and to the Soviets. Be that as it may, with Nasser's proclamation of his intent to block the Straights to Israeli shipping and Prime Minister Eshkol's precautionary military shifts, Pres. Johnson reacted to the increased pressures produced by the Egyptian cordoning off of the waterways by asserting that the government of the United States of America is very much distressed, unequivocally with three theoretically volatile matters of the present friction. He said the government is distraught by the speedy expulsion of the United Nations Emergency Forces after over ten years of dedicated and effective aid in maintaining the peace, it admonishes the recent magnification of military forces and considers it vital that troop intensities be reduced and is disturbed that the apparent closing of the Gulf of Aqaba to Israeli shipping has produced an increased and unstable dimension to the emergency.

Pres. Johnson affirmed that the United States sanctions the right of open and safe transit of the international waterway and that this is of crucial import to the entire international community. He acknowledged that the United States regards the Gulf to be an international waterway and judges that blocking Israeli shipping is unlawful and hypothetically shattering to the basis for peace.

Israeli diplomats jumped into the fray and started functioning in all ways. Israel invited UN Observer Odd Bull to the north to verify that troops were not there, making an effort to convey to Egypt that Israel was not fixated on war and imparting to the world the significance of Egypt's acts. See: Odd Bull, *War and Peace in the Middle East* by Leo Cooper, London, 1976, pp. 72-78. Cooper, also, revealed terrorist movement emanating from Jordan. "Infiltrations from Jordan and assaults on civilian villages inside Israel added to Israel's anxiety." Fatah, the Palestinian terrorist organization, set off more than a dozen outbreaks on Israel and put mines and explosives in the ground on Israel's borders with Syria, Jordan, and Lebanon. On May 5, antagonisms increased as Palestinian fighters shot at Kibbutz Manara. A month later on April 7, Syrians fired at two Israeli tractors in the Demilitarized Zone located between Syria and Israel. Israel returned the fire. The clashes on land then amplified into one in the air when Israeli planes commenced a strike on Syrian military installations and confronted the Syrian Air Force. A big skirmish pursued over Damascus entailing approximately one hundred and thirty aircraft. Four Syrian MiGs were shot down and "Israeli Mirages did a victory loop around the city to rub it in."

The Egyptian blockade of the Straits of Tiran to Israeli shipping on May 22, 1967 was considered an act of war under international law. This was the only time since the 1956 war that the Straights had been blockaded. Nasser's resolve to block the Strait got events going throughout the Arab world. Lebanon, Kuwait and Saudi Arabia activated their militaries. Iraqi troops advanced toward the Syrian and Jordanian borders and Jordan sent tanks towards the West Bank.

Israel's Foreign Minister, Abba Eban, was implementing what turned out to be a failed diplomatic operation to France, Britain, and the United States while all this was going on. Even though Pres. Johnson had denounced the obstructing of the Straights of Tiran as "illegal" and "potentially disastrous to the cause of peace" and had informed Egypt that its aggression would generate the "gravest international consequences," Johnson, nonetheless, adhered to his disapproval of any independent Israeli activity. The French and Soviets, likewise, cautioned Israel against starting the war.

A former close friend of Nasser's whose growing influence ultimately began to intimidate the president, Egyptian Field Marshal Abd al-Hakim Amer managed to seize rule over his country's military from the Supreme Headquarters. He devised a war strategy which he termed "Dawn." Dawn's purpose was to capture the whole Negev desert, far and away surpassing the more restrained strategy to simply cut Eilat off and to bombard clearly recognized targets. Nasser didn't interfere in Amer's orders, regardless of the circumstance that they generated chaos among the poorly-equipped troops teeming into the Sinai and undid Egypt's established three-pronged security policy, called "Conqueror."

After the war on June 9, 1967, Āmir was fired and stripped of his rank as field marshal following Egypt's shattering defeat. According to *Encyclopedia Britannica,* Field Marshal Abd al-Hakim Amir was arrested on September 5 and indicted for directing a coup to oust the government. Booked to appear before a court-martial convened to consider the justifications for the June defeat, he, allegedly, imbibed a deadly dosage of poison immediately before he was to render his testimony.

Prime Minister Eshkol, in a nerve-racking summit meeting of Israeli leadership, endorsed the mobilizing of the remaining reservists despite the fact that he and Rabin were yet resolute in their determination not to go to war. Allowing for a different option, they were supportive of pausing for a while, hopeful of the affirmative outcome of Abba Eban's continuing diplomacy undertaking. In France, Eban got a stern admonishing from Prime Minister Charles de Gaulle to desist from attacking. Britain's reaction was less threatening and with promises that Britain would attempt to achieve an end to the blockade.

While Eban was in Washington, on May 25th, he received a communiqué from Jerusalem stressing that Israel was encountering a serious threat. "An all-out Egyptian-Syrian attack is imminent and could occur at any moment," the cable stated. Despite that, and deeply to the dismay of his associates in Israel, Eban moderated the Egyptian and Syrian menace in his dialogues with American statesmen. Conceivably soothed by Eban, Washington, at first, delayed in extending any clear-cut assurances or agreements and carried on pledging headway vis-à-vis assembling an international convoy to traverse the Straights.

Ostensibly endeavoring to placate the Israelis, it appears that Pres. Johnson assumed that he could gain time to possibly untangle the predicament by way of the United Nations or, perhaps, convince Israel to assent to the consignment of UNEF (United Nations Emergency Force) on her terrain, an unconceivable possibility to Israel. On May 26, Eban met with Johnson who told him the U.S. "will support a plan to use any or all measures to open the Straits." At the same time, Johnson continued to caution Israel not to become involved in any proactive, defensive action.

The Soviet ambassador in Cairo informed Nasser of a cable emitted from Washington about an indication of an impending Egyptian assault and insisted Nasser not attack.

This Day in History, June 11, 1967 On May 30, (now, a week before the war) "King Hussein of Jordan and Nasser signed a mutual defense pact in which Egypt gained joint command of the Jordanian army." Simultaneously, Iraq formed a military coalition with Syria, Egypt, and Jordan. In the framework of this agreement, Jordan allowed the reopening of the formerly shuttered PLO offices in Amman and, in essence, surrendered control of its army to the Egyptians who moved two Egyptian battalions to Jordanian territory. At this point, Israel was enveloped by some five hundred thousand troops, more than five thousand tanks, and almost a thousand fighter planes.

Yielding to public stress and because he was stunned and tormented by this occurrence, Prime Minister Eshkol give up his position as Defense Minister on June 1 and chose the recognized war hero, Moshe Dayan, to be his alternative.

Egyptian troops continued to stream into the Sinai and, on the Jordanian front under the command of Egyptian General 'Abd al-Mun'im Riyad, battalions of the Arab Legion were split up all over Palestinian villages in the West Bank. In no doubt of victory, the Jordanians were steadfast in their determination to sever western Jerusalem by breaking into Israeli positions both in the north and the south of the city. Nevertheless, with no regard to their defense pact, Syria did not synchronize with Egypt, or with Jordan. The Syrians elected, instead, a blitz-type offensive. Saudi Arabia, Libya, Morocco, and Tunisia all dispatched troops to the Sinai.

In response to the Arab nations having combined forces like never before, association oil companies vouched to boycott any country that buttressed Israel, and Nasser warned that he would close down the Suez Canal to them. The alliance, too, joined together to transfer ten warships to the eastern Mediterranean.

Furthermore, Israel's main munitions supplier, France, notified her that De Gaulle had approved an absolute embargo on weapons sales to Israel. In addition, in the course of a June 4 Israeli cabinet meeting, the new cabinet got a cable from President Johnson appearing to reverse the prior American moderating on the topic of defensive action. It asserted that "Israel will not be alone unless it decides to go it alone." In spite of that, the Israeli cabinet in a twelve-to-two vote resolved for war, slated to commence early the following morning, Monday, June 5, 1967.

Let's briefly recap: in the weeks leading up to the war Voice of the Arabs radio station mimicked previous language, announcing that "the sole method we shall apply against Israel is total war, which will result in the extermination of Zionist existence." The same five Arab nations that had attacked in 1948, plus Kuwait, Saudi Arabia, Tunisia, Libya, and Morocco were mobilizing.

1. Egypt blockaded the Straits of Tiran to shipping destined for Israel, a violation of the 1949 Armistice Resolution signed by Egypt and Israel.
2. United Nations Secretary General U Thant moved to censure the Arabs, opposed by the Soviet Union.
3. In response to the Arab troop buildup, Israel invited UN Observer Odd Bull to confirm that its troops had not mobilized.
4. Israel's Foreign Minister Abba Eban was on a diplomatic campaign to France, Britain, and the United States where Pres. Johnson condemned the blocking of the Straights of Tiran as "illegal."
5. Egyptian Field Marshal Abd al-Hakim Amer developed a plan to capture the whole Negev desert
6. By May 30, Israel was surrounded by some five hundred thousand troops, more than five thousand tanks, and almost a thousand fighter planes.
7. Egyptian troops poured into the Sinai. On the Jordanian front, battalions from the Arab Legion were spread out across West Bank Palestinian villages. The Jordanians cut off western Jerusalem by attacking Israeli positions in the north and south of the city. The Syrians opted for an offensive operation. Morocco, Libya, Saudi Arabia and Tunisia all sent troops to the Sinai. The Arab nations were united like never before.
8. The Soviets, too, lent a hand of support by way of ten warships which arrived in the eastern Mediterranean.
9. The Israeli Cabinet in a twelve-to two vote opted for war, scheduled to begin early the next morning, Monday, June 5, 1967. The Prime Minister had sought power to go to war without full government approval, approval of only the security cabinet and not the full cabinet. Eschol's purpose was to avoid information leaks.

Not only generals cannot declare war, the Prime Minister of Israel could not, on his own, declare war but needed to obtain the approval of his cabinet in order to declare war just as Pres. George Bush, decades later, had to get the approval of the US Congress to declare war on Saddam Hussein's Iraq.

And, in the same aforementioned "Synopsis" handout, Peled states "...the Six Day War in which Israeli forces launched a highly successful ***surprise*** attack on Egypt..."!

Peled had said there was no reason for that war, that the generals had gotten together in a secret meeting and conjured up reasons to go to war. As though generals can start wars! They were generals and they weren't aware of the situation! How stupid could these same military leaders *who defeated those numerous attacking enemies in six days* have been! Imagine soldiers being mobilized, taken from their jobs and businesses, from their homes and families and students from the universities along with their professors only to arrive at the front and--nothing—nothing! A hoax! This is where Peled should have asked, "Who were they going to fight?"

Remember that ice cream tree with the doggy biscuits and pickles? Well, maybe it's time to pick a pickle from the ice cream tree.

On June 6, 1967, Israeli Foreign Minister Abba Eban addressed a meeting of the United Nations Security Council in New York. He spoke for well over an hour portraying Israel's case, Israel's anxiety over what was then happening and her hesitancy to engage in that which would be certain, inescapable, should assistance not come from the United Nations and from the great powers of the world. Mr. Eban began by thanking those convened for giving him the opportunity to speak to the Council. He told the distinguished body that he had just arrived from Jerusalem to inform the Security Council that Israel, by its autonomous determination and sacrifice, had gone from a state of severe vulnerability to a state of effective forbearance.

He said that two days prior, Israel's condition had become cause for much concern across the western world. A bleak time had been reached and he would attempt to bring the world's attention to the precarious situation that, presently, existed. Mr. Eban described the force that had been assembled in the Sinai. He said that a force greater than any ever before assembled was at Israel's southern frontier and that Egypt had dismissed the United Nations peace-keeping forces which had symbolized the international interest in the maintenance of peace in the region.

Nasser had, provocatively, brought five infantry divisions and two armored divisions up to Israel's very border, a force consisting of eighty thousand men and nine hundred tanks, and they were poised to move. Jordan, he stated, against her better interest, has been browbeaten into joining a defense pact with Egypt which is not a defense pact at all but instead an aggressive pact which caused, yesterday, shells to fall upon institutions of culture and on hospitals in Jerusalem. Mr. Eban said that with Jordan's participation in this pact of aggression with Egypt, every street and every home in City of Jerusalem is now within the range of fire, as is the heavily populated, constricted coastal strip in which much of Israel's life, culture, and industry are massed.

Now, there can be no doubt about what is intended for us, Mr. Eban warned. In President Nasser's speech on May 26th, he said *"We intend to open a general assault against Israel. This will be total war. Our basic aim will be to destroy Israel."* And on June 2nd, the Egyptian Commander in the Sinai, General Mortagi, published his Order of the Day calling on his troops to wage a war of "destruction against Israel." Here, then, was a systematic, overt, proclaimed design at politicide, the murder of a State. The policy, the arms, and the troops have all been brought together and the State of Israel, the last sanctuary of a people which saw six million of its sons and daughters exterminated by a more powerful dictator two decades before, is thus threatened with collective assault!

The question, now, widely asked in Israel and across the world is whether we have not already gone beyond the most extreme point of danger. Is there any precedent in world history for a nation to passively suffer the blockade of a vital port, its means of access to nearly all its vital fuel when such acts of war, legally and internationally, have always provoked resistance? This is a most unusual condition. It exists because we acceded to the suggestion of some of the maritime states that we give them the opportunity to concert their efforts in order to find an international solution which would ensure the maintenance of free passage in the Gulf of Aqaba for ships of all nations and of all flags.

As we pursued this avenue for an international solution, Mr. Eban told the Security Council, we wanted the world to have no doubt about our readiness to exhaust every prospect, however fragile, for a diplomatic solution, and some of the possibilities that were suggested were very fragile, indeed. But as time went on, there was no doubt that our margin of security was becoming smaller and smaller. Thus, on the morning of June 5th, when Egyptian forces attacked us by air and land bombing the villages of Kissufim, Nahal-Oz and Ein Hashelosha, we knew that our limit of safety had been reached and, perhaps, had been passed. In accordance with its inherent right of self-defense as formulated in Article 51 of the United Nations Charter, Israel responded defensively and with full strength. Never in the history of nations have armed force been used in a more blameless or urgent cause.

Even while engaged with Egyptian forces, we still hoped to contain the conflict, Mr. Eban informed the Security Council. He told the Council that Egypt was blatantly bent on Israel's destruction, but Israel still hoped that other nations would not join this offensive. Prime Minister Eshkol, who for weeks had carried the heavy burden of reckoning and decision, communicated a message to other neighboring States proclaiming, *"We shall not attack any country unless it opens war on us. Even now, when the mortars speak, we have not given up our quest for peace. We strive to repel all menace of terrorism and any danger of aggression to ensure our security and our legitimate rights."*

In accordance with this policy of attempting to restrict the conflict, yesterday, Mr. Eban stated, he had invited General Bull, the Chief of Staff of the Truce Supervision Organization, to inform Jordan that Israel had no desire to expand the conflict beyond the regrettable scope that it had already assumed and that if Israel were not attacked by Jordan, it would not attack and would act only in self-defense.

This message was properly and accurately conveyed and received, he told the Council but, nevertheless, Jordan joined the Egyptian position against Israel and opened artillery attacks across the whole long frontier, including on Jerusalem. Those attacks are still in progress as we are meeting.

In direct answer to the appeal by Prime Minister Eshkol to avoid any further extension of the conflict, Syria, at five minutes past twelve yesterday morning bombed Megiddo and Degania and thirty-five minutes later shot artillery fire at Kibbutz Ein Hammifrats and Kibbbutz Kurdani. And Jordan embarked on a much more total assault by both artillery and aircraft along Israel's entire eastern front, with special emphasis on Jerusalem. Having been in Jerusalem, yesterday, I bear heart-wrenching, personal witness to these atrocities.

There was the bombing of houses; the great, new National Museum of Art was struck; there was a hit on the University and on Shaare Zedek, the first hospital ever to have been established outside the ancient walls of Jerusalem's Old City. Is this not wreckage that deserves the condemnation of the entire world? And in the Knesset building, whose construction had been stirringly celebrated by the entire democratic world ten months ago, the Israeli Cabinet and Parliament met precariously because of the heavy gunfire, the main Knesset hall reverberating at the end of the meeting with Hatikvah, our national anthem of hope. Thus throughout the day and night of June 5th, Jordan, whom we had expressly bade to abstain from this uncalled-for carnage became, to our surprise, the most intense of all the belligerents; and death and injury, again, as so often in history, stalks the streets of Jerusalem.

When the Egyptian aircraft approached Israel's border quickly followed by artillery attacks on villages near the Gaza Strip, Mr. Eban stated, he instructed Mr. Rafael to alert the Security Council, in accordance with the provisions of Article 51 of the Charter. Mr. Eban acknowledged that he was aware that this would cause the President of the Council to be awakened at a most disagreeable hour of the night, but he felt it urgent that the Security Council should be immediately informed. He said that he would be less than frank if he did not state that the Government and people of Israel have been disappointed by some positions the United Nations has taken in this conflict. The abrupt departure of the United Nations Emergency Force was not accompanied, as it should have been, by proper international discussions on the effects of that withdrawal. Israeli interests were affected; they were not sufficiently investigated. No attempt was made to help Israel to surmount grave tribulations to its vital interests because of that withdrawal. And, a new confrontation of forces suddenly arose and had to be met at Sharm el-Sheikh at the entrance to the Gulf of Aqaba, the Strait of Tiran. Legality exited, but blockade ensued. The peace of the world quivered. The United Nations was put into a position of leaving the Sinai exposed to belligerency.

Mr. Eban went on to say that a question of sovereignty was involved. The United Nations should, rightfully, assume that when it adopts a position, the termination of that position shall not take place in conditions that would lead to situations directly in opposition to its Charter. He said he was not raising this point in order to linger upon what has passed but because of Israel's general position on the peace-keeping functions of the United Nations. He stated that his own attitude and those of his colleagues and of his fellow Israeli citizens to the peacekeeping roles of the United Nations have been traumatically affected by the current aggressions. The United Nations Emergency Force had for a decade provided great service. Nothing became it less than the mode of its withdrawal. He acknowledged that gratefulness and appreciation are owed to the individuals who sustained this peace-keeping action and gave recognition to the fact that in the course of the recent conflicts, some of these United Nations personnel had been killed or wounded, and all those they were there to protect express a most sincere remorse. I join with them, Mr. Eban declared.

Mr. Eban questioned the future role of the United Nations in conflicts such as these. He said that we must ask ourselves a question that has arisen as a result of this experience. People, not only in Israel but, also, in many other countries are asking the following question: what is the use of the United Nations being there if it is only an umbrella which is taken away as soon as it begins to rain? Future arrangements for any peace-keeping force of necessity must depend on the agreements and the enactment of the parties themselves rather than on procedures which are totally at the mercy of the host country so as to be the instrument of its policies, whatever those policies may be.

Exasperated, he declared that Israel has lived through three histrionic weeks. These three weeks have made clear the current stresses but, also, the potential of considerably less stress in the future. First, a series of sabotage acts emanating from Syria took place. As early as October of 1966, the Security Council had been aware of this problem, and a majority of its members drew attention to the Syrian Government's responsibility to revise this situation. Almost every single day, a mine, a bomb, a hand-grenade, or a mortar exploded on Israel's soil, at times with deadly or crippling effects, always with a disturbing psychological impact. Easily, around fifteen such incidents would accumulate before Israel considered a response necessary. These continual terrorist sabotage incidents which were called the popular war along with the predictable responses were for quite a long time the main core of apprehension in the Middle East.

Mr. Eban went on to state that then, in the month of May, there came an even more severe source of tension when atypical troop build-ups were detected in the Sinai Desert. For the ten years of relative stability beginning in March 1957 and ending in May 1967, the Sinai had not seen Egyptian troops. The Sinai Peninsula had been a physical, topographical barricade, a largely empty, unpeopled space separating the two sides. Obviously, in terms of dominion and of law, any State is able to put its armies in any part of its territory as it sees fit. But this is not a legal issue: it is a political problem and a security problem.

Experience in many parts of the world and, certainly, in this region demonstrates that substantial forces in close juxtaposition to each other in an environment of belligerency and threats by one nation to annihilate the other, sets up a provocative condition. And we, in Israel, he stated, are mystified by the virtual lack of concern of friendly governments and international agencies with this unusual troop build-up which found its reflection in precautionary concentrations on our side. Several weeks ago, the Israeli Government proposed the reduction of forces on both sides of the frontier. No response to this proposal was forthcoming.

To these terrorist actions and acts of sabotage coming mostly from Syria and the heavy troop build-ups with the unnerving, macabre threats in the Sinai, in May there came the most electrifying shock of all, the closing of the international waterways, specifically the Strait of Tiran and the Gulf of Aqaba. In 1957, the United Nations General Assembly had declared the doctrine of free and innocent passage through the Strait. Therefore, it is understandable why shutting down these international waterways had a more far-reaching effect than any of the other hostile actions. And when this doctrine of free and innocent passage through the Strait was pronounced, it was not challenged by Egypt or Egypt's current allies in the present controversy, Mr. Eban reminded the Council. To Israel, this doctrine has held enormous but still unfulfilled promise, not yet actuality.

Speaking further of this doctrine of free and innocent passage through these international waters, Mr. Eban stated that during the ten years in which Israel and other States have relied upon this free passage and upon the recognized usage of these waterways, many hundreds of ships under the flags of many nations sailing through these waterways uninhibited has solidified this doctrine. The doctrine has facilitated the development of commerce and industry, and of communication. The world's means of communication has been greatly expanded, and on that new avenue of communication, Israel established her bridge with the welcoming states of Asia and Africa, a web of associations which is an essential part of Israeli commerce and communication in this, the second decade of her independence.

This effectual usage of these waterways under the United Nations flag has been established during these past ten years, Mr. Eban stated and questioned whether Pres. Nasser really thinks that he can indiscriminately cancel this firmly established, legal usage granted by the Doctrine.

He called Mr. Nasser's actions acts of malice stating that the closing of the Strait of Tiran did not benefit Egypt but only gave Egypt the deviant pleasure of imposing harm on Israel. It was a lawless act showing absolute disdain for the law, this law which has not been challenged for ten years. And it is a superciliousness act as other nations in Asia and East Africa sail through the Strait of Tiran and across the Gulf of Aqaba to the Port of Eilat to trade, which is perfectly legal. Other nations, including Japan, Thailand, Cambodia, Madagascar, and even landlocked Uganda and Ethiopia have the right to decide for themselves whether they want to do business with Israel or have no inclination to do business with Israel. These are sovereign countries. They are not under the jurisdiction of Egypt. They can either trade with Israel or not depending on whether or not this trade would be beneficial to each of them. Mr. Nasser is not the President of these and other African and Asian States and has no right to inhibit their trade.

Mr. Eban told the Council that Pres. Nasser was maliciously intruding in the rights of other nations of the world to make the decisions themselves whether or not they wish to trade with Israel or with Jordan's port at the tip of the Gulf of Aqaba. So, obviously, the shock of the closing of these international waterways was great. But by far the main reason for this shock is that such blockades of international waterways have traditionally been regarded as acts of war. To blockade is, actually, to attempt to strangle; and independent nations should not have their trade choked off at the whim of another nation.

Mr. Eban suggested that the Council imagine, for instance, a foreign power forcibly closing the Port of New York or of Montreal, or Boston or Marseille, Toulon or Copenhagen, Rio or Tokyo or Bombay harbor. He asked those assembled at the Council how they thought those governments would react? What would they do? What should they do? How long would they wait? He said that Israel waited because she was confident that the other countries which had been benefiting from this new trading pattern would assert pressure in order to enforce the law and to seek the dissolution of this blockade. Let it be known, he said, that there will never be an Israel without the Port of Eilat. Israel cannot be expected to face to the Mediterranean alone, its passage to the eastern part of the world cut off. Throughout history, peace and blockades have never co-existed. A complete blockade of the Port of Eilat and a lessening of stress in the Middle East can never be synchronized.

Mr. Eban, then, elicited the three main fundamentals of this conflict: the acts of terrorism and sabotage; the blockade of the international waterways; and, certainly the most impending, the massive, armed encirclement of Israel interposed with Pres. Nasser's statement that the objective of this encirclement is the devastation and the annihilation of the State of Israel. These acts taken together with the dismissal of the United Nations Emergency Force have unsettled the status quo as it has existed for ten years which had confirmed a relative stability on the Egyptian-Israeli border.

Although those elements in the Egyptian-Israeli relationship have subsisted, there has not been even one solitary, violent incident between Egypt and Israel for ten years. But, suddenly, this stability is shattered. Now, it must be the duty of these governments to articulate just how they intend to co-exist. Because of what has transpired, and to assure tranquility in the Middle East, we must have stronger assurance than before of peaceful co-existence. Is there any reason to believe that such assurance may be forthcoming? I am, to a certain extent, he said, optimistic about this because I do believe that men and nations do behave wisely once they have expended all other options. Assuredly, the other choices, war and belligerency, have now been expended. And what would be achieved by more war except devastation? So that a new procedure for relationships in the Middle East may flourish, stronger tenets must be applied far beyond the Security Council-endorsed cease-fire.

Mr. Eban stated that Israel welcomes the petition for the cease-fire as conveyed in this Resolution. But, he pointed out, that the execution of this Resolution depends on the total and sincere adherence to the form of the Resolution and on the co-operation of the other parties who, by their multiple belligerent actions, are responsible for the current state of affairs. However, he stated that he must point out that the other governments have not, as yet, made clear their intents.

He went on to affirm that the conditions to be implemented after the cease-fire must, of necessity, depend on certain tenets. The major tenet, unquestionably, must be the recognition of Israel's existence, her sovereign statehood, and the complete eradication of the nonsense of Israel's non-existence. After three thousand years, it is time, now, he avowed, to accept Israel's statehood for this nation, Israel, is the only nation in the entire world which has existed in the same territory, which speaks the same language, and which maintains the same religious belief as it did three thousand years ago. And if, as not only this Council but the entire membership of the United Nations and, indeed, the entire world knows to be the true fact, in the last several weeks the moral conscience of the world has been most violently shaken at the prospect of the mortal danger to Israel not only because there seemed to be the danger to a sovereign nation but, also, because it is the State of Israel with all that this ancient name conjures up, imparts, signifies and arouses. How distorted would a universal society be which accepts one hundred and twenty-two sovereign nations but does not recognize the autonomy of the nation which has given nationhood its deepest meaning and its most persistent grace.

Is it any wonder, then, that when we were endangered, a thunder of outrage bellowed and traversed the world? Men in enlightened societies and associates of the scientific and humanistic circles bound together to broadcast their distress about a matter that crucially affects the very ethics of humanity. And is it any surprise, congruently, that a deep and universal sensation of contentment and respite has come with the news of Israel's brave, successful forbearance. However, the need to secure a true and reliable acknowledgement by neighboring Middle Eastern countries of Israel's profound roots in the Middle East is profound. It is intellectually inconceivable that Arab leaders have failed to accept, to come to grips with, however grudgingly, the depth of Israel's authenticity based on her ancestral roots in the life, the history, the spiritual experience, and the culture of our part of the world!

The first truism, Mr. Eban stated, must be a much more mindful and unconstrained recognition of Israel's statehood. Know this to be true, he said, there will never be a Middle East without an independent and sovereign State of Israel. The second axiom must be the diplomatic, non-violent resolution of differences between the nations of the Middle East.

The present Resolution contains the hypothesis of the peaceful resolution of disputes. As I have already stated, he said, that advancements would be enhanced if the governments in the area would agree to direct contact. They must find a way to speak with each other. When there is conflict between them, they manage to come together. Why should they not come together to solve these very same conflicts? And, would it not be a good idea, through discourse, to reach a solution and, therefore, avoid the conflict altogether? When the Council discusses what is to happen after the cease-fire, we hear many formulas: go back to the 1956 borders, go back to 1948. I'm sure, he said, that our neighbors have aspirations to turn the clock back to 1947. However, clocks move forward, not backward; and this will be the case with the clock of the Middle East. It will move forward to peace, not backward to animosity, and warfare.

Mr. Eban quoted the representative of Argentina who said: the cease-fire should be followed immediately by the most intensive efforts to bring about a just and lasting peace in the Middle East. The representative of Canada cautioned against simply replicating the old postures of opposition without endeavoring to settle the essential problems of Arab/Israel co-existence. It is necessary and inevitable that in order to establish amicable rapports, the neighboring states of the Middle East should join together in diplomacy. All of the neighboring states of the Middle East must join in a collaborative quest for peace and make their voices known against constant war. They must issue a call for free trade and the diplomatic, peaceful resolution of differences and violent threats through diplomacy.

These states must employ an even-handed backing for the integrity of independent states and for the privileges of these states under the Charter of the United Nations and other foundations of international law.

Mr. Eban asserted that no state in the Middle East—he named specifically the United Arab Republic, Iraq, Syria, Jordan, and Lebanon--has more right to be a state than the State of Israel with its ancient roots in the area and, in addition, asserted that nations outside the Middle East, also, employ this same even-handedness and that they not manipulate any frictions that arise, that they not attempt to enhance their own positions by exacerbating transient disputes, and that they make an attempt to enhance cooperation and co-existence in the area.

Many speeches were given at this emergency meeting of the Security Council by the members of the Council and Mr. Eban declared that he would not reply to the reflections and remarks expressed as each member could judge for himself the validity of the statements, but he did single out the rhetoric of the Representative of the Soviet Union stating that what this representative told the Council is exactly what he, himself, had been told by the Soviet Ambassador to Israel several days before and that he questioned the authenticity of the Soviet Ambassador's and the Soviet Representative's fervent, prejudiced admonition. But, he said, this world body can judge for itself who had endeavored to eradicate a neighboring State in 1948.

Was it Israel, or was it a neighbor of Israel? What state has, now, closed an international waterway blocking the route to the port of a neighboring state? Is it Israel who is adamantly opposed to negotiating a peace settlement with her neighbors, or do Israel's neighbors refuse to negotiate with her? Is Israel currently surrounding the entire area of the Middle East or are Egypt, Syria, Jordan, Iraq, Lebanon, Kuwait, and Algeria surrounding Israel at this very moment?

Mr. Eban referred to the fable by La Fontaine, "*La Raison du plus Fort est Touours la Meilleure*" that children read and said that unlike in that story, the members of this renowned Council adhere to the concept of autonomous equivalency, that no member is more effective on this Council than any other but that it is the duty of each to substantiate by irrefutable proof any accusation one makes of another member of this esteemed society.

Mr. Eban concluded his lengthy, emotional speech stating that these are, of course, somber times. But nonetheless, he reflected, the happenings of the last three weeks may, conceivably, awaken in those who have disrupted the relative tranquility we in the Middle East enjoyed for a decade a realization of what their aggressive actions have achieved. What advantages have accrued to the perpetrators? What are left are destroyed planes and tanks, destroyed hopes and aspirations. So, what did Pres. Nasser and the heads of the other belligerent nations achieve? Only discord, conflict, and the disapproval of enlightened societies throughout the world. Through what Israel has experienced these past three weeks, she has demonstrated her resoluteness and stamina. Israel is now ready to demonstrate her willingness for peace. Mr. Eban called for a vision of peace, a new order of relations in the Middle East leading to a bright future for the region. He drew attention to the Syrian Government's responsibility to revise the current situation.

Experience in many parts of the world and, certainly, in this region demonstrates that substantial forces in close juxtaposition to each other in an environment of belligerency and threats by one army to annihilate the other, set up a provocative condition. And we, in Israel, he stated, are mystified by the virtual lack of concern of friendly governments and international agencies with this unusual troop build-up which found its reflection in precautionary concentrations on our side. Several weeks ago, the Israeli Government proposed the reduction of forces on both sides of the frontier. No response to this proposal came.

Through what Israel has experienced these past three weeks, she has demonstrated her resoluteness and stamina. Israel is now ready to demonstrate her willingness for peace. Mr. Eban called for a vision of peace, a new order of relations in the Middle East leading to a bright future for the region.

So, who was it who decided to go to war in 1967, the generals at a secret meeting that they subsequently blabbed about because there was no reason for the war? No, it was the Cabinet of Prime Minister Levi Eshkol in a twelve-to-two vote that made this decision. And what was the reason? The reason was the impending Arab attack as Israel found itself surrounded by a three-week buildup of half a million Arab troops, five thousand tanks, and almost a thousand fighter planes.

From *Miracles of the Six Day War*, according to all the military analysts and pundits, it was to be a lopsided match. At that point in time, the Israel Defense Forces (IDF), contained two hundred and seventy-five thousand troops, in contrast to the five hundred thousand soldiers of the combined Iraqi, Syrian, Jordanian and Egyptian armies. The merged Arab forces also had an indisputable advantage in the number and types of weaponry and military equipment. They enjoyed more than double the number of tanks, and nearly four times the number of combat aircraft.

The Lemon Tree by Sandy Tolan, Bloomsbury Publishng, NY, NY 2006, p. 135, 330 "On March 28, The Voice of Cairo dared Israel to strike, 'We challenge you, Eshkol, to try all your weapons. Put them to the test. They shall spell Israel's death and annihilation'…Israeli Gen. Matitiahu Peled would call it, 'unheard of foolishness.'"

What! Israeli Gen. Peled! Miko Peled's father! Gen. Peled was aware of the state of affairs, of the three-week buildup of nine Arab armies ready to pounce on Israel and Israel's superb military to where he could call the Egyptian bravado "unheard of foolishness…Nasser's army, which, with unheard of foolishness, had exposed itself to the devastating might of our army"!

Gen. Peled hadn't been in a secret meeting of Israel's generals to declare war when there was no reason for a war! He knew what was going on, as far back as Mach, 28th, *two and a half months before the breakout of the war*? The war didn't actually start until June 5th! And how did Eshkol put the army on high alert, move tanks to the south, and mobilize the reservists without his generals, including Gen. Peled, knowing? Did he authorize nineteen-year-old privates first class affect the mobilization?

From *The History of Learning*, UK 26 May, 2015 "Rather than wait to be attacked, the Israelis launched a hugely successful military campaign against its perceived enemies." The combined air forces of Egypt, Jordan, Syria and Iraq were just about annihilated on June 5th, the day the war started. By June 7th, innumerable Egyptian tanks had been destroyed in the Sinai Desert and, on the same day, Israeli forces approached the Suez Canal. The entire west bank of the Jordan River was emptied of Jordanian forces, also, on that day.

"The Golan Heights were captured from Syria and Israeli forces moved thirty miles into Syria itself." The war lasted from June 5 to June 10.

From *Encyclopedia Britannica* "The UN Security Council called for a cease-fire on June 7 that was immediately accepted by Israel and Jordan. Egypt accepted the following day." In spite of the alliance Syria had with these countries, Syria did not agree to the cease-fire and continued bombarding villages in northern Israel. Israel inaugurated an offensive on the buttressed Golan Heights on June 9, capturing it from Syrian forces after one day of significant combat. Syria agreed to the cease-fire on June 10. The Arab states' mortalities in the war were calamitous. Egypt's killed were in excess of eleven thousand, six thousand for Jordan, and one thousand for Syria juxtaposed against only seven hundred fatalities for Israel.

The Arab Press was still in denial about the causes of the 1967 War on June 7, 2007, the fortieth anniversary of the War. In the *Canadian Arab News*, there is a harangue against Abba Eban on his speech to the United Nations Security Council immediately before the war. The writer calls Eban a "liar," alleges that he "invented history…stood history on its head" in his petition to the UN.

Let's explore what Abba Eban "lied" about, according to this article, in his speech. Eban spoke of Nasser's evicting the UN Peacekeeping Force that had been in the area for ten years without even notifying the United Nations, ten years that had been peaceful thanks, in great part, to this peacekeeping force, and Nasser's closing of the Straights of Tiran, an act of war under international law. The writer of the article in the *Canadian Arab News* did not deny these facts but labeled Eban "a liar" because his stressing these facts "was a masterpiece of rhetorical fraud that established the twin myths of Israeli vulnerability and Arab provocation…these were marginal actions" as though Abba Eban was lying because Israel had no reason to consider the dismissing of the very effective UN Peacekeeping Force and the three-week buildup in the Sinai of five hundred thousand troops, more than five thousand tanks, and almost a thousand fighter planes, a numerically very far superior force to her's, a threat.

The writer, also, states that Nasser had "sent one hundred thousand of his best troops to fight in Yemen's civil war and was in no position to start hostilities." Being a student of this war, the writer was, surely, aware that Nasser had recalled these troops and they had been re-deployed in the Sinai during the three weeks of the troop buildup, there.

The writer, also, claims that "Israel's roots have no depth or authenticity—it is an artificial, un-Semitic, Western creation… unlike the United Arab Republic, Iraq, Syria, Jordan, and Lebanon."

Although Jewish habitation of the area goes back more than a thousand years before the birth of Christ, the *New York Times*, April 12, 2016 article "Ancient Grocery List May Shed Light on when the Bible Was First Written" states, "Eliashib, the quartermaster of the remote desert fortress (the Arad fort) received his instructions in writing for provisions to be sent to forces in the ancient kingdom of Judah." Scrutiny of the writing shows that the list, containing wine, flour, and oil, was "composed in Ancient Hebrew around 600 B. C., toward the end of the First (Jewish) Temple period."

So, the Jews were there and, already, had an army with a quartermaster corps filling requests for supplies for the forces at least six hundred years before the birth of Christ. And Mohammed wasn't born until six hundred years after the birth of Christ. "Israel's roots have no depth or authenticity" is the rebuttal to Abba Eban's speech to the United Nations?

Nineteen years of Jordanian control over the Old City of Jerusalem came to an abrupt end when Israel liberated the city on June 7, 1967. Israeli Defense Minister Moshe Dayan made this proclamation: "To our Arab neighbours, we extend our hand in peace. And to our Christian and Muslim fellow citizens, we solemnly promise full religious freedom and rights. We did not come to Jerusalem…to interfere with the adherents of other faiths, but in order to safeguard its entirety, and to live there together with others, in unity."

Jews, Israelis, and others had not been allowed to go see their holy sites and cemeteries while Jordan controlled the Old City and Christians, including Christian tourists, were forced to show baptismal certificates to gain entry to Jerusalem's Old City. Israel, also, declared that Gaza, the West Bank, the Golan Heights, and the Sinai would be *returned in exchange for Arab recognition of the right of Israel to exist and guarantees against future attack.* The Arabs did not agree.

Peled spoke of Israel restraining prisoners for fourteen years without a trial and, of course, the audience responded as Peled was steering it to, with disgust. But Peled must have been confused. He was, obviously, thinking of another country. Could it have been the United States of America that Peled was thinking of? Had this audience in Santa Fe, NM, never heard of a place called Guantanamo (Gitmo) where prisoners considered a threat to the US have been held for fourteen years? There are prisoners in Israel being held under administrative detention but unlike in the US, the maximum amount of time they can be held without being charged and brought to trial is six months, in some cases as little as forty-eight hours, although this can be extended.

The legal basis for Israel's use of Administrative Detention is the 1945 British Mandate Defense Emergency Regulations which was amended in 1979 to form the Israeli Law "Authority in States of Emergency." Administrative detention is often used for detention of Palestinian political prisoners. It is mainly used by Israel against individuals not engaged in violent activities. Administrative detention is also used in cases where the existing testimony is based on intelligence obtained by the security services (particularly the Shin Bet), and where a trial would reveal secret security information, such as the identities of informers or infiltrators.

Although Administrative Detention is usually used with alleged Palestinian militants, it has sporadically been employed with Jewish Israeli citizens, including Jewish right-wing public figures and activists (e.g. in the aftershock of the assassination of Yitzhak Rabin) and more recently, now and again, with settlers.

In Israel, the Defense Minister has the right to issue Administrative Detention commands for up to six months in situations where there is a genuine chance that the individual could trigger harm to the security of the state. The same Minister has the capability of repeating the orders. The Chief of the General Staff is able to instigate such orders, but his orders would be in force for just forty-eight hours. As of April 2012, three hundred and eight Palestinians were being detained under administrative detention by the Israel Prison Service (IPS) and data on those being held by the IDF were beyond reach.– Israel was holding two hundred and eighty-five Palestinians in administrative detention in June 2012 out of four thousand and seventy-six political prisoners. As affirmed by IPS numbers for December 2012, one hundred and seventy-eight Palestinians were being detained in administrative detention (without charge or trial). As of December 2013, one hundred and forty Palestinians were being held under administrative detention by the IPS.

The Israeli government endorsed the system of administrative detention against Israeli terror suspects in an attempt to decrease the swelling of "Price tag" tussles, feats of physical force by Israeli youths mostly against Palestinians as payback for strikes on Israeli victims in August 2015. The price tag pattern has been openly disowned by Israeli officials, including Prime Minister Benjamin Netanyahu, who has instructed that those responsible be brought to justice. Administrative detention--indefinite detention without trial--even though the right of habeas corpus is still exercised (a legal action through which a prisoner can petition the court against unlawful imprisonment) is currently used by the United States. Inappropriate confinement of American colonists by Brittan was a major factor leading to the American Revolutionary War. During WW11, the United States restrained in excess of a hundred thousand Japanese Americans in administrative detention in internment camps; fewer numbers of German Americans and Italian Americans were, also, kept in administrative detention.

The United States also utilizes administrative detention as a counter-terrorism means and as a method to control illegal immigration. There are in the region of a hundred thousand individuals in deportation actions at any time, and about thirty-one thousand held in detention for the period of these proceedings.

Following the September 11 attacks, the US Patriot Act was passed. The Act expanded the capacity of law enforcement agencies to employ administrative detention for the declared underlying principle of thwarting terrorism in the United States. Under the Act, any person (citizen or alien) believed to have terrorist contacts can be administratively detained for up to seven days and denied the benefit of a habeas corpus proceeding. The Attorney General, at his discretion, may extend this seven-day period to six months, and this extension itself may be reinstated indefinitely, legally creating the possibility of lifetime imprisonment in the US lacking the prospect of ever facing charges. One of the denunciations of the Patriot Act is that the Attorney General's decision is not bound by any judicial review.

U.S. forces apprehended hundreds of terrorists who were accordingly incarcerated without trial at the Guantanamo Bay detention camp as a function of the War on Terror, mostly in the course of the war in

Afghanistan. The U.S. at first refused to permit these detainees prisoner of war status arguing that they were illegal enemy fighters because they did not meet the stipulations laid down by the Third Geneva Convention. Of the seven hundred and seventy-five detainees interned at Guantanamo, four hundred and twenty have been freed without charge, and only one has been prosecuted and found guilty.

In Israel, law enforcement authorities are obliged to show cause within forty-eight hours (in a hearing behind closed doors). Administrative Detention orders can be appealed to the District Court and, if rejected there, to the Supreme Court of Israel. The District Court can dissolve such orders if it uncovers the administrative detention arose for grounds other than security (e.g., customary crimes, or the application of freedom of expression). General supervisory authority on the use of the relevant law is under the control of the Minister of Justice.

Any Israeli district army commander within the West Bank and the Gaza Strip has the authority to issue an administrative detention order, and the order can be appealed to the Israeli district military court, or, if rejected there, to the Supreme Court. At this juncture, also, an administrative detention order is lawful for at most six months but can be restarted by the proper authority. Israel submits that its use of administrative detention in the occupied territories is authorized by Article 78 of the Fourth Geneva Convention of 1949 which states, "If the Occupying Power considers it necessary for imperative reasons of security to take safety measures concerning protected persons, it may, at the most, subject them to assigned residence or to internment."

At this time, twelve countries employ the use of administrative detention. Israel is the eighth guiltiest abuser of this practice which human rights groups judge to be unlawful. The United States is number twelve, the worst abuser, as per these groups.

Administrative detention procedures have been harshly censured with opponents maintaining that it violations human rights. Amnesty

International considers that administrative detention contravenes Article 9 of the International Covenant on Civil and Political Rights (ICCPR) which "makes clear that no one should be subjected to arbitrary detention and that deprivation of liberty must be based on grounds and procedures established by law." The ICCPR does permit a government, under restricted conditions such as a public emergency endangering the life of a nation, to briefly derogate from its duty not to take part in arbitrary detention.

One might concur with the human rights groups that administrative detention is an insult to civil liberties, but twelve countries together with the United States and Israel have held this practice to be essential to their populaces' security. We would all like it better if this type of internment were not necessary. In vindication of both the United States and Israel, let's not overlook the humanitarian advantages both provide to the world, the US's contributions so diverse and benevolent that they don't have to be substantiated here and as far as Israel is concerned, we can focus on the hundreds of thousands of its enemies, predominately its enemies' children, that are treated in Israeli hospitals, in contradiction to Peled's, "Once in a while they take a child, and they charge hundreds of thousands of dollars to treat the child."

Also, dear reader, if you haven't noticed before, at any major natural disaster such as the earthquakes in Haiti and Nepal and the huge tsunami in the Pacific, the first to be there to help those who are devastated is Israel. Always, Israel. Israel has extended worldwide humanitarian assistance to in excess of hundred and forty countries, including to nations that do not maintain diplomatic relations with the Jewish state, countries such as Indonesia. Israel not only was one of the first to extend help to Sierra Leone in its disastrous mudslide in August 2017 but sent food, ten thousand meals, to this Muslim-majority country.

July, 2017, Bloomberg Press reported that Montenegro's Interior Ministry has asked for international aid to put out the ravaging, strong, wind-swept fires that were destroying that nation's coastline. Montenegro had deployed its navy to evacuate the area, including tourists. Israel sent firefighters and its Air Force Fire Squadron which achieved fast results in containing the devastating fires, winning great enthusiasm and admiration from the locals.

Israel, by unfortunate circumstance, is perhaps the world's leading expert in bulk injured person conditions. She has achieved immense expertise in reacting to such circumstances halting from the relentless defensive situation she has unendingly been in leading to the fostering of exceptionally effective techniques for speedy and positive reaction in the event of crisis. This proficiency meets the criteria for Israel to rapidly post field hospitals and medical and search and rescue teams to countries in the direct aftershock of both natural and man-made catastrophes. Reasonably, it's simpler for Israel than for other nations to be almost immediately meting out medical care as Israel has these mobile hospitals prepared constantly. The United Nation's World Health Organization credited the Israeli army's field hospital, which is repeatedly sent abroad to offer aid at natural disaster sites, as "the number one in the world."

All of us would like to believe that there will be no more shattering natural disasters, but we all realize that more will come. Observe who is there, directly, to assist. It will be Israel. It will be interesting to see if some of the world's richest nations, such as Saudi Arabia, Kuwait, Bahrain, Qatar, United Arab Republic, etc., noted for their continued absence in response to natural disasters, will join Israel rendering in immediate humanitarian aid.

"I left Israel when I was thirty-nine years old and I never had an Arab friend."

Miko Peled lived in Israel until he was thirty-nine and he never had an Arab friend! Why not? Didn't everyone see "Exodus" where Ari's (Paul Newman) father, Barak ben Canaan, in the Galilee village with the young orphan Jews speaking with his friend, the young sheik from the neighboring Arab village, says of the young sheik's deceased father, "Speak that name, always, with respect."

Decades later, the strong affiliation between like-minded Arabs and Jews continues. On Sept. 27, 2017, in the mourning tent of the Arab village of Abu Ghosh surrounded by fellow Muslims and many Jews, Suheir, father of Youssef, stood wearing a white shirt and holding an Israeli flag and a picture of his son and spoke passionately, "My son, who was killed by a terrorist while protecting the Jewish town of Har Adar, is a hero and he died fighting for the right side: Israel…Israel is the side which stands for justice and is constantly seeking peace." Dozens of Israeli-Arab Muslims nodded their heads in agreement.

Twenty-five year old Yousef, one of three security officers killed in a terrorist attack was being mourned by hundreds of friends and family, including residents of the Arab Israeli town of Abu Ghosh, former Israeli Border Police colleagues, and members of the Jewish West Bank settlement he died protecting, Har Adar. Youssef was described as friendly and intelligent, and a man who had finished his three years of service in an elite unit of the Israeli Border Police with distinction. The burial ceremony was conducted by the town's Mayor, Issa Jaber, in both Hebrew and Arabic and was attended by police officials, Knesset members, and a government minister. Youssef's father, Suheir, said of his son, "He stopped the terrorist from getting into the village at the time children were just going to school. He jumped on the terrorist and got a bullet in the chest that took his life." The father added that he "shares in the sorrow of the other families who lost their children this day." A twenty-one year old cousin of Yousef's said they had grown up together, described the former police officer as "intelligent" and "understanding" and said that Youssef was working as a security guard to save up money to go to university and had talked about becoming a dentist.

Until Hamas was voted into power in Gaza and the terrorist attacks on Jews forced Israel to close the border and not allow Gazan workers into Israel, the construction industry, amongst others, was manned by Arab workers. (We noted, earlier, the massive unemployment in Gaza, *the highest rate of unemployment in the world!)* Arabs built Israel, the high rise residential and commercial buildings, the universities, the factories, the roads. Arabic wasn't taught in Israeli schools, so how did they communicate? How were the Israeli construction companies able to hire Arab construction workers from the West Bank and Gaza? How were Israeli shopkeepers able to hire Arabs to work in their shops? There was much interaction between Jews and Arabs. Now, Israel has been forced to replace the Arab construction workers with workers from Romania, the Arab farm workers with workers from Thailand, and the Arab household workers by those from the Philippines. More unemployment for the Arabs while Israel has developed a very successful foreign worker program, one that the United States would be wise to emulate.

If Peled didn't have any Arab friends--and with everything else he said, why should one believe this?—it had to have been because he didn't want Arab friends. Or, maybe, he displayed the same degree of truthfulness and hatred when he was younger and so neither Arab nor Jew would associate with him. Is that why Miko Peled left Israel?

Peled spoke of the affluent Arabs of Jerusalem. In *The Lemon Tree* by Sandy Tolan, p.10, Tolan states, "...the degree of interaction was undeniable. The well-to-do of al-Ramla traveled to Tel Aviv to have suits cut by Jewish tailors, fezzes cleaned by Jewish dry cleaners, or portraits taken by Jewish photographers...Women had their dresses made by Jewish seamstresses. One of the Khairi family physicians, Dr. Litvak, was Jewish...At the Schmidt Girls Collage in Jerusalem, many of the (Khairi) girls' classmates were Jewish. 'They were there, like us.' Mr. Solli, a Jewish architect and builder (who would work with Ahmed Khairi to build the Khairi house) spoke Arabic...and coexisted comfortably among the town's Christians and Arabs."

It's obvious that Miko chose not to coexist. Among Peled's constant themes throughout his talk: the Jews started the war because they wanted it all, all the land, not just what had been allotted to them by the UN partition plan; apartheid state; ethnic cleansing; and also, the term "massacre," allegations that the Jews committed countless massacres. Although he did not mention any specific massacres in his talk, in the same handout mentioned before, "A Synopsis of the Israeli-Palestinian Conflict," Peled writes of the Dier Yassin "grisly massacre" in which, he claims "over one hundred men, women, and children were massacred." I refer the reader to the following link:

http://best-hoaxes.blogspot.com/2009/12/deir-yassin-massacre-hoax-originated-by.html "Best Hoaxes and Pranks: it's pretty easy to hoax people. We all want to be deceived, but only up to a point. Some hoaxes are fun and pleasant, others malicious an unpleasant. We'd like a way to tell the difference." (Robert Carroll)

Here is an abbreviated account of the Dier Yassin massacre by "Best Hoaxes and Pranks."

Several days before the attack on Deir Yassin, the presence there of foreign fighters was depicted made up of Iraqi soldiers and irregular forces. An Arab research study implemented at Bir Zeit University (an Arab university near Ramallah) relates that the men of Deir Yassin took a dynamic role in cruel acts against Jewish targets, that trenches had been dug at the entry to the village, and that more than one hundred men had been trained and armed with rifles and Bren guns. A local guard force had been created and forty occupants safeguarded the village through the night.

On Thursday, April 8, 1948, between 4: and 5: am with the objective of unblocking the road to Jerusalem where Arab forces had cut Jewish supply lines and hunger was worsening and there was insufficient water, the *Hagana* launched an attack on Deir Yassin. A loudspeaker fixed to an armored car warned the Arabs of the pending attack and entreated them to send away their women and children. Hundreds left, but hundreds stayed. A ferocious fight ensued and when it was over, one hundred and ten to one hundred and twenty Arabs were dead, forty Jews were seriously wounded, and four Jews were dead. The number killed has been confirmed by Palestinian Arab researchers such as Bir Zeit University Professor Sharif Kanaana who sets the figure at no more than one hundred and twenty Arab men killed. An additional concurrent Arab spokesperson decreases the number killed to under a hundred, asserting, after a count, "that there were no more than forty-six corpses."

Exacting commands (documented) were issued in advance to the Israeli commanders and fighters not to harm the elderly, women, and children. Also, stipulated clearly was that any Arab who surrendered was to be taken prisoner.

The loudspeaker's usage to warn the civilians to evacuate is a key point, indisputably not the action of soldiers intending to assassinate the people. The loudspeaker is not in contention. A publication of the Arab League titled *Israeli Aggression* states, "On the night of April 9, 1948, the peaceful Arab village of Deir Yassin was surprised by a loudspeaker, which called on the population to evacuate it immediately."

The village was not peaceful. There were foreign fighters there, Iraqi soldiers, and the men of Deir Yassin had taken part in violent deeds against Jewish targets and trenches had been dug in preparation for battle, but the fundamental part of this quote matches the Jewish version: a loudspeaker alerted the populace to evacuate.

The massacre allegation, the killing of defenseless people, has been completely disproved not only by the Israeli government but by every historical analysis. The fabrications survive because pro-Arab speakers repeatedly restate them, frequently raising up the number of dead to two hundred and fifty or more. There are thoroughly untrue versions published about Arabs being led to the mosque and shot down against the walls, or even grislier fabrications of torture, rape, or any other contemptible feature the storyteller invokes. To state there is not a shred of evidence for these embellishments is giving them too much credit.

There are eyewitness reports to the contrary, both Jewish and Arab, about what really ensued. For instance, according to the *Daily Telegraph*, April 8, 1998, an Arab inhabitant of the village and a survivor of the fighting there called Ayish Zeidan avowed, "The Arab radio talked of women being killed and raped, but this is not true... I believe that most of those who were killed were among the fighters and the women and children who helped the fighters." He said that the Arab leaders made a big error. By overstating the made-up carnages, they presumed they would motivate people to push back with more frenzy. In its place, the people became terrified and ran away."

Deir Yassin was a reasonable military target for Jewish forces, there was warning given in advance of the battle, and then a fierce battle took place with fatalities on both sides. No mutilations, no atrocities, no massacre.

Palestinian Arab eyewitnesses have admitted that a number of their statements about Deir Yassin were intentional fabrications. The issue of the Jerusalem Report dated April 2, 1998, mentions a BBC television program in which Hazem Nusseibeh, an editor of the Palestine Broadcasting Service's Arabic News in 1948, revealed that he was told by Hussein Khalidi, an notable Palestinian Arab leader, to construct claims of brutalities at Deir Yassin with the objective of encouraging Arab governments to attack the projected Jewish state.

According to a Jerusalem Report, Nusseibeh, in a happenstance meeting at the Jaffa Gate of Jerusalem's Old City with Deir Yassin survivors and Palestinian leaders including Hussein Khalidi, queried Dr. Khalidi in what way he should cover the story. Dr. Khalidi responded, "We must make the most of this." So Mr. Nusseibeh composed a press release asserting that "at Deir Yassin, children were murdered, pregnant women were raped. All sorts of atrocities."

BBC Report "Israel and the Arabs: The 50 Year Conflict" The BBC program shows an interview with Abu Mahmud, who was a Deir Yassin inhabitant in 1948, who said, "The villagers objected to the atrocity claims. We said, 'There was no rape.' Khalidi said, 'We have to say this, so the Arab armies will come to liberate Palestine from the Jews." Khalidi was one of the architects of the "massacre" claim in 1948.

Nusseibeh, who now lives in Amman, Jordan, and is from one of Jerusalem's most renowned Arab families disclosed to the BBC that the concocted atrocity stories about Deir Yassin were "our biggest mistake" because "Palestinians fled in terror." He articulated that

Palestinians departed the country in massive numbers after hearing the atrocity assertions.

Pres. John F. Kennedy said years later, "The great enemy of truth is very often not the lie—deliberate, contrived and dishonest—but the myth—persistent, persuasive and repeated."

The audience at the Universalist Unitarian Church in Santa Fe, NM was not necessarily Church members. Peleds's talk was open to the public, as are the multitude of such talks by the pro-Palestinian/anti-Israel organizations.

*****

PBS Hosts Extremist Miko Peled on Talk Show

On February 2, 2017, PBS's Tavis Smiley hosted Miko Peled on his talk show. It was obvious that Mr. Smiley had not researched his subject as what he conducted was not an interview as the public tends to expect, a give and take with the interviewer striving to get the truth for his or her audience, the purpose of an interview. From the day that Donald Trump first announced this bid for President of the United States, not only the US but the world through CNN and Fox News have been subjected to fiery exchanges between interviewer and interviewee. But, Travis Smiley gave Peled a platform from which to espouse his vehement hatred of the country he was born in and which his father served, attaining the rank of general, without any challenge to his guest's assertions.

We will not go into and refute Peled's caprices on this program as we are, already, fully familiar with Miko Peled's truthfulness, or lack thereof. We know his act: Gaza with its four thousand year history never existed, just a line in the sand drawn by Israel; the Balfour Declaration came about through a bribe to Lord Balfour, not because of Britain's dire need for the fuel brought from the Mosel oilfields in the, then, Ottoman Empire and refined in the Haifa refineries to power the newly converted (from coal to oil) British navy; generals get together in secret meetings and start wars; etc.

We will, at this point, repudiate only one amongst the myriad of denunciations of his motherland Peled espoused, unchallenged, on the program: he called Jewish history a "myth." Even though Miko Peled grew up in the Jewish State of Israel, there are not only Jews and Arabs in Israel, there are Christians and a multitude of Christian churches and holy sites that are visited, continuously, by Christian groups. It is hardly possible that Miko Peled had never learned of a Jew named Jesus Christ who was born in this Jewish land two thousand and seventeen years ago to Jewish parents named Joseph and Mary who had traveled to Bethlehem, Jesus's birthplace, from their hometown, the Jewish town of Nazareth which was, at that time, over a thousand years old.

Travis Smiley's interview was reminiscent of interviews conducted during the 2014 war, Operation Protective Edge. The networks tended to interview both an Israeli spokesperson and a Palestinian spokesperson each time they conducted interviews. The Israeli would answer the questions, typically about what was occurring at the precise time in the war. The Palestinian spokesperson would, typically, totally ignore the question and espouse his propaganda. A Palestinian interviewee attempted this with CNN's Don Lemon. Mr. Lemon cut him off tersely with an emphatic, "I ask the questions!" and let the spokesperson know that he would answer the questions posed to him or the interview was over.

The Palestinian spokesperson was stunned. He didn't know how to react. The *modus operandi* was to ignore the interviewer. He had been prepared for what he was going to promote and didn't know how to handle Don Lemon.

Smiley and PBS should avoid hosting radicals such as Peled in the future, unless the interviewers are prepared to aggressively challenge their narratives and false claims.

Travis Smiley, you're no Don Lemon.

We know what Miko Peled's agenda is, but one might wonder exactly what his motivation is.

CHAPTER 7

Water, Electricity, And Stupidity

Restraint and cease-fires get Israel into wars: how dumb can smart people be?

WAR! And the UN and the United States urge restraint on Israel's part. Hamas leaders signal their willingness to consider a brokered cease-fire, as long as their terms are met. Israelis are considered to be smart: a multitude of Nobel Prize winners, one of its largest exports medical technology, and an intelligence force perhaps the best in the world; so how dumb can smart people be?

As of the war in 2014, it had been twelve years that rockets had been raining down on southern Israel from Gaza, even though Israel had returned the Gaza Strip in a "Land for Peace" deal. *What peace!* And each year, the rockets from Iran were becoming more sophisticated with longer range and greater accuracy. The Sinai went back to Egypt in this agreement, but Egypt refused to take Gaza back. It wanted no part of Gaza. They, the Egyptians, are the smart ones.

When Israel pulled out of Gaza in 2005, James Wolfensohn, President of the International Finance Committee and of the World Bank, contributed $500,000 of his own money towards the $14 million these two institutions paid to the Israeli government to leave the modern, computer-run hothouses the Israelis had built where vegetables, fruits, and flowers were being grown so this industry could continue to provide jobs for Gazan workers and products not only for domestic consumption but for export, necessary for the Gazan economy. The first thing the Palestinians did after the Israeli withdrawal was to loot the hothouses stripping them of their pumps, plastic sheeting, and glass, and then burned them down. They burned down their places of employment!

On page 362 of *City of Oranges* by *Times of London,* international correspondent Adam Le Bor, states, "The Israeli departure from Gaza brought neither peace nor comfort to its inhabitants. It was, also, a missed opportunity." Le Bor described how the (Israeli) settlers had left an extensive, complex system of computer-controlled, state-of-the-art greenhouses where they had grown tomatoes, strawberries, and flowers, which comprised a major portion of Gaza's meager exports. This could have furnished the basis for a flourishing agricultural industry. Instead, within hours of the Israeli evacuation, Gaza's inhabitants devastated the greenhouses stripping off their glass, pipes, and irrigation apparatus. They, then, burned what was left of these modern, computer-controlled greenhouses to the ground. So much for the forty-three percent unemployment in Gaza, and for the $14 million paid to Israel, including Mr. Wolfensohn's $500,000, to leave the greenhouses intact!

Had Gaza become a vibrant economy, conceivably also turning into the beautiful seaside resort that it could have and should have become, Israel could not be blamed for the resultant dreadful condition that the Gazans, purportedly, live in now. (Doesn't anyone watch the news on TV? Are they dressed in rags? Do they look hungry? The young men wear shirts and jeans like any young American and they look firm and strong, the older men hardy and a bit overweight. Do they live in shacks or in the high rise apartment buildings we see on TV? Look on the Internet. They have seven universities and a long Mediterranean coast that could be developed into beautiful beach resorts.) Let's examine if the Palestinians would sacrifice their own people to wage *jihad* on Israel.

Rockets rained down on Tel Aviv and a rocket even targeted Jerusalem, Jerusalem, which houses the *Al Aqsa* Mosque, the third holiest site in Islam! Arabs live in Jerusalem. The Palestinians are risking destroying one of their holiest sites and killing their own people! Are they restraining from attempting to kill Israelis to avoid putting their own people in harm's way? No. Israel uses surgical strikes to take out top military officials and caches of the weapons that are stockpiled to use against her. But where have these stockpiles been purposefully stashed? They are under apartment complexes and adjacent to hospitals, just as the mortar launchers which they know Israel will target are strategically set within residential areas. The Gazan leaders are using their people as human shields for their propaganda value when these human shields are killed or wounded.

Israel has a choice: be humanitarian and don't destroy the stores of rockets for fear of killing the human shields and don't bomb the stockpiles of weapons stored in residential buildings but, instead, leave these weapons so they can be used to destroy Israel's own residential buildings with sleeping Israeli children in them. And speaking of sleeping children, what about the innocent but naive Gazans who are offered money for the rental of a room in their apartment which, they are told, will be no trouble as the room will be used only for storage. Are these innocent people told that what will be stored in that room are arms, rockets, which Israeli intelligence will seek out and Israel will have to destroy, unfortunately but most probably, along with that man's family or risk these rockets destroying Israeli families? No. He only knows that with this money he can buy food for his family and gas for his car. He may or may not know that he is paying inflated prices for these food and gas necessities, his own leaders enriching themselves at his expense.

But those who set him up will show the mutilated child which, it will be said, Israel killed and will loudly extol, "And how will this help Israel? Are Palestinian children expendable? They should be charged with murder for this!" The Israelis will be charged, not the renters of the room in their fellow Gazan's flats and Hamas, their duly elected government which is supposed to help and protect its people, not set them up to be killed in Hamas's propaganda war.

It's hard to imagine in the midst of these hostilities, but Gazans are being treated in Israeli hospitals, specifically the Rambam Medical Center in Haifa; the Hadassah Medical Center in Jerusalem; the Sheba Medical Center outside Tel Aviv, including an Arab boy who was hit by a Gazan rocket that fell in the Israeli town of Kiryat Malachi; Tel Aviv's Sourasky Medical Center; and other hospitals throughout Israel. Rambam Medical Center Director-General, Prof. Dr. Rafael Beyer when asked why his hospital was treating the enemy said, "We at Rambam are taking care of children and adults, and we are not looking at their religion or where they come from…We are very far away from politics."

But not all rockets hit where they are intended to hit. A syndicated article by Liat Collins on Dec. 22, 2017 was about a rocket heading for Israel like the recent rocket that hit a kindergarten in Sderot but fell short of its target and instead hit an UNWRA school in Gaza. No outcry form from the UN, or from the Palestinians. Why not?

At the same time, Hamas was warning that it would start another suicide bombing campaign. Hamas had been posting on the Internet photographs from various, other conflicts claiming these were victims of the Israeli offensive in Gaza; for example, a photograph of a weeping sixty-year-old father with his dead, bloody six-year-old child in his arms while doctors look on. Twitter followers have pointed out that this photo was taken at the Dar al-Shifa Hospital in Aleppo, Syria, the child a casualty of the conflict in Syria, not in Gaza.

It would not be unusual for that sixty-year old father to have fifty children. It is a misnomer that Arab men can have four wives. They can have four wives *at a time!* When his first wife dies in childbirth having their eleventh child at the age of thirty-four and he is left with only three wives, he can take another. Even with fifty children, one cannot afford to lose one. But that is the explanation of a man who, in a different society, would be a grandfather, or even, possibly, a great grandfather at the age of sixty; and he may be all of those as well as a grieving father of a six-year-old.

Another photograph was posted of an injured infant held by a rescue worker in Gaza. Facebook and Twitter users identified the photo as one previously posted as a baby wounded by a Hamas rocket attack. Today, one has online research tools to dig into and reveal the truth. Not that Palestinian children have not been and will not continue to be harmed by Israeli fire as long as they are being used as human shields with rockets and other weapons being stored in and fired from their midst.

Israeli Arabs with that many and fewer children receive government subsidies, welfare, to raise their children as do Israeli Jews with more children than they can support; although among Jews, eight children, not fifty, would be an extreme number. All Israeli citizens, Arabs and Jews, are treated alike. They vote in elections and they receive the benefits they are entitled to. The difference today, as contrasted with former years, is that many of the government workers in the Welfare and other government offices are Arab young women who, under Israeli law, have been educated; so they now work in offices instead of tending sheep or they are university educated and work in the professions.

Numerous TV reporters have brought up the fact that at a point in the war in 2014, early in the conflict, Israel had three casualties while Gaza had suffered ninety, referring, perhaps, to some sort of inequality in this battle. And we all know that Americans are for the underdog. What is to be expected, especially in view of this strategy of placing weapons and their launchers in populated areas? Does Israel use its people in this manner? No. The Israeli people are as protected as their government can keep them.

For at least the past decades, all new Israeli residential buildings are required to be constructed with one room built to be a bomb shelter, usually one of the bedrooms in a house or an apartment. Older buildings have the shelter in the basement. Very old buildings do not have shelters and residents are instructed to go into the stairwells at least two floors down from the top of the building as the stairwells are in the center of the building and reinforced. When a rocket is fired from Gaza, it is tracked; and along its course, sirens sound warning the Israelis to enter the shelters, and safety. Those outside who cannot reach a building know they are to huddle against a wall and cover their heads. If riding in a car or bus, passengers emerge from the vehicle and lie down on the ground on the side away from Gaza, also covering their heads.

The "Iron Dome," the Israeli anti-missile system, has been effective in intercepting eighty-five percent of incoming rockets, those that are headed towards a populated area. If the rocket is headed into the unpopulated desert or out to sea, it is ignored. Is it any wonder that Israelis have suffered so few casualties? The three casualties that Israel suffered should not have been. They were in an old building without a shelter but those who were living in the apartment did not follow the safety instructions, as Israelis tend to do. They did not take their children and go into the stairwell at least two stories down from the top floor of their building. Instead, they remained in their top floor apartment where a rocket made a direct hit. They were killed and the two children they did not protect, injured.

Perhaps some of the blame should go to Israeli mothers. For years, they have been sending their children off to school knowing full well that although rockets strike at any time of the day or night, the peak time for Palestinian rockets to strike Israel is around 8: in the morning and 3: in the afternoon when the children are going to and coming from school. Were the usual times at 8: in the morning and 5: in the afternoon, one could reason that they were set for peak rush hour times to target working adults. At 3: pm, children are coming home from school, not parents from work.

What kind of mother sends her child out into imminent danger? Perhaps the kind who, finally, should say to her government, "Stop this or we'll call a general strike here in the south of Israel where we have been suffering and exposing our children to rockets from Gaza, daily, for twelve years! For twelve years a thousand rockets a year have been shot at us, most when our children are out on the streets. Enough! It's time for a general strike to get our government to stop appeasing, showing more and more restraint as the US, the UN and others demand it to, and agreeing to another cease-fire and then another to give Iran time to supply more rockets to Gaza which, again, are fired on us, and on and on for twelve more years! No. It's time to shut down the south, not only schools but businesses, too."

The Israeli government has the obligation to protect its citizens. Now that insulated Tel Aviv is being bombarded, and even Jerusalem, and rockets are intercepted close to the international airport, Israel's lifeline to the outside world, perhaps the Israeli government will not be so willing to use the restraint it is always told to use and to accept the cease-fires that lead to more wars.

Not all mothers react to their children's safety in the same way. In most of the world, mothers are totally protective of their children, as we'd all like to believe Arab mothers, also, are. Following is a link to a YouTube video of a young Palestinian suicide bomber and his mother's reaction. But caution; the video is disturbing, grotesque. It is not for the faint hearted. You may choose to only read the text that accompanies the video: http://www.youtube.com/watch?v=PPU4UN03t7E It is about Hussam Bilal Abdo, a fourteen-year-old Palestinian boy, a suicide bomber who was arrested at the Nablus (Shem) checkpoint.

Hassam was not well-liked in school and he was spurned by his classmates, according to his family. A good means to become accepted, to be liked by his classmates, was to become a martyr, he had thought. An older boy he knew was acquainted with some bomb makers. This buddy managed to set up a meeting for Hussam with them. The bomb makers gave Hussam one hundred Israeli shekels for performing the deed (about twenty-four US Dollars at the time). Hassam began running in the direction of the checkpoint, soldiers commanded him to halt, but he did not and the soldiers grabbed him. He is currently in an Israeli jail, even more brainwashed for martyrdom than before as his jail companions all come from the same backward 'Muqawama' (popular resistance/eternal conflict enrichment) viewpoint.

Hassam's parents were alive at the time and "his mother, Tamam, said of her son that if he were over eighteen, she might have encouraged him to do what he did."

A teenager attempting to come into Israel from Arab territory with an explosives belt on him says a whole lot about the value of life for the Palestinians. Life is cheap, as cheap as $24. This boy was not only paid one hundred shekels to blow himself up, he had grown up knowing that seventy-two virgins would be waiting for him in heaven to provide him with the 'best time of his life' (or is it the best time of his death?).

And where do these explosive belts and vests stem from? Not long ago, an Arab in an Israeli prisoner earned a PhD in chemical engineering from Hebrew University in Jerusalem. Who instructs the Palestinians on precisely how to devise the explosives they will use to kill themselves and as many Israeli as they can take with them if not chemical engineers? Who furnishes these chemicals to youths so that they can blow themselves up? And what country offers jailed terrorists serving time in its prisons the potential to obtain bachelor's, master's, and doctorate degrees, especially in subjects like chemical engineering so that they can create and communicate how to make explosives that can be employed against them? Why not give the prisoners the capability to become plumbers and carpenters, electricians, or even teachers?

It is hard for the western mind to understand a mother celebrating her son's suicide by maintaining that if he were eighteen years old, she would nurture him to commit suicide. A quote from *Newsweek*, March 8, 2016, by a mother of a slightly older youth, a twenty-one year old who was crushed when a tunnel Hamas was constructing to gain access to Israel as militants had done before in Israeli army uniforms and fitted out with guns and explosive belts to kill or kidnap Israelis, "This is an honor for me and my family."

It is not only adolescents implementing these suicidal attacks and their mothers glorifying them. On January 8, 2017, Fadi al-Qunbar, a twenty-eight year old married Palestinian, the father of four, butted his speeding truck into a group of young, Israeli soldiers who were on an educational tour of Jerusalem killing four and injuring another eighteen. Al-Qunbar was shot to death on the spot. His sister, Shaida, said of her brother and his performance, "Praise the Lord for him becoming a martyr. It is the most beautiful, saintly death." She affirmed that her brother was a devoted religious man. Hamas spokesperson, Abdul-Latif Qanou, proclaimed it a heroic act and heartened other Palestinians to do the same.

Since the beginning of 2016, nearly a dozen tunnels have collapsed on the Palestinians as they were digging them, killing at least ten.

A more heart-breaking tale from "Cult of the Suicide Bomber" is that of Wafa Al-Biss who misused the benefit of the pass she had that enabled her to enter Israel. Wafa had been severely burned in her kitchen by a gas explosion and had her life saved in an Israeli hospital. Afterward, she tried to carry a bomb into Israel, resolved to detonate it, to blow herself up in the very hospital that had saved her life and which had treated her as it treated everyone else. She related her account in a documentary. (Also see: Arabs treated in Israeli hospitals in "The Miko Peled Speech.")

More recently, a sixteen year old (although there is speculation that she is really eighteen, but that wouldn't make such good propaganda against Israel should Israel choose to retaliate against her), Ahed Tamimi continued her crusade—a crusade her parents started her on when she was a mere three years old--to try to provoke Israeli soldiers. Previously, she had been filmed biting the hand of an Israeli soldier; now, she was filmed slapping and punching a young soldier. He stood his ground and did not respond to her provocations. Ahed had been reared in a culture of martyrdom, promised fame and family fortune, much of it through the courtesy of unknowing American taxpayers. This is a new kind of warfare against Israel, the camera war. To facilitate this new battlefield, there is a huge operation of actors, extras, camera crews, directors, and logistical support. Israeli

Lt. Peter Lerner arrived on the scene of Ahmed's barrage against the eighteen-year-old soldier and decided not to arrest her biting, screaming at, and hitting the soldier, as caught on camera.

"In psychological warfare, words and images kill." But it must not, also, be forgotten that rocks and stones, also, kill.

The weapons supplied to Gaza get more sophisticated at each cease-fire. Until not too long ago, Hamas's rockets didn't have the range to strike the center of Israel with its most populous cities of Tel Aviv and Jerusalem. Now, they do. But still, the rockets are not accurate. They are aimed on the track of the city they supposed to reach and, maybe, some few will attain the anticipated objectives and not merely drop into empty space, like the desert or the sea. Like the outdated B52 bombers, shove a sufficient number of bombs out the bomb bay door and, with a bit of luck, several will, in fact, hit the target.

The Palestinians, today, have considerably longer range rockets. So, what will more cease-fires achieve? Time for them to achieve greater accuracy, precision missiles which can cause greater destruction? Iran has now outfitted the Palestinians with Qassam M75 rockets which have a range of around fifteen miles and the Fajr-5 missile which has a range of almost fifty miles, able to reach Tel Aviv and Jerusalem. Does one's common sense dictate that Israel should keep on agreeing to additional cease-fires to allocate time for the Palestinians' regrouping and resupplying? Only if one is an idiot! And, of course, Hamas wants its military leaders safe so they can continue to direct the assaults on Israel.

And does the world know that smart Israel, also, is Gaza's electricity supplier? According to treaty, Israel supplies this enemy with a major portion of its electric power. In fact, as of Sunday, Nov. 18, 2014. the fourth day of fighting in Operation Protective Edge, Israel was still supplying one hundred and twenty-five megawatts of electricity to the Gaza Strip from the power station in Ashkelon despite the rocket attacks on Israel's population, *and on Ashkelon, itself!* The treaty is broken as Gaza has not paid for this electricity, as agreed. When an Israeli household does not pay its electric bill, service is terminated. Isn't that the same in the U S? But if Israel would dare to refuse to keep on bankrolling Gaza's electric supply, wouldn't there be, immediately, another campaign of vilification against Israel? So, Israel supplies its enemy which is sworn to destroy it with electricity *which the Israeli civilians, the targets of Gaza's rocket attacks, pay for through their taxes.* Judge Israel on that one! Ask an Israeli why Israel doesn't simply cut the power supply. His reply is that there are children there. Really, while his own children are exposed to death! Sheer stupidity!

On September 13, 2016, two years after Operation Protective Edge while Israel was still continuing to supply Gaza with electricity with rockets, intermittently, falling on Israel's southern towns, Israel and the Palestinian Authority signed an agreement that will erase well over a hundred million dollars of the debt which, at that date, stood at $530 million. The Palestinian Authority agreed to pay $130 million to the Israel Electric Corporation (IEC) immediately and agreed to pay the remainder of the debt over an extended period of time except for the final $130 million, which will be forgiven. Banks both in Israel and the United States, perhaps all over the world, tend to make this type of concession in order to recoup at least a portion of what is owed them. The US Internal Revenue Service, also, is known to negotiate amounts owed to it.

Since the amount of electric power supplied by Israel and by Egypt plus the amount Gaza's own electric power plant can supply is insufficient to meet the needs in Gaza, "brownouts" are a matter of daily life which means that, for many years, Gazans have only had electricity for from eight to twelve hours a day, insufficient for their needs but enough to allow them to moderately heat their houses and carry out much of their daily functions. The Gaza power plant, which was bombed by Israel in 2006 shortly after Israel pulled out of Gaza in a "Land for Peace" deal during fighting between Israel and Hamas, has been operating at half capacity since. Contributing to the additional cuts in electricity are disagreements over taxation between Hamas and the Palestinian Authority. The Palestinian Authority had been reducing vital tax exemptions that it had formerly been conferring on Hamas to purchase fuel for the Gaza power plant.

Infighting between Hamas and the Palestinian Authority has been taking its toll on the residents of Gaza.

The *New York Times* reported on Jan. 17, 2017, that electric power in Gaza had been reduced to three to four hours a day triggering, "in a rare display of defiance against the Hamas authorities," the first riot by over ten thousand Gazans who "took to the streets in the Jabaliya Refugee Camp in Northern Gaza." The protesters riled against Hamas leader Ismail Haniya and against Mahmoud Abbas, Pres. of the Palestinian Authority/Fatah. The demonstrators burned tires and threw stones. Hamas police fired into the air in an attempt to diffuse the rioters.

Not only can businesses not operate to capacity on the scant amount of electricity they receive, students cannot study in the cold and the dark. A Gazan comedian, Adel Al-Mashoukhi, was arrested by Hamas police and taken from his home the in southern Gaza town of Rafah for ranting against Hamas because of "no jobs, no border crossings, no food, no water." Al-Mshoukhi had posted a video of himself blaspheming Hamas for these deprivations and yelling, "Enough, Hamas! Enough!" In almost no time, the video had almost three hundred thousand views.

The Israeli newspaper, *Haaretz* reported that Norwegian Foreign Minister, Borge Brende, was instrumental in negotiations concerning the debt owed to Israel due to the unpaid electric bills. The debt which had been growing from month to month had led the IEC to temporarily cut power in various locations. These power outages created heavy international pressure on Israel. The agreement reached in these negotiations allows Israel to deduct some of the money the IEC is owed from the taxes Israel collects for the Palestinian Authority.

Of course, the $130 million that is forgiven and not paid by the Palestinian Authority for electricity already consumed will be picked up by the Israeli taxpayer, both Jewish and Arab, in the form of higher electric bills.

Two years after Operation Protective Edge, On September 6, 2016, Prime Minister Netanyahu was in Holland negotiating a deal whereby Holland would assist Israel in improving gas and water supplies to the energy-strapped Gaza Strip. Both Reuters and the Associated Press reported, "Netanyahu said that while the government is in conflict with what he called 'terrorist forces,' in the Gaza Strip which is controlled by the Islamist Hamas movement, Israel still wishes to improve the quality of life for most people living there." Mr. Netanyahu spoke of laying a gas pipeline and that he was "publicly committed to making this happen," although he did not elaborate on the details of the gas pipeline plan.

The report by Reuters and the Associated Press went on to say, "Currently, the Gaza Strip has electricity less than half the time using an eight hour on, eight hour off rationing system. The power in the territory is supplied by Israel, Egypt, and a single generating plant in the Strip that is insufficient to meet the population's needs." The report stated that Hamas has accused the Palestinian authority of intentionally preventing supplies of diesel fuels from reaching the Strip. The gas pipeline from Israel that Mr. Netanyahu is advocating for the Gazan people would allow Gaza's power plant to double (its) generation.

What's that? Hamas, the governing body of Gaza, accuses the Palestinian Authority, the governing body of the West Bank, of preventing supplies of diesel fuel from reaching Gaza so Israel, whom all the Palestinian factions have pledged to destroy, is not only supplying electricity and water to Gaza but is soliciting the help of Holland to lay a gas pipeline to Gaza to make it more energy self-sufficient! Lunacy?

Israel is continuing the yearly supply of five million cubic meters of water (1,320,860,250 gallons) to Gaza. On Feb. 24, 2017, the New York Times, again, reported on the Palestinians' water shortages, that they were getting as little as twelve hours of water a week. The Palestinians' water is controlled by the Palestinian Water Authority so the oft claimed admonition that Israel is allowing the Palestinians only twelve hours of water a week is, simply, a libel. Israel supplies the water from Israeli wells and has laid hundreds of kilometers of new water mains and connected hundreds of Palestinian villages and towns to the newly built water system, and the Palestinian Water Authority dispenses the water. Israel has nothing to do with how much water, or on what schedule, the Palestinian people get water.

Palestinian policies waste water, whether deliberate or not, and water shortages that they suffer are the result. The Palestinians have declined to develop their own underground water resources. They have not built a water desalination plant, they have refused to fix substantial leakage from their municipal water pipes, build sewage treatment plants, irrigate land with treated sewage effluents, or utilize modern water-saving devices and techniques. They refuse to use the drip irrigation to increase agricultural yield with not only less water but with less fertilizer, also, that half the world uses because it was developed on an Israeli kibbutz. Nor do they bill their "customers" for consumer water usage. Palestinians get their water free (like all of us in the U. S. do, right?) leading, obviously, to enormous waste. No need to limit showers to three minutes as much of the United States does during drought conditions, or to fix a leaky faucet.

Let's recap: Israel supplies the Palestinian Water Authority with water from Israeli wells, under treaty, and has laid hundreds of kilometers of new water mains and connected hundreds of Palestinian villages and towns to the newly built water system; but Israel has not been paid for the water, so this treaty is broken; but Prime Minister Netanyahu goes to Holland to arrange for gas lines for the Palestinians, like he thinks he's going to be paid for whatever payments would be due according to treaty. The Palestinian Water Authority gives its people twelve hours of water a week and the world blames Israel for its mistreatment of the poor, defenseless Palestinians. Defenseless against their own leaders! Obviously, things haven't changed much since Yasser Arafat was stealing billions from the people he was leading as revealed by Leslie Stahl when she hosted a segment on "60 Minutes: Arafat's Billions" on November 7, 2003.

Moreover, Palestinians have drilled, illegally, into Israel's water resources, and they dispose of their sewage by letting it flow into the streams in central Israel. The Palestinian Authority is, actually, using water as a propaganda weapon against Israel. There are practical solutions to solve the Palestinian people's water shortages which could be done if the Palestinian leadership were interested in this but, apparently, they would prefer to perpetuate the shortages and besmirch Israel rather than help their people by providing them with this basic necessity of life.

On AUG 13, 2017, REUTERS Geneva wrote "A crisis in Gaza is depriving two million Gazans of electricity, vital medical care, and clean water in sweltering summer temperatures" due to the feud between Hamas and the PA which is attempting to pressure Hamas to give up control of Gaza. PA Pres. Mahmoud Abbas vowed to keep up sanctions against Hamas-run Gaza where electricity during the hot summer is limited to four hours a day and is having an impact on health care, water, and sanitation services. Meat and dairy products cannot be refrigerated and sewage cannot be processed.

What is the title of this chapter, "Water, Electricity and Stupidity"?

Gaza is not experiencing food scarcity as Israel is not blocking the entrance of goods into Gaza except for weaponry and dual-use materials. Construction materials can be imported into Gaza under the supervision of international organizations.

From January through October 2014, approximately fourteen thousand five hundred patients and their accompanying chaperones entered Israel from Gaza for medical treatment. Ninety-nine percent of the medical requests by Palestinian residents of Gaza are approved by Israel. Israel is not blocking the entrance of medical supplies into Gaza. Requests submitted by the international community are answered within twenty-four to seventy-two hours, almost always positively. At present, there is a shortage of some medical supplies in Gaza due to disagreements between Hamas and the Palestinian Authority and budgetary difficulties of the Palestinian Authority, not because of Israel.

There is a simple cure to this problem and end to the hostilities: Hamas stops firing rockets into Israel and there will be no need for further Israeli responses, including another ground invasion; therefore, a total end to the hostilities.

But the Palestinians refuse to stop the rockets pouring into Israel. So, what do they expect, or want? Do they expect that they can continue to fire their weapons into Israel for another thirteen years and Israel will stop doing what it must do to protect its citizens? Does this even make sense? Does the world expect this? A Gaza spokesman when asked what they want to end this strife replied, "End the occupation." *Where has he been since the 2005 "Land for Peace Agreement" which Gaza signed and Israel pulled out of Gaza? There is no occupation of Gaza! There hasn't been for twelve years!* Is he simply stating that there is no compromise: Israel must be destroyed or is he, simply, being as truthful as the pictures taken from the Internet and presented as theirs?

As Nazralla, the head of Hezbollah stated during the 2006 Lebanon war with the Hezbollah, "We will win and they will lose because they love life and we love death."

The Palestinians say that they will not submit to Israel. Submit to what? What is it that Israel is asking of them? To allow its children to walk to school and home safely, and to get a decent night's sleep? The world says today that there is no military solution, only a diplomatic one. A diplomatic solution with an adversary that will settle for nothing less than Israel's demise? That is incorrect. There is a military solution: stop the rockets pouring into Israel and Israel will stop its counterattacks.

CHAPTER 8

Thorns On the Lemon Tree

I was given a copy of *The Lemon Tree* by Professor Sandy Tolan by a very astute, highly educated, worldly woman, the widow of a navy admiral, a man who, on his retirement from the navy, held a high post in the administration in Washington, D C. *The Washington Post* wrote of this book, "A sweeping history of the Palestinian-Israeli conundrum." It is that, a humanly touching tale of two diverse individuals, Dalia, who was brought to Israel from war-torn Europe by her Jewish parents when she was an infant and Bashir, a Palestinian born in the house that his parents fled and Dalia, subsequently, grew up in. In her late teens and his twenties, Dalia and Bashir met and forged a friendship that would last for the rest of their lives. *The Lemon Tree* is skewed shamelessly towards the Palestinian protagonist's point of view.

I met with Dalia in her home in Jerusalem after sending her a copy of the letter (below) I had written to Sandy Tolan pointing out many of the discrepancies in his novel. An unexpected pleasure was that her son, Raphael, who is, also, in the novel was with her at the time. I was hoping that Dalia would confer with me on a sequel to *The Lemon Tree* both to continue her story and contest some of the blatant deceits which people tend to believe, especially since this book was written by a university professor. Dalia had no interest in pursuing this, perhaps because of her friendship with Bashir.

The Lemon Tree is 264 pages long with 66 pages of notes in type so small, the notes are barely readable; therefore, virtually as much in notes as text. Bashir tells of explosives in booby-trapped toys that the Israeli army would leave for little children to pick up, a toy that he, allegedly, picked up that exploded in his hand taking the palm of his hand and four fingers off.

Nowhere in the extensive notes, notes filled with interviews, historical documents, recollections of family members, memoirs, and personal diaries is there any mention of this grotesque attack on the seven-year-old Bashir, or on any other Palestinian child. Bashir does have a deformed left hand, but this could have happened any time during the violent life he led, or it could have been a birth defect.

Bashir and Dalia, the Palestinian and the Israeli Jew, agreed on the use of the house with the lemon tree in the back yard that had been planted, with love, by Bashir's father when neither were any longer going to live in it. The house is, today, a preschool for Arab children, a community meeting place for Jews and Arabs to get together to talk over what interests them, and a summer camp for Arab and Jewish teens.

CHAPTER 9

The Lemon Tree:

A Synopsis and Critique

(All references signified by page only are from *The Lemon Tree* by Sandy Tolan, Bloomsbury, NY, NY 2006.)

Ordinary citizens, members of Parliament, and officials of the Orthodox Church in the mountainous Republic of Bulgaria defied their King, Boris 111, who had aligned with Hitler's Axis in the Final Solution to the Jewish problem and prevented the deportation of Bulgaria's forty-seven thousand Jews to the Triblinka death camp, benevolent Christians whom Dalia was brought up to revere. Vice President of the Bulgarian Parliament, Dimitur Preshev, presented the Prime Minister with a petition to prevent the expulsion of the Jews. Bishop Kiril, the Orthodox Bishop of the Bulgarian province of Plovdive, said to the fifteen hundred Jews who had been amassed in a schoolyard for deportation to the death camp, "My children, I will not let this happen to you. I will lie on the railroad tracks and will not let you go." p. 36 Thus, the King capitulated and the forty-seven thousand Jews of Bulgaria were spared the fate of almost all of Europe's Jews.

After the war, tens of thousands of Bulgarian Jews made their way to what was to become Israel. In this multitude were Moshe Eshkenazi, before the war a garment salesman in Sofia, the capital of Bulgaria, his wife, Solia, and their eleven-month-old daughter, Daisy, who would change her name to Dalia.

After the Arabs' crushing defeat in the Six Day War in 1967, the government opened the boundaries within Israel and Palestinians from the West Bank were allowed to enter Israel.

Three cousins who had been born in al-Ramla, now the Israeli town of Ramla, boarded a bus in Jerusalem to the town their parents had fled when the boys were very young hoping to visit the homes in which they had been born. Yasser, excitedly, spotted his old home only to be rebuked and screamed at by its Jewish inhabitant with a threat to call the police if the boys didn't leave. They were admitted to Ghiath's boyhood home, now a school, by the principal who gave them tea and told the boys they could walk through the building after the class period ended. After much wandering in the now unfamiliar neighborhood, they found the house where Bashir had been born, and he rang the bell. The bell at the gate Bashir's father had set for his family, with love, was answered by Dalia.

Bashir Khairi's father, Ahmad, laid the first stone of the house he would build for his family outside the Khairi extended family compound--Ahmed wanted to feel independent--in al-Ramla in 1936. The house went up during the year. He built a car port and planted a lemon tree in the back yard. Ahmed and his, again, pregnant wife, Zakia, had four daughters and Ahmed longed for a son. He wanted to pass on the inheritance in the way of his ancestors. Then in 1942 after six daughters, Zakia gave birth to a boy. They named him Bashir.

The year in which Ahmed Khairi's house was built, "Arab farmers in Palestine would produce hundreds of thousands of tons of barley, wheat, cabbage, cucumber, tomato, figs, grapes, and melons…oranges, olives, and almonds." p. 8, 286.

These figures are documented in the extensive notes to *The Lemon Tree*, but how was it possible for such a massive amount of produce to grow in a desert? Olives and figs are documented as having grown in the desert in biblical times and, perhaps, they were growing there long before that. But vegetables require water to grow. The Jews turned the land green, their part of the land. Isn't that how the term "the green line" came into existence? One side, the side irrigated by the Jews, became a lush green and the Arab side remained barren sand, a distinct demarcation. The Arabs called the irrigation systems installed by the Jews "Jewish rain." So how did all the bountiful crops, *hundreds of thousands of tons of grains and vegetables*, grow before the "Jewish rain"? They couldn't. The vegetation described here requires water, water from the irrigation the Palestinians didn't have, except for some small amounts from springs and the local wells to water the kitchen gardens and some small farms to produce enough produce for themselves and to sell at their local markets where Arabs and their Jewish neighbors both shopped on market days.

Had these figures been accurate and hundreds of thousands of tons of produce been produced, what was done with the excess over the meager domestic consumption considering the small population and that families tended to have their own kitchen gardens? There was no infrastructure to allow the movement of this produce to markets outside the neighboring Arab villages and towns. There were a few small railways, mostly to facilitate the passage of Arabs to Mecca, but these, certainly, didn't have the refrigeration capacity to transport hundreds of thousands of tons of perishable vegetables to markets in Europe and Asia.

> "A telegram from the American Consulate in Jerusalem on August 12 (1948) …'Refugees entirely dependent on springs for water, standing in line hours for turn to fill cans…Definitely possible that water supply will give out completely before end of August.'" p. 87.
>
> And this was the water supply that produced the hundreds of thousands of tons of barley, wheat, cabbage, cucumber, tomato, figs, grapes, and melons…oranges, olives, and

> almonds! One hundred thousand refugees had descended upon Ramallah, but the water supply that had allowed these hundreds of thousands of tons of vegetables to grow was not sufficient to supply even the barest needs of these refugees. "Additional description comes from an interview with eyewitnesses Abu Issam Harb (and) Palestinian folklorist Dr. Sharif Kanaana of Bir Zeit University, 'Sanitation practically nonexistent…no water available for bathing or laundry.'" p. 315

On November 29, 1947, the United Nations voted to partition Palestine into two states, one for the Arabs and one for the Jews. "Reaction...was swift. Palestinians, backed by other Arab leaders, immediately rejected the partition and pledged to fight it…Egypt's Minister of War boasted, 'The Egyptian military is capable on its own of occupying Tel Aviv, the capital of the Jews, in fifteen days.' It appeared that Arab armies could eliminate the Jewish State before it was even established." p. 51.

Attacks and counterattacks ensued, including the destruction of the headquarters of the ex-mufti's commander right outside al-Ramla by the *Hagana.* "The people of al-Ramla grew increasingly worried. If the mufti's commander could not guard even his own headquarters, how could he protect the city's residents?" p. 52.

Then the terrifying news of the massacres and rapes by the Jewish militia at the nearby village of Dier Yassin reached the people of al-Ramla, including Ahmed and Zakia Khairi with their nine children, seven of them girls. Egyptian forces were attacking in the south, Syrian and Iraqi forces were entering from the north, King Abdulla's Arab Legion was crossing the Jordan River and marching west, and al-Ramla was under attack. A bomb went off in the Wednesday market while Ahmed was there, but he wasn't hurt.

Ahmed moved his family into the family compound, but he had had enough. In forty-eight hours, the British would be leaving and whatever order their presence had provided would be gone. Despite pleas not to abandon al-Ramla, Ahmed hired two cars and took his family to Ramallah.

What Ahmed Khairi and other Palestinians did not know was that the story of Dier Yassin, the massacres and the rapes, was a hoax perpetrated by Palestinian leaders to inveigle additional Arab forces to invade but instead incited fear and caused much of the local population to flee. I refer the reader to the following link: http://best-hoaxes.blogspot.com/2009/12/deir-yassin-massacre-hoax-originated-by.html "Best Hoaxes and Pranks." Here is an abbreviated account of the Dier Yassin massacre by "Best Hoaxes and Pranks."

On April 8, 1948, the *Hagana* commenced an attack on Dier Yassin between 4: and 5: am in an attempt to open the road to Jerusalem where the Jewish population was enduring severe shortages of food and water. The *Hagana* mounted a loudspeaker on an armored car and warned the Arabs, asking them to evacuate their women and children. A ferocious battle took place and when it was over, one hundred and ten to one hundred and twenty Arabs lay dead, forty Jews were gravely wounded, and four Jews had been killed. The total killed has been validated even by Palestinian Arab academics such as Bir Zeit University (an Arab university near Ramallah) Professor Sharif Kanaana who places the number at no more than one hundred and twenty Arab men killed. A different contemporaneous Arab resource decreased the total put down to under one hundred, affirming, after a count that "there were no more than forty-six corpses."

"An Arab research study conducted at Bir Zeit University relates that the men of Dier Yassin took an active part in violent acts against Jewish targets," that more than a hundred men had been trained and equipped with rifles and Bren guns and that forty inhabitants guarded the village every night."

Strict orders (documented) were given, in advance, to the Israeli commanders and fighters not to harm the elderly, women, and children. It was also ordered, unequivocally, that any Arab who surrendered was to be taken prisoner.

"The use of the loudspeaker to warn the civilians to evacuate is a key point, certainly not the action of soldiers planning to murder the population." The use of the loudspeaker has been confirmed. An Arab League publication titled *Israeli Aggression* states: "On the night of April 9, 1948, the peaceful Arab village of Deir Yassin was surprised by a loudspeaker, which called on the population to evacuate it immediately." The village was hardly peaceful, but the fundamental part of this quote agrees with Jewish accounts.

The slaughter of powerless people, the massacre assertion, has been totally brought into disrepute by abundant historical investigations. The story endures because pro-Arab spokespersons continuously restate it, frequently increasing the amount of dead to two hundred and fifty, or more. There are totally untrue versions scripted about Arabs being walked to the mosque and opened fire on against the walls, or still baser falsehoods of torture, rape, or any other outrageous aspect the storyteller contrives. To articulate that there is not a sliver of proof for these aggrandizements is awarding them too much credit.

There are eyewitness accounts from the time, both Jewish and Arab, which relate the story as it actually occurred. For instance, as stated in the British *Daily Telegraph*, April 8, 1998, a resident of the village and a survivor of the fighting there, Ayish Zeidan, stated: "The Arab radio talked of women being killed and raped, but this is not true…most of those who were killed were among the fighters and the women and children who helped the fighters." Apparently, a big mistake was committed by the Arab leadership. They thought they would encourage people to fight back harder by exaggerating the atrocities. But this attempt backfired. Instead, they generated panic and people fled.

Dier Yassin was a realistic military target for Jewish forces, there was notice given in advance of the battle, and then a brutal battle was waged with fatalities on both sides. No atrocities, no massacre, no mutilations. Palestinian Arab observers have lately acknowledged that certain of their accusations about Dier Yassin were purposeful fabrications. The edition of the *Jerusalem Report* dated April 2, 1998, tells of a BBC television program in which an editor of the Palestine Broadcasting Service's Arabic news in 1948, Hazem Nusseibeh, acknowledged that he was instructed by Hussein Khalidi, a renowned Palestinian Arab leader, to concoct allegations of brutalities at Dier Yassin so as to incite Arab regimes to attack the anticipated Jewish state.

According to the Jerusalem Report, Nusseibeh told of a chance meeting at the Jaffa Gate of Jerusalem's Old City with Deir Yassin survivors and Palestinian leaders, including Hussein Khalidi. He said that he asked Dr. Khalidi how he should write the story. Nusseibeh said that Dr. Khalidid told him, “We must make the most of this.” So Nusseibeh wrote a press release stating that at Deir Yassin children were slaughtered, pregnant women were raped. “All sorts of atrocities" said a BBC Report, “Israel and the Arabs: The 50 Year Conflict”

The BBC program then shows a recent interview with Abu Mahmud, who was a Dier Yassin resident in 1948, who said “the villagers protested against the atrocity claims. We said, ‘There was no rape.’ [Khalidi] said, ‘We have to say this, so the Arab armies will come to liberate Palestine from the Jews.’” Khalidi was one of the inventors of the "massacre" assertion in 1948.

Nusseibeh, who comes from one of Jerusalem's most renowned Arab families and presently lives in Amman, Jordan, told the BBC that the invented massacre stories about Dier Yassin were “our principal biggest mistake because Palestinians fled in terror and left the country in huge numbers after hearing the atrocity claims.”

Fearing for their seven daughters because of the stories of the rapes, Ahmed and Zakia Khairi decided to take their seven daughters and their two youngest, six year old Bashir and his younger brother, Bhajat,from al-Ramla based on these fabrications of Hussein Khalidi, a prominent Palestinian Arab leader, who was determined to "make the most of this."

Ahmed and his family arrived in Ramallah several months before the rest of the Khairi clan who, on their arrival, jammed in and shared the house Ahmed had rented, as many as ten to a room.

Zakia was, now, in charge of the family finances selling her jewelry to fend off family hunger with the bread, olives, cooking oil, and vegetables she was able to purchase with the proceeds. The Red Cross and King Abdullah of Jordan sent trucks loaded with bread and "the occasional sack of tomatoes or eggplants…to prevent starvation" of the one hundred thousand refugees who had fled to Ramallah. p. 88

Gen. John Bagot Glubb, the British-trained commander of the Arab Legion arrived in Ramallah and was stoned by the destitute and furious refugees. Gen. Glubb had refused to advance to protect al-Ramla and neighboring Lydda fearing that such a redeployment of troops would have allowed the Israelis to advance in other strategic spots such as Latrun and Ramallah. However, the now starving refugees who had been promised protection and promised that they would be able to return to their homes in fifteen days felt betrayed by King Abdullah and Gen. Glubb. They demanded that the lost towns be recaptured at once.

Amid the chaos, the misery that was surrounding them and the grim prospects in Ramallah--Ahmed had not found work--Ahmed and Zakia decided to move the family to Gaza where they had relatives with property and where, perhaps, Ahmed would be able to find work. Not only the Khairi family, but two hundred thousand Palestinian refugees poured into Gaza "more than tripling its population" and causing a density of "two thousand people per square mile…Wages plummeted by nearly two-thirds." p. 96-97

With his furniture-making skills, Ahmed was employed by UNRWA (the newly formed United Nations Relief and Works Agency) making furniture for refugees for which he was paid in additional rations of flour, rice, sugar, and fat. UNRWA was created "to generate jobs and housing for the hundreds of thousands of Palestinian refugees in Jordan, Lebanon, Syria, the West Bank, and Gaza." p. 97

And unthinkable in their society, Zakia and the elder daughters would work. They "made extra money embroidering Palestinian table covers and pillows and by knitting sweaters and scarves…Zakia, only months removed from a life of servants, perfumes, and private baths had become crucial to the families survival."

She removed her veil. p. 98

In November of 1948, the government began to resettle the remains of the European Jews who had arrived in Israel from the transit camps that had been established as temporary housing for them along the Mediterranean coast near Haifa. Moshe and Solia Eshkenazi with their infant daughter who would be one year old the following month were on the first busload to arrive in the abandoned town of Ramla. They had been told they could choose any house. Moshe and Solia found a house with an open layout and plenty of space. It had a lemon tree in the back yard. Dalia went to school in an Arab house. She learned how the Arabs had invaded to throw the Jews into the sea. She learned that other European Christians "did not show the courage of the Bulgarian Orthodox Church." p.114 In 1966, Dalia graduated from high school and prepared to enter Tel Aviv University.

June 1967 Bashir Khairi, twenty-five years old and recently graduated from Cairo University, now a lawyer, advocates force to return his people to their homes. "Force expelled us from our land, he reasoned, and only force will get it back." p. 123 *Herein lies the crux of the entire matter*! Bashir was only six years old when his parents fled from their lovely home with the lemon tree in the yard. He was not privy to the fear his parents, who had seven daughters at the time, felt on hearing of the fictional rapes in the neighboring village of Dier Yassin. He, certainly, didn't learn in school that Hussein Khalidi, a prominent Palestinian Arab leader, had perpetrated this hoax and had fabricated claims of atrocities including the rapes that Bashir's parents so feared at Dier Yassin in order to encourage Arab regimes to invade the impending Jewish state, but that instead Khalidi had created panic *and the people ran away! His parents took their children and ran away! The Ahmed Khairi family was not forced out; they had run away!*

This and more Bashir, certainly, had not learned in school. He, surely, hadn't learned that his family and the hundreds of thousands of other refugees had been used by their leaders, that Jamal Husseini, a member of the Arab Higher Committee in Palestine in response to the British High Commissioner Sir Alan Cunningham's expressed concern for the welfare of the ordinary Palestinian people had threatened *jihad* stating that not only was he prepared to die but the ordinary Arab population was prepared to die, too.

Jamal Husseini, certainly, had not conferred with Ahmed Khairi regarding Mr. Khairi's feelings about sacrificing his family's wellbeing by taking them from their lovely home in the community where they lived and he earned his living in *jihad,* or if Khairi was prepared to totally sacrifice his family and let them die. Was Bashir taught in school that Azzam Pasha, Secretary-General of the Arab League announced to the Secretary-General of the United Nations, "It will be a war of extermination. It will be a war of annihilation. It will be a momentous massacre in history that will be talked about like the massacres of the Mongols or the Crusades"?

Was Azzam Pasha even concerned with the welfare and security of Ahmed Khairi's family during this war that would take place where Khairi was living with his family of eleven, about what could happen to them during this war that he, Pasha, was willing to wage where the Khairis lived, thrusting them into the midst of the war?

Why does Bashir say that he was forced out of his home? In all the years of his growing up, had the circumstances of their leaving the house his father had built, with love, for his family in al-Ramla outside the Khairi extended family compound with the lemon tree in the yard never been discussed? Ahmed Khairi was an honorable man. He would not have fabricated a story of being forced from his home. He would have said that out of fear of his daughters being raped, he took his family to what he thought would be out of harm's way. Ahmed Khairi had been duped by the Palestinian officials, just as Bashir was duped all the years he was growing up. Now, as he enters his adult years, finished with university, what can we expect of the misguided, angry Bashir Khairi?

Ramallah, where Bashir had returned to after completing is studies and had started practicing law, was under military occupation, the justice system administered by occupation judges. The Palestinian lawyers went on strike against the new order. "The strike was organized…by a young West Bank lawyer named Bashir Khairi." p. 141 "Bashir began to believe that his people would go back to their homeland only through the sweat and blood of Palestinian armed struggle." p. 142

How brainwashed had intelligent Bashir, an attorney, become? How could he not be aware that the reason his people were under occupation was because they had instigated two wars, both to drive the Jews into the sea, and had been defeated in both!

And what did Israel want in return for leaving the lands it had captured with the blood of its sons and daughters? Recognition and the guarantee that it could live in peace, simply live in peace. The Palestinian leaders who were so willing to sacrifice their people, to wage a war where Ahmed Khairi lived with his family and where hundreds of thousands other Palestinians lived refused to agree to such outlandish Israeli demands, demands for peace.

Flashback: Dalia welcomed the three cousins into the house and showed them around. She and Bashir had shared the same bedroom, at different times. Dalia mentioned Bashir's family leaving the house. "Bashir wanted to explode, to yell, *We didn't leave the house. You forced us out!*" p. 147

He didn't know! He really didn't know that his father had hired two cars and left, voluntarily, because Dr. Hussein Khalidi, a prominent Palestinian Arab leader, had fabricated claims of atrocities at neighboring Dier Yassin in order to encourage Arab regimes to invade the projected Jewish state and wanted to "make the most of the situation." Ahmed Khairi took his family away from the house "so his daughters wouldn't be raped."

It appears that Bashir didn't know the real cause of the *nakba*, or the causes for the '67 War. He was angry at the refugee problem, but he wasn't angry at the neighboring Arab states that kept the refugees in squalid camps or, simply, in poverty, as he had grown up in poverty. Why not? Why wasn't Bashir angry that his fellow Arabs didn't integrate their refugees into their society as Israel did with the refugees who came to her into her society? Bashir Khairi knew only what he had been taught, and he was angry about that. *The makings of a terrorist!*

But, can we completely blame Bashir? Schoolbooks used in UNWRA (United Nations Relief and Works Agency) in Gaza and the West Bank show extreme anti-Israel and anti-Jewish sentiments and state that there is no hope for peace in the region. The textbooks show indoctrination to violent struggle instead of peace. The books convey that the Jews have no right to be in Palestine and have no holy places here, the Western Wall, the Cave of the Patriarchs, and Rachel's Tomb presented as Muslim holy places.

Israel is not a legitimate state according to the books studied in UNWRA schools. The name, "Israel," is just about completely erased from these textbooks. Even the name, "the Arab-Israeli conflict" is called, "the Arab-Zionist" conflict. According to these texts, Jews first arrived here in 1882, not thousands of years ago. A Molotov cocktail attack on a civilian Israeli bus is described as a "barbeque party," and a Palestinian female terrorist who killed more than thirty civilians in another bus attack is exalted. The UNWRA schools not only propagate non-peaceful lines but, also, advance the preparing of the young pupils for war against Israel.

Now, after the Six Day War, when Israel lifted the boundaries that Jordan had imposed when it controlled the West Bank from 1948 till 1967, many Palestinians returned to view their former homes, just like Bashir and his cousins. The longing to return, a return that would never occur, grew. "The sudden nearness of the lost gardens made exile even more intolerable." Yasser Arafat, George Habash, and other revolutionaries had been launching attacks into Israel since 1965 vowing "to recover their dignity and their lost lands, to get justice," p. 150 Justice, for having started two wars and suffered devastating defeats in both? This, no doubt, is what was fuming in angry, budding terrorist, Bashir Khairi.

Dalia accepted Bashir's invitation to visit his family in Ramallah. She arrived, unannounced, on a cold, dark winter day and was, almost immediately, overwhelmed by the warmth and hospitality flowing towards her from Bashir's family. But as Bashir spoke of his beliefs about the Palestinians' right to the land they both coveted, she was forced to think, "What am I doing here…What is the point of continuing this conversation?" p. 162

Bashir told Dalia that "Israel first came to the imagination of the Western occupying powers for two reasons…to get rid of you in Europe (and) to rule the East through this government and to keep down the whole Arab world. And then the leaders started remembering the Torah… " p. 160

Where had Bashir, who didn't even know how his own leaders, his own Palestinian leaders, had willingly sacrificed their people to a cause they are unable to win come up with such felonious reasons for the Jewish people returning to their ancestral land, a land that has had a continuous presence of Jews living in it, speaking their native tongue, for more than three thousand years? Is this what he was taught in school, what he learned at his university in Cairo or from his equally uninformed friends, or is this, simply, what he conjured up because it is what he wants, in the deepest depths of his soul, to believe?

Is Bashir Khairi, who doesn't know the true cause of the plight of the Palestinians, his own people, to be considered an authority on the desires of Western powers, European Jews, *or on the Torah*? Foolishness! Bashir can be considered an authority on hatred, hatred born out of the deplorable condition he finds his family and the hundreds of thousands of other sacrificed Palestinian families in because he was ignorant of the cause of this depravity brought on by Azzam Pasha, Secretary-General of the Arab League, Jamal Husseini, a member of the Arab Higher Committee in Palestine, and Dr. Khalidi, a prominent Palestinian Arab leader, one of the originators of the fabricated "massacre" allegation in 1948.

But Bashir should have been aware that his people were lied to by their own leaders. On hearing that the 1967 war had started, Bashir, excited, rushed home to find "Ahmed, Zakia, Nuha, and other siblings transfixed before the radio. Egyptian aircraft fire had shot down three-quarters of the attacking Israeli jets, the Voice of the Arabs reported from Cairo…Israeli forces had penetrated Sinai, but the Egyptian troops had engaged the enemy and taken the offensive. Jordan, the Voice of the Arabs announced, had captured Mt. Scopus, a strategic hill in Jerusalem...We thought victory was in our hands…It was an illusion.

"By the time Bashir and his family heard the reports of the Egyptian advances, Gamal Abdel Nasser's entire air force lay smoking on tarmacs in Cairo, Sinai, and the Nile delta…Israel had destroyed virtually all of Egypt's Soviet-built fighter jets." p. 136 Triumphal messages from Jordan did not relay the facts. "By midafternoon of June 5, the air forces of Jordan, Syria, Iraq, and Egypt had all been demolished…the Six Day War was, essentially, decided in six hours." p. 137

Had the family switched to the Syrian radio station, this is what BBC reported, "Radio Damascus reports a 'massive Egyptian victory over the Zionist aggressor…with forty-seven Jewish planes already shot down. No Egyptian losses are reported.'"

In the entire war, Israel lost two planes.

And Bashir never came to the realization that all was not as his teachers, Arabic radio, and Arab leaders claimed, that his people were, in fact, being lied to! Bashir, an educated man, a lawyer trained to depict what an adversary would say, never questioned what he was told even after he became aware that "Egyptian aircraft fire had shot down three-quarters of the attacking Israeli jets" and a "massive Egyptian victory over the Zionist aggressor...with forty-seven Jewish planes already shot down. No Egyptian losses are reported" were lies!

Bashir, also, told Dalia, "We have a history here: Lydda, Haifa, Jaffa, al-Ramla. Many Jews who came here believed they were a people without a land going to a land without a people. That is ignoring the indigenous people of this land...Why did this happen, Dalia?" p.161

Bashir, again, your hatred is born out of ignorance which, perhaps, you are not accountable for. No, the Jews did not think they were going to a land without a people. They knew you were here, and they were willing to accept less than they thought they were entitled to, less than they wanted, and were willing to share the land with you according to the division of the land by the United Nations. It was your leaders who were willing to sacrifice you in their greedy quest for all the land.

Were you not taught that you are the interlopers? No, of course not. You, undoubtedly, were not taught that the Jews were here in this land more than a thousand years before a Jew whom the whole world knows and much of the world worships, a Jew named Jesus Christ, was born in this Jewish land, born of Jewish parents. You use Jaffa as a testament to your "history" here. Jaffa!

Walk down to the big tourist plaza in Jaffa from the main road. On your walk on the right side you will see a building with an overhang protecting Hebrew writing that is *four thousand years old*!

Where was Mohammed four thousand years ago? He wasn't born, yet. Mohammed lived only in the sixth century, fourteen hundred years ago, much less than half the time that the Jews have inhabited this land. Jews inscribed that writing three thousand years before Mohammed was even born! And al-Ramla, named "from the Arabic word for sand, *raml.*" p. 8 *That*, certainly, had to be thousands of years after there is recorded Jewish history, here. Your own descendants came in the sixteenth century when Khair al-Din al-Ramlawi came from Morocco. p. 8. Is that where the name al-Ramla really came from, from your ancestor al-Ramlawi, in the sixteenth century, four hundred years ago? Well, the Jew, Jesus Christ, was born in this Jewish land two thousand and seventeen years ago.

Haifa? Haifa has a history three thousand years old. You offer Lydda and al-Ramla as historical basis for your claim to this land? Well, what about Jerusalem, Tiberius, Be'er Sheva where one can go today to visit Abraham's well, or Nazareth, the then thousand-year-old city from where Joseph and his pregnant wife, Mary, traveled to Jerusalem? Didn't you ever hear that "Joshua fought the battle of Jericho and the walls came tumbling down?"

No, Bashir, you are not the indigenous people. The American Indians are the indigenous people in the Americas. They were there a thousand years before the first European looked westward towards that land. The Native Americans had a rightful claim on their land. *You do not!*

There was a people in this land long, long before you came. They are called "Jews." In fact, to a large extent, you are squatters. Your family, Bashir, was bequeathed its land by a rightful owner, but most of the Palestinians simply lived on land they did not own. Much of the land was purchased by the Jews from absentee Arab owners who weren't at all concerned that the squatters on the land they sold would be dispossessed by the new owners.

The Slate Gist: A Cheat Sheet for the News, May 18, 1997 "Selling Land to Jews" by Franklin "Jews acquired huge tracts of farmland from absentee Syrian and Lebanese landlords." The Jewish National Fund, founded in 1904 for the purpose of buying land from Arabs, was effective in purchasing land, mostly from absentee Arab landholders who hadn't the least bit of compunction about evicting the Palestinian peasants that had been living on the newly sold plots. The Palestinians said the "evictions destroyed their way of life, forcing them to move from rural Palestine to crowded cities in search of work." The Zionists purchasers of the lands maintained that the land purchases benefited all the territory's peoples. Jewish immigrants brought modern agricultural technology to the land which heightened productivity and helped fill the markets with food to feed the growing population, both Jewish and Arab.

But the Arabs claimed that at the time of the Zionist land purchases "Arab farmers in Palestine would produce hundreds of thousands of tons of barley, wheat, cabbage, cucumber, tomato, figs, grapes, and melons...oranges, olives, and almonds." p. 8, 286.

The Arab markets should have been full, overflowing, before the introduction of modern agricultural technology, including irrigation, which the Arab farmers did not have and dubbed "Jewish rain," to increase productivity. Zionists also maintain that Jews became a lucrative market for Arab-manufactured goods.

Wildolive, November 2010 documents a 1937 report of the British Palestine Royal Commission which states that the Hula Valley in the north of the country was infested with mosquitoes. "The landowners were Syrians in Damascus who leased out the marshes to Arab or Egyptian peasants (*fellahs*) who lived in primitive mud huts and inevitably fell sick with malaria."

In 1934 when the Jewish National Fund purchased fifty-one square miles of marshland for $4.5 million, it set up twenty Jewish settlements on the land and the first thing they did was to drain the swamps in an attempt to battle the malaria and yellow fever that was prevalent, there, and that had killed so many Arabs farmers and their families, and reclaim the land. "The Arab landlords, who lived abroad and owned large estates, had done nothing to solve these problems." The wealthy Arab landowners from Syria, Egypt, and Lebanon, simply, kicked out the *fellahs* and Bedouins from their enormous tracts of real estate. "Then they made a huge profit by selling the land to Jews from Europe and America."

The wealthy, absentee landowners had been extracting onerous interest rates of *up to sixty percent* from the Arab farmers who leased the lands and many tenants were left destitute, losing their farms and their homes. "Ultimately, the Arab landowners drove out their Muslim brothers so that they could sell the land for large amounts of money to the Jews...What was to happen to the renter from whom the land was sold from under his feet concerned the landowners very little." The renter was just thrown out, thrown off the land. In northern Jerusalem, at least seven hundred illegal housing units were constructed by Arabs on land purchased for Jews by the Jewish National Fund (JNF).

An article published in July 1911 by Mustafa Effendi Tamr, an Arab teacher of mathematics at a Jerusalem school reads, "You are selling the property of your fathers and grandfathers." The article states that the Zionists bought the land from Arab landholders who were either absentee landholders or who took the money and moved to cities, or even left the country. It says that the Arab landlords were all too willing to sell because the price paid by the Zionist purchasers was often many times more than anyone else would or could pay. The landowners made a killing, with no regard for the Arab *fellahs* and the Bedouin whom they had been living off of.

King Abdallah of Jordan complains several times in his memoirs about Jews acquiring land in Palestine. Not once does he accuse the Jews of stealing it from the Arabs. Each time he mentions it, his protest is the vast amount of land the Jews are "buying" and that the land policy of the Zionist movement in the pre-state era was grounded on purchase of land on the open market by Jewish institutions (mainly the JNF) and then freezing its ownership so as to guarantee that the purchased land would be in Jewish hands in perpetuity.

Not only was the land being legally purchased, it was being purchased at drastically inflated prices. Arab land owners were making a killing selling their land during the waves of Jewish immigration in the late nineteenth and early twentieth centuries. It, simply, made good economic sense for landlords to sell while they could exploit the thriving market the Jewish demand was creating. Sometimes the land being purchased was nothing more than sand dune, malarial swamps and marshes, or other unattractive plots of waste. Even so, it was payday for many landlords, a day many hadn't seen in a long time and one that, they were aware, would never come again.

Bashir, also, insisted to Dalia that only Jews who were in Palestine prior to "1917, the date of the Balfour Declaration and the beginning of the British Mandate in Palestine, have a right to be here...But anyone who came after 1917...cannot stay." p. 161 Bashir did not explain why he picked that historical date rather than another; but if his reason is as uninformed as the rest of his reasoning, it makes no difference.

Bashir said, "...cannot stay"! What does he think he can do, start yet another war where his fellow Arabs live so that they can, again, lose wreaking even more havoc on his brethren? Bashir's bravado echoes The Voice of Cairo daring Israel to strike just before the Six Day War, "We challenge you, Eshkol, to try all your weapons. Put them to the test. They shall spell Israel's death and annihilation" which Gen. Peled deemed "unheard of foolishness."

Bashir's "cannot stay" is exactly that, "unheard of foolishness." How about this? Only Arabs who were here prior to the fourteenth century have a right to be here. Anyone who came after the fourteenth century cannot stay. Since the Jews have by far the historical claim to the land, doesn't that make more sense?

Dalia was unnerved by Bashir's statement as she had not even been born in 1917, and also because Bashir had said that Dalia's people "stole" the country from his people. (How, by first purchasing the land from Arab landowners who were willing to line their pockets at exorbitant prices at the expense of their brethren who had been living on the land and paying these landlords extortionate amounts to do so and then winning the two wars the Arabs had started in their attempt to drive the Jews into the sea, or to massacre them?)

By now, Dalia should have realized that Bashir was not interested in facts, that he could conjure up any bizarre fiction to support his, very unlikely unknown to him, ill-founded desires. In answer to Bashir's insistence that Jews who were not here before 1917 leave, Dalia, the kind-hearted young woman of nineteen, a considerate guest in this warm and welcoming home and out pitted by this lawyer, asked the wrong question, "Where shall we go?" She could have said, "No, we were here first, by many millennia. You go." Instead, respectful, caring Dalia's innocent question appeared to give credence to Bashir's outlandish thesis.

Bashir's reply was that this was not his problem.

The visit was over. Dalia left. During her well-intentioned visit and while she was experiencing Arab hospitality at its finest, Dalia had been exposed to Bashir's philosophy of the reasons the Jews were sent to Palestine from Europe, the Palestinians historical claim to the land, that the Palestinians were the indigenous people in the land, and that all Jews not there by 1917 "must go."

Actually, the term "Palestinian Nation" is something that was created in the recent past, as is the term "Palestinian children." This is, in point of fact, a non-existent nation, not a legal and historic entity such as Israel is. History speaks of the nation of Israel, of the sons of Israel (*Bnei Israel*). Charles Krauthammer has said, "the Jewish people have maintained a well-documented, unbroken presence in Israel for well over three thousand years beginning in the second millennium B.C.E. and continuing under a long series of Jewish kingdoms and foreign rulers through to the modern State of Israel. Conquerors, diplomats, and pilgrims throughout the millennia have left an abundance of references to the Jewish communities living there. Israel is filled with archaeological and historical sites, many of which testify to Jewish life over the centuries. Even the Muslim Qur'an refers to the Jewish people as the 'Children of Israel.'"

Israel is the very embodiment of Jewish continuity: it is the only nation on earth that inhabits the same land, bears the same name, speaks the same language, and worships the same God that it did three thousand years ago. You dig the soil and you find pottery from Davidic times, coins from Bar Kokhba, and two thousand-year-old scrolls written in a script remarkably like the one used today.

But nowhere in the annals of mankind is there a Palestinian state or nation. Nowhere in history was there ever a country called Palestine. Nowhere is there a book documenting the "History of the Palestinian People." In 2017, a book on the history of Palestine *consisting entirely of empty pages* became a bestseller on Amazon.com. The Koran does not speak of Palestine. It is another writing, the so-called "Palestinian Doctrine," which is instilled in Arab children from birth that teaches them that their goal in life is to kill Jews even it means blowing themselves up, though they still have their whole lives before them.

One side's revolutionary is the other side's terrorist. But one is only a revolutionary if he believes that his cause is just. Bashir's hypothetical analogies appear to show that he is determined to drive the Jews out of the land. He wants what he wants without even considering that the other side, the side that was willing to share the land with the Palestinian people, may have a claim on this land, also; and he is determined to get what he wants by whatever means necessary.

February 21, 1969, a bomb exploded in a Supersol market in Jerusalem. Two dead and others grotesquely mutilated, some with limbs blown off. Bashir Khairi was accused of taking part in the bombing. He was a member of George Habash's Popular Front for the Liberation of Palestine (PFLP) which had hijacked a plane and killed several people. Bashir would be tried by an Israeli military court. He was tried and sentenced to fifteen years in prison. Palestinian informers testified about Bashir's participation in the bombing.

Dalia had opened the Eshkenazi family home to Bashir and his family and had experienced the Khiari family's warmth and hospitality in return. With Bashir's conviction, he had confirmed a prejudice, "…Arabs kill Jews simply because they are Jews. Yeah, everything stopped…The door she had opened was closed…

"In September 1972, eight Palestinian gunmen snuck into the Olympic village at Munich shooting two Israeli athletes dead and capturing nine more. In a subsequent shootout at a military base with German police, fourteen people died, including all of the Israeli hostages." p. 180

The PFLP hijacked more airplanes. In September, 1970, Arab faction fought Arab faction, mostly in Jordan. "When Syria crossed the Jordanian border to fight on the side of the Palestinians, the king secretly contacted Israel asking for air support against the Syrians…it was Arab against Arab…killing thousands of Palestinians…the month would be known to Palestinians as Black September" p. 175

In Israel, the Palestinians bombed busses, busses that Palestinian children often rode on. Later, in 1976, the PFLP would hijack the Air France plane in Athens, Greece, and take it to Entebbe, Uganda, where Israeli forces would perform its daring liberation of the plane and almost all its passengers.

Dalia still thought of Bashir, thought of making contact with him. She, also, waited for some signal from Bashir, hoping for a letter from him, a letter which never came. Of the long-awaited Khairi son, born after seven daughters, Bashir's oldest sister, Khanom, would say he gave the family pleasure two times, the day he was born in September 1942 and on the day he was released from prison after serving his fifteen year sentence.

Although "Khairis rarely married outside the clan…Ahmed was an exception." p. 9

Bashir's sister, Nuha, married their cousin, Ghiath who was one of the three who had ventured to Ramla and visited the school housed in his childhood home before the three young men rang the bell that was answered by Dalia. Bashir married his cousin, Scheherazade, and had a child who he named after his recently deceased father, Ahmed. That same year, 1985, Moshe Eshkenazi died, eight years after his wife, Solia, had passed away. Dalia had married and was living in Jerusalem; and now the house with the lemon tree in the back yard, the house that Ahmed Khairi had built for his family, with love, outside the family compound, the house that had sheltered two diverse families and which, now, belonged to Dalia was empty.

It had been eighteen years since the friends, Dalia Eshkenazi and Bashir Khairi had seen each other. Dalia arranged a meeting in Ramallah to discuss what was to be done with the house that held the memories, the histories, of two families. Dalia was willing to sell the house and give the money to Bashir, but Bashir would not hear of selling his "patrimony." It was decided: the house would become a preschool for Arab children, according to Bashir's wishes. Bashir wanted the children to have the childhood in that house that he never had. "What I lost there, I want to give to them." Dalia declined Bashir's suggestion for a name, "Dalia's Kindergarten for the Arab Children of Ramla" p. 191 "and a center for Arab-Jewish coexistence…They would call it 'Open House.'" p.222 By its fifth year, Open House, also, housed "summer peace camps for Arab and Jewish children." p. 230 Food was served and Dalia and her husband gave the blessing in Hebrew.

1987, the start of the first *intifada*. After only three years from his release from prison, Bashir was convicted by a military court of being a leader and instigator of the ongoing disturbances in the West Bank and Gaza by Yasser Arafat's Fatah and the newly formed Hamas which decreed "no recognition of Israel and no compromise on the right of return…an Islamic state in all of historic Palestine. Its charter described the Jews as conspiring 'to rule the world.'" p. 194

Bashir and three others would be deported. Although blindfolded, Bashir was aware that he was being taken by helicopter. The helicopter landed in the demilitarized zone of southern Lebanon where cars were waiting to drive the four deportees north, further into Lebanon.

Dalia's husband, Yehezkel Landau, suggested to her that she write about Bashir and the house in an effort to help Bashir. Dalia was too weak to consider this.

Dalia, at the age of forty, kept abreast of the uprisings as she lay in her hospital bed. Diagnosed with cancer and against the advice of her doctors, Dalia was determined to have the baby in spite of the warnings that she was risking her life. As the deportation loomed, Dalia had a change of heart. The January 14, 1988, edition of the *Jerusalem*

Post carried Dalia Landau's "Letter to a Deportee."

"Dear Bashir,

"Dalia recounted for the Israeli readers the story of the Eshkenazis, the Khairis, (how she and Bashir met), and the house in Ramla; Bashir's visit to the house after the Six Day War; Dalia's visit to Ramla and the 'warm, personal connection' they established across the gulf of political differences; and her understanding, ultimately, that the house that she, Moshe, and Solia moved into in November, 1948, was not, simply 'abandoned property…'

"It was very painful for me, as a young woman twenty years ago, to wake up to a few then well-hidden facts. For example, we were all led to believe that the Arab population of Ramla and Lod had run away…in a rushed and cowardly escape…But after 1967, I met not only you, but also an Israeli Jew who had personally participated in the expulsion from Ramla and Lod. He told me the story as he had experienced it, and as Yitzhak Rabin later confirmed in his memoirs.

"(Dalia) then recounted the 'unforgettable day' of Ahmed Khairi's only visit to the house he had built, with love, for his family and the moment when he stood at the lemon tree, tears rolling down his face, as Moshe Eshkenazi plucked a few lemons from the tree and placed them in Ahmed's hands…"

Dalia had come to the realization that "that home was not just my home. The lemon tree which yielded so much fruit and gave us so much delight lived in other people's hearts too. The spacious house with its high ceilings, big windows and large grounds was no long just an 'Arab house,' a desirable form of architecture. It had faces behind it now…

"Dalia described a 'strange destiny' that connected her family to Bashir's. Though the plans for turning the house into a kindergarten and a center for Arab-Jewish dialogue had long been delayed…Dalia questioned whether genuine reconciliation could be possible across the chasm as wide as the one between herself and Bashir. She recounted Bashir's conviction and prison term in the aftermath of the explosion that killed three civilians and mutilated others in the Supersol market…and then pleaded with Bashir to transform his politics.

"Dalia told Bashir that his support of George Habash and the PFLP—support he had never acknowledged, but which she assumed—represented a 'refusal to accept the Jewish state in even a part of Palestine,' a position she said 'will alienate all those Israelis who, like myself, are prepared to support the Palestinian struggle for self-determination…'"

Dalia described the differing points of view, Israeli and Palestinian, of terrorism and acknowledged that some of Israel's present leaders had been terrorists, or freedom fighters, depending on one's point of view, in the past.

"What we consider our right to self-defense, when we bomb Palestinian targets from the air and inevitably hit civilians, you consider mass terror from the air with advanced technology. Each side has an ingenuity for justifying its own position. How long shall we perpetuate this vicious circle?"

Dalia described her objection to her government's action "in deporting Bashir, which she called a 'violation of human rights,' which 'creates greater bitterness and extremism among the Palestinians' and allows the deportees 'greater freedom to plan actions against Israel from abroad...'

"You, Bashir, have already experienced one expulsion from Ramla as a child. Now, you are about to experience another from Ramallah forty years later. You will then become a refugee twice. You may be separated from your wife and your two small children, Ahmed and Hanine, and from your elderly mother and the rest of your family. How can your children avoid hating those who will have deprived them of their father…?"

Dalia's view was that by her government's deporting Bashir, it was "actually empowering (him). I appeal to you to demonstrate the kind of leadership that uses nonviolent means of struggle for your rights…

"I appeal to both Palestinians and Israelis to understand that the use of force will not resolve this conflict on its fundamental level. This is the kind of war that no one can win…

"Our childhood memories, yours and mine, are intertwined in a tragic way. If we cannot find means to transform that tragedy into a shared blessing, our clinging to the past will destroy our future. We will then rob another generation of a joy-filled childhood and turn them into martyrs for an unholy cause. I pray that with your cooperation and God's help, our children will delight in the beauty and bounties of this holy land.

"Allah ma'ak - May God be with you."

Dalia" p. 200-203

Bashir was, now, in a PFLP training camp deep inside Lebanon. Palestinian rebel factions had left Jordan for Lebanon and this was a major concern to Lebanon's Christian population who "fought a proxy war for Israel against the Palestinian factions." p.203

From Lebanon, Bashir would relocate to Cyprus and then to Tunisia where he would live for years, away for his small children and his wife, his mother and his siblings.

Bashir had told Dalia that if one plants a tree in the wrong place, it (Israel) cannot grow. While in Tunisia, Bashir had read Dalia's letter many times, and he decided to answer her. "He who plants barley, Dalia, will never reap wheat…your ability to see things the way they are in reality, not the way they were told to you." p. 217

Dalia can see things the way they are in reality, not the way they were told to her! What enormous irony from one whose people were used by their leaders, people who left their homes in fear of the improvised massacres and rapes of Dier Yassin and the invasions of non-Palestinian armies to drive the Jews into the sea, invasions that backfired on them causing the refugee problem! "Not the way they were told to you"! Dalia had reached some realization, but Bashir, gullible Bashir, lived on, or chose to live on, in deception, not in reality.

Let's take a look at this, additional, Bashir philosophy that a tree (Israel), planted where it should not be, cannot grow. Let us examine Bashir's "tree," now, close to fifty years after his dire prediction. Did the tree wither and die during these intervening years because it was where it should not be, or did it grow and flourish in the soil of its ancient homeland? What is Israel's condition today?

Welcoming Israel's main domestic industry, tourism, into this thriving land through its beautiful, new airport, tourists can then proceed into Israel via its limited access, super highways or modern, high speed trains. The land's well-maintained antiquities are open to all since their recapture from Jordan in the 1967 War before which not only Israelis were not allowed to visit them but Christians from all over the world had to show baptismal records to gain admission to the sites. Israel's gross domestic product, three hundred percent greater than that of the United States, is evident in its well-maintained infrastructure, public buildings, hospitals, and schools.

Travel north out of Tel Aviv and one would think he were in Stanford, CT, with its modern, glass buildings which house Israel's extensive computer industry. The major American computer firms such as IBM, Cisco Systems, Qualcom, and Microsoft are all there providing employment not only for Jews but for Israeli Arabs who, highly educated in Israel's schools and universities, comprise a portion of the country's computers scientists. All along Israel's pristine beaches are a myriad of American and European hotel chains, as they are in all Israel's major cities, the Waldorf Astoria having recently opened a magnificent hotel and residence complex in Jerusalem. (Read "Why isn't Gaza the Monaco of the Middle East?")

Israeli farmers utilize high tech farming techniques to assure a year round supply of produce for domestic consumption and for export. A big disappointment to this writer was, when traveling in Spain recently, orchards were pointed out where Jaffa oranges grow under license from Israel! The aforementioned computer industry now stands along the Sharon Valley where Jaffa oranges used to grow. The land is, now, much too valuable to be used for agriculture. The Ramat haNegev Research Center in the Negev Desert just south of Be'er Sheva not only researches and develops desert farming techniques but its mission affirms its intern program to teach these modern techniques to students from underdeveloped countries. How a Palestinian State living in peace besides technologically advanced Israel would have benefited from Israeli technology, and this agricultural program!

From Wikipedia: "Science and technology in Israel are some of the country's most developed sectors. The percentage of Israelis engaged in scientific and technological inquiry and the amount spent on research and development (R&D) in relation to gross domestic product (GDP) is the second highest in the world...In 2009, Israel's percentage of the total number of scientific articles published worldwide was almost ten times higher than its percentage of the world's population.

"Israeli scientists have contributed to the advancement of agriculture, computer sciences, electronics, genetics, health care, optics, solar energy, and various fields of engineering. Israel is home to major players in the high tech industry and has one of the world's most technologically literate populations. In 1998, Tel Aviv was named by *Newsweek* as one of the ten most technologically influential cities in the world. Since 2000, Israel has been a member of Eureka, the pan-European research and development funding and coordination organization and held the rotating chairmanship of the organization for 2010–2011. ..Google 's Chairman, Eric Schmidt, complimented the country during a visit there, saying that "Israel has the most important high-tech center in the world after the US."

From *The Global Cleantech Innovation Index 2014*, "Israel places first on the overall index, with extremely high evidence of emerging cleantech innovation drivers. The country has demonstrated the greatest density of high-impact cleantech start-ups, as well as a high level of business sophistication and entrepreneurial attitudes, strong venture capital activity, and a good number of environmental patents."

Israel has the eighth longest life expectancy in the world: eighty-two years. More than the United Kingdom, the United States, and Germany.

Israel has more Nobel Prizes per capita than the United States, France, and Germany.

Israeli scientific research institutions are ranked third in the world.

Israel is ranked second in space sciences.

Israel produces more scientific papers per capita than any other nation by a large margin--one hundred and nine per ten thousand people--as well as one of the highest per capita rates of patents filed.

Israel has the third highest rate of entrepreneurship amongst women in the world.

Israel leads the world in patents for medical equipment.

Israel has more NASDAQ listed companies than any other country besides the US, more than all of Europe, India, China, and Japan combined.

In proportion to its population, Israel has the largest number of startup companies in the world. In absolute numbers Israel has more startup companies than any country besides the US.

Israel has the highest number of museums per capita in the world and the second largest per capita of books.

Israel is the eighth happiest country on Earth.

According to the Organization for Economic Co-operation and Development (OECD), Israel has the highest standard of living in the Middle East, and the third highest in Asia.

Israel is among the top three countries in cyber-attack defense.

A US State Department report cited Israel as being No. 1 in the world for the sixth year in a row in the fight to stop human trafficking and prostitution.

Israel is the country which offers the best conditions for clean technology startup companies after Denmark.

Israel has the highest ratio of university degrees to population in the world.

Twenty-four percent of Israel's workforce hold university degrees ranking third in the world behind the US and Holland. Twelve percent hold advanced degrees.

Israeli universities are among the best of the world. Three Israeli universities ranked among the world's one hundred most innovative: Hebrew University, Tel Aviv University, and Technion. Reuters identified these universities as doing the most to advance science, new technologies, and to power new markets and industries. These were the only Middle East universities that made the list. And Israel's Weizmann of Science placed sixth in an in international ranking of the world's top two hundred research institutions and first outside of the US.

Israel is the second-most educated country after Canada.

Israel's $300 billion economy is larger than all of its immediate neighbors combined.

Israel has the highest percentage in the world of home computers per capita.

The cell phone was developed in Israel by Israelis working in the Israeli branch of Motorola, which has its largest development center in Israel.

Voice mail technology was developed in Israel.

The proportion of women among R&D workers in Israel is approximately twenty-three point four percent. This puts Israel in second place behind Denmark.

Women earned thirty-seven percent of all degrees granted in science and engineering in Israel, one of the highest proportions in the world.

Israel has a world-class symphony orchestra which performs in the beautiful, new Habima Theater and was conducted, for years, by Maestro Zubin Mehta.

Established in 1982, by Stef Wertheimer, a German-born businessman, philanthropist, and former member of the Israel Parliament, the Tefen Industrial Park materialized from a holistic perception of economic development similar to The Rockefeller Foundation's "Catalyst for Change: Paths out of Poverty." Through the Tefen Industrial Park, Israeli Entrepreneurship Incubator, Wertheimer emphasizes the importance of economic development as a process for developing a country. Under the original direction of Arieh Baron, PhD University of California at Berkeley, Tefen Industrial Park offers space for entrepreneurs who are able to demonstrate that their creation will be globally competitive and self-sustainable when marketed.

The industrial park provides these entrepreneurs space to start up their businesses with no overhead costs. All external facilities such as banking, strategic advice, internet and other communication technologies are, also, made available to them in the park, most at a subsidized rate or, at times, free of charge for a specific time frame. In this way, the park is an accommodating business incubator that supports entrepreneurs at the initial phases of business development and allows them to center their energies on their major interests, specifically, the manufacture and marketing of their products.

So much for Bashir's tree planted in the wrong soil analogy. Israel's tree not only grew because it was rooted in its ancestral ground but it has blossomed and provided a beautiful life for Israel's population, including the refugee masses that huddled to its shores. How the Palestinians that Bashir so loves could have benefited from an amicable association with their willing neighbors!

What roots did the Palestinian people put down? After all, Bashir says they are the indigenous people, so the Palestinian tree should flourish in this land, a tree planted where it should be. Why did his people forgo the opportunity to put down roots in the portion of the land that the United Nations bequeathed to them? They planted no tree. There are no roots. Instead, they are like a vine with shallow roots that can be pulled up by a child with one hand spreading out to all their neighboring countries where they are not allowed to inhabit the land, where they are, almost three-quarters of a century later, crammed into refugee camps, even in the West Bank and East Jerusalem which was to be their portion of the partition. Their own people keep them in refugee camps on their own land! Their innovations: the Qassam rocket and the suicide vest.

From the Miko Peled speech analysis: Gaza has a forty-three percent unemployment rate, seven universities, and a ninety-two percent literacy rate. On May 11, 2015, the World Bank reported that *Gaza has the highest unemployment in the world rate at forty-three percent, with youth unemployment at sixty percent.* The report was to be presented to the Ad Hoc Liaison Committee (AHLC) at its bi-annual meeting in Brussels on May 27, 2015. Amongst other recommendations, the report recommended the easing of the blockade to allow construction materials to enter in sufficient quantities.

(On what planet had they been living? Construction materials have been entering Gaza in large quantities and were used instead of to build schools, roads, and hospitals, to reinforce tunnels in order to infiltrate Israel, even via kindergartens.) There were, also, tunnels to Egypt which Egypt discovered and filled in.

With seven universities and a ninety-two percent literacy rate, why has the tree not taken root, certainly not as it could have had the Palestinian leadership not deceived its people by leading it into wars that they could not win, "*unheard of foolishness*"?

Back to Bashir's letter to Dalia. Bashir asked, "Why am I exiled from my homeland? Why am I separated from my children, Ahmed and Hanine, from my wife, from my mother, from my brothers and sisters, from my family?" p. 218

One might ask," Why was Bashir given a fifteen year sentence for his part in the Supersol market bombing?" People died and were maimed, severely mutilated with limbs, arms and legs, blown off in that bombing. Why wasn't he given a life sentence? And then, within three years of his release from prison, to be an instigator of attacks where more people were killed, and he asks why he is exiled! Bashir, most certainly, had been aware that if he were caught, he would be separated from his wife and young children if not by exile, then by another prison term. He, willingly, made this sacrifice. He had told Dalia of her "ability to see things the way they are in reality." But Bashir has lived in a life of his desires and neither truth nor reality would interfere with what he wants, demands!

Bashir wrote to Dalia, "Do you know, Dalia, that in 1948, with childhood innocence, I played with one of the booby-trapped toys that were scattered by the Zionists...the gifts of the terrorist Zionist organization to the children of Palestine? The family was in Gaza, Bashir explained, late in 1948, shortly after arriving from Ramallah. Bashir, Nuha, and other brothers and sisters were playing in the dirt yard outside their cement-block house. They saw something gleaming in the sun. It was bulbous, with a wick protruding. It looked like a lantern. The children brought it inside. Bashir held the new toy as the other children gathered around. A clay water jug stood on the kitchen counter; one of the children bumped into it, and it crashed to the floor. The other children scattered. Bashir was left alone with the toy in his hands. Suddenly, there was an explosion.

"The booby-trapped toy exploded in my left hand to crush my palm, to scatter my bones and flesh and shed my blood, to blend it with the soil of Palestine, to embrace the lemon fruit and the olive leaves, to cling to the dates and flowers of the fitna tree…In the explosion in Gaza, six-year-old-Bashir lost four fingers and the palm of his left hand." p. 218-219

Dalia was powerfully shaken by Bashir's revelation of how he lost his fingers and the palm of his hand, and rightfully so, had Bashir's emotional appeal to her to help him return to his homeland and to his wife, his children and elderly mother, to his siblings, and to the palm of his hand and his blood supposedly soaked into Palestinian soil been true. Who would not be shaken by such a revelation, by such an appeal?

But Bashir was a true terrorist, not a freedom fighter like the French freedom fighters in the Second World War who were fighting for the land that an invading force was trying to conquer and take from them. Bashir was, all his life, determined to wrest the land, the entire land, from those who had a rightful claim to it and were willing to accept a portion of what they felt should, rightfully, be theirs, those who were willing to compromise and to live in peace besides the Bashirs of Palestine. Bashir lost the palm of his hand and four fingers due to the explosion of a shiny toy, one of many, left for the Palestinian children but only he, Bashir, picked up a shiny toy and nothing in *The Lemon Tree* with its constant verifications confirms this, not through all the resources used to compile this book nor through the myriad of interviews and personal recollections, mainly by his sisters *who were there at the time!*

The Lemon Tree is 264 pages long 66 pages of notes in font considerably smaller, almost as much in notes as in script. There are, also, several pages of Acknowledgements citing the archivists, scholars, journalists and editors, etc., who tracked records. There are over two hundred and fifty archives, electronic sources, newspaper and magazine articles, pamphlets, government publications, unpublished works, and books, and, perhaps, equally as reliable, interviews with and memories of the participants, the protagonists and their immediate families and yet, not one note, not one recollection or affirmation of any sort of this supposed accident caused by the pretty toys left for the little Palestinian children to be maimed by, nor is there any indication of any child other than Bashir being injured by such a toy. The international press was there, but they "missed" the distribution of shiny toys left for children that would explode in their hands just as the press had "missed" the Deir Yassin massacre.

The notes to most of the chapters start off with the statement that much of the material in the chapter is based on, amongst other sources, firsthand accounts including interviews and personal accounts and recollections. Details of the Khairi family meals and Ahmed's social life…were described by Khanom" p 288 as was the celebration on the completion of the family home. "To celebrate, the family butchered a lamb and prepared a huge feast: chicken stuffed with rice and great piles of lamb…handmade couscous, date-filled cookies made with soft, buttery dough, and *kanafe*, a hot, pistachio-covered sweet that is shaped like a pizza and looks like shredded wheat." p. 13 Bashir's release from prison was recalled by Nuha and Khanom, "The house was full of well-wishers. Relatives from Gaza sent large bags of oranges for the celebration…Mom was cooking; everybody is welcoming." p. 188

In a section based on, amongst other sources, family recollections, here specifically Nuha and Ghiath Khairi and Khanom, speaking of Bashir, "He never bought anything expensive, shirt, shoes, nothing for himself," Khanom recalled… "Bhajat, Bashir's younger brother by a year, was completely different…We used to call Bashir the son of a beggar and Bhajat the son of a lord. People couldn't even believe they were brothers." p. 124

Not all the recollections were of family feasts and clothes. Khanom recalled the family's return to Ramallah after their years in Gaza. "After nearly nine years in Gaza, Ahmed and Zakia Khairi decided to move the family back to Ramallah. They had come into a family inheritance and would be able to buy a modest property in the West Bank and think about higher education for the children. It was 1957." p. 103

This book is based to such a large extent on personal recollections that hundreds of examples could be cited here, but not one recollection, not even by the sisters who were with Bashir at the time of the alleged explosion that took the palm of his hand and four fingers! Not only no recollection by the family is cited but no documentation in all the sources used to compile this book is quoted as having verified that he or any other child was wounded by a shiny toy left by the Zionists. Not one!

Ok, never mind documentation or recollections. Family feasts are described in detail, so how about tending to such a severe wound? Was Bashir taken to a doctor, if not a hospital? Did Khanom or Nuha remember rushing to an apothecary shop for a salve? How was the blood stopped so this little child wouldn't bleed to death? Did they use a tourniquet? What did they make it from? Did such a severe wound become infected? Did they have bandages or did Zakia or Khanom tear up shirts or a sheet to bandage the wound? How was he bathed, and dressed? Was Bashir in school or a kindergarten at six years old? Did he stay home? Who tended him? No details, no records, no recollections of such a family trauma! Food, they remember, like chicken stuffed with rice and home-made couscous and they recall the fact that Bashir never bought clothes but Bhajat dressed like a dandy but losing the palm and four fingers of a beloved child's hand is not as important as pistachio-filled pastries that looked like shredded wheat and were shaped like a pizza to be recollected by any member of the family.

No, it wasn't recollected, or documented, not Bashir's trauma caused by the shiny, explosive toy nor other children's maiming because there never were such toys. The international press that was throughout Israel and the Palestinian areas reporting on what was happening missed children being maimed by toys left to deliberately harm them and rushed to hospitals, or their wailing mothers, just as Zakia would have been wailing? No! Bashir led a life of violence, embroiled with explosives in the Supersol bombing and in how many other cases that we don't even know about during which he could have been maimed. Or, perhaps this was, simply, a birth defect.

Bashir, from your very first encounter with Dalia, she treated you and your family, including your revered father, with nothing but kindness. She deserved more from you than such deceit that caused her such anguish.

Cry baby, Bashir. "Why am I exiled from my homeland? Why am I separated from my children, Ahmed and Hanine, from my wife, from my mother, from my brothers and sisters, from my family?" Bashir wrote to Dalia.

You suffer anguish Bashir, because you are separated from your children! But your children are healthy and in the bosom of their mother, their grandmother, and your extended family. You, who were a cause of the bombing where people were killed and others had limbs blown off! You, who instigate! You are separated from your children, from your wife, your mother and brothers and sisters and from the wonderful homeland your land could have been if not for the "Bashirs" in its midst. Your people are not stupid. The Palestinians who chose to remain in Israel see how their brethren are treated in the West Bank and Gaza, and yes, in the miserable refugee camps in the surrounding Arab countries. While the Israeli Arabs live at a high standard of living, well educated, well dressed and well nourished, with good jobs and with excellent medical care.

Were you a freedom fighter, you would deserve some consideration, but you are not. You are a terrorist. You are an intelligent man, Bashir, a lawyer, and while you served out your fifteen year prison sentence you read "Hegel, Lenin, Marx, Jack London, Pablo Neruda, Bertolt Brecht, the Egyptian novelist Naguib Mahfouz, Gabriel Garcia M`arquez and his *One Hundred Years of Solitude*, and John Steinbeck's *Grapes of Wrath*." p. 182 Was your time spent in forced hard labor? No, no mention of this, and if so, how did you have the time to do all this reading and have discussions about these works with your fellow prisoners if they, also, spent their time in hard labor? Perhaps not then, but today, Arab prisoners have the opportunity to become educated while in prison. Recently, an Arab received his PhD in chemical engineering while in an Israeli prison.

Again, you, possibly, are not aware even today of the treachery against their own people of Azzam Pasha, Jamal Husseini, and Dr. Hussein Khalidi and how many other of your leaders that turned you into a terrorist? Do you know about the billions of dollars, yes, I said *billions* of dollars, that Yasser Arafat stole from his people, your people, (the Lesley Stahl segment on "60 Minutes," November 7, 2003)? What could have been done with that money to help your people, your own mother, Zakia, working in Gaza, the antipathy of what her life had been shortly before and should have continued to be had your people not been deceived by your leaders, affected daily by this deception?

Did you know that Arafat's finance minister, Salam Fayyad, a former World Bank official, told "60 Minutes" that Arafat would control commodities, such as flour and cement, which he would hand over to his cronies who then turned around and fleeced the public? Who were the public? The housewives of Gaza, the Zakias of Gaza who, you said, along with your sisters worked constantly were paying much more for the flour and the bread that they bought than they should have been paying, and for how many other staples that they worked so hard for to provide for their families?

But the biggest commodity Arafat controlled knowing that his people were being fleeced was through his General Petroleum Corporation, the one for gasoline. The corporation purchased fuel "and watered it down with kerosene, not only defrauding the Palestinian drivers, (your father, Bashir?) but wrecking their car engines. Fayyad says the

Petroleum Corporation "charged exorbitant prices, and Arafat got a hefty kickback." How else did he become a billionaire?

Fayyad dismantled the corporation after which "the Palestinian drivers paid twenty percent less for gas and *eighty percent less* for diesel fuel"!

Even if you were unaware of how your people were duped and defrauded by their leaders causing their despicable condition, with all your reading it is hard to believe that you do not know of the Jewish rabbi, Jesus Christ, and that the Jews have been in this land for thousands of years before your people arrived here, before your people were even a people. You know this: you are not the indigenous people and you, also, are cognizant of the magnificent society the Jews have built in Israel, of the tree that flourishes in its proper soil.

And you should know (but, perhaps, you have blocked this out of your mind just as you are in denial about the reasons for your exile) that young people, other peoples' children, have a right to go out to a pizza parlor and enjoy time with their friends just as your father enjoyed his time with his friends in the coffee shop in al-Ramla and not be blown up, parents separated from their children for good, for forever, because their children were blown to smithereens by a bomb that you instigated. You are separated from your family, Bashir, as you should be and, hopefully, will remain.

Based on the Oslo Accord concessions, in 1996 Palestinian fighters began to return. In this group after eight years of exile, was Bashir Khairi. Nuha recalled, "Mom prepared food." p 226 "As a result of Oslo, Bashir would soon be seeing his mother, his wife, and his two small children. He would be in Palestine for the first time since his deportation to Lebanon in 1988. *But he would not be all the way home to al-Ramla.*" p. 226 A portent of things to come?

Among those who returned from Tunisia when Bashir returned were cohorts who came back with Yasser Arafat. 224 "The Chairman, himself continued to live modestly." p. 228 In later years while the refugees he represented were still being held in deplorable refugee camps in Palestinian areas as well as in neighboring Arab countries, CBS's 60 Minutes' November 7, 2003, program reported, "Arafat may have $1 billion, but he sure isn't spending it to live well. He's holed up in his Ramallah compound which the Israelis all but reduced to rubble a year-and-a-half ago. Arafat has always lived modestly, which you can't say about his wife, Suha…She gets $100,000 a month from Arafat out of the Palestinian budget, and lives lavishly in Paris on this allowance."

"But some of his (Arafat's) longtime cohorts in exile built mansions in Gaza, all the more striking for their juxtaposition against the squalor of the refugee camps on one of the most crowded places on earth. One of the mansions, estimated to cost $2 million, was built for Mahmoud Abbas, known as Abu Mazen, who would later succeed Arafat as leader of the Palestinians." P. 228 *Cost two million dollars utilizing Palestinian labor paid in extra rations of flour, rice, sugar, and fat!* The "60 Minutes" segment reported that "the conservative Gazans were stunned at the appearance of seaside nightclubs with belly dancers and alcohol catering to the wealthy arrivals from the diaspora. It was not uncommon to see a black Mercedes with VIP plates streaking through a red light in Gaza City leaving donkey carts literally in the dust."

This "60 Minutes" broadcast also documented that "Yasser Arafat diverted nearly $1 billion in public funds *($1 billion!)*, but a lot more is unaccounted for." Lesley Stahl reported that Jim Prince's team (American accountants hired to scrutinize Arafat's books) "determined that part of the Palestinian leader's wealth was in a secret portfolio worth close to $1 billion--with investments in companies like a Coca Cola bottling plant in Ramallah, a Tunisian cell phone company, and venture capital funds in the U.S. and the Cayman Islands…the money for the portfolio came from public funds, Palestinian taxes, *and virtually none of it was used for the Palestinian people.*"

Arafat took your money, money from Gaza, and used it for venture capital in the United States? Why? What about venture capital in

Gaza? Why didn't he buy some embroidery machines and provide work for the women of Gaza, the Zakia Khairis of Gaza, by starting a factory to turn out the embroidered linens the Arab women so like? These could have been exported to neighboring Arab countries bringing money into Gaza, to the families of the women just a few months removed from their maids and perfumed baths who would be earning money to feed their families.

Maids and perfumed baths do not mean wealth as we think of wealth, today. In poor societies, an unskilled worker, a maid, often works for very little or simply for the food she eats on the job and, perhaps, her employer's leftover food to take home to her family.

What about venture capital funds to rebuild the hothouses the Gazans burned down destroying their places of employment so they could, again, grow vegetables and flowers for their own consumption and for export?

Salam Fayyad, a former World Bank official whom Arafat was forced to appoint finance minister the previous year reported, "There is corruption out there. There is abuse. There is impropriety."

Martin Indyk, a top adviser on the Middle East in the Clinton administration and now head of the Saban Center, a Washington think-tank, says of Arafat, "He's accumulating hundreds of millions of dollars…Arafat accumulated another $1 billion…Under the Oslo Accords, it was agreed that Israel would collect sales taxes on goods purchased by Palestinians and transfer those funds to the Palestinian treasury." But instead, Indyk says, "that money is transferred to Yasser Arafat." Dennis Ross, who was Middle East negotiator for the first President Bush and President Clinton, and now heads the Washington Institute for Near East Policy, says Arafat financed a vast patronage system…like a Chicago ward boss, he still doles out oodles of money; Fayyad says he pays his security forces alone $20 million a month, all of it in cash.

"All told, U.S. officials estimate Arafat's personal nest egg at between $1 billion and $3 billion…

"Both Israeli and U.S. sources say that Arafat has spent millions to support terrorists and purchase weapons.

"Did he steal from his own people? He defines himself as being the embodiment of the Palestinian people," Ross answers. "So what's good for him is good for them. Did they benefit? The answer is no. Did they lose? The answer is yes."

How did Zakia, whom Bashir said was always working in their cinder block house in Gaza embroidering linens and knitting sweaters, benefit from Arafat's getting richer by making her pay more for basic commodities such as bread and for other foods items and his father pay more for gas for the family car, and for repairs for the damaged engine?

Mohammed Rachid, Arafat's economic adviser, referred to "the investment portfolio he managed for Arafat. He opened that account at the Leumi Bank in Tel Aviv…Rachid says that 'transfers to the Leumi Bank account never stayed. It was receiving the revenues and transferring these revenues to the Palestinian Authority's account in the Arab bank in Gaza…and from there, much of it was sent to Switzerland, to the prestigious Lombard Odier Bank, for yet another secret investment account that held over $300 million…'

"Rachid says that the funds came from Palestinian 'taxes' and 'customs revenues.' The account was under a code name, 'Ledbury'--not the Palestinian Authority--and Minister Fayyad says that this pot of money, too, was available only to Arafat. The Swiss account was closed out in 2001. No one really knows where that money is today…

"There's yet another stash of money Arafat might be asked about: the funds he collected when he was chairman of the PLO in exile. The PLO's former treasurer told us he saw Saddam Hussein hand Arafat a $50 million check for supporting him during the first Gulf War. And there were other large gifts from the KGB and the Saudis…

"Fayyad is trying to make sure it's the people's money, but many say his one-man reform effort is having only limited success. Arafat recently sent armed men to prevent Fayyad from replacing the head of the civil service who runs Arafat's patronage apparatus...Indyk says, 'Other people who have dared to call for transparency of all these finances have been beaten up, shot, and silenced.' Indyk says, Fayyad 'has upset so many powerful people, and his offices have already been ransacked more than once.'"

But the Ad Hoc Liaison Committee (AHLC) at its bi-annual meeting in Brussels on May 27, 2015, recommended the easing of the blockade (of Gaza) to allow construction materials to enter in sufficient quantities as a cure for the dire economic conditions in Gaza. How naïve!

The "60 Minutes" report states, "He (Arafat) defines himself as being the embodiment of the Palestinian people...So what's good for him is good for them." Would Zakia agree that she and her older daughters should work all the time because her paying more for basic food and kerosene-laced gasoline was good for them because it was good for Arafat? Bashir might want to look to see who is causing the problems for this family, his people.

"When Arafat returned to Gaza in July, 1994, delirious throngs welcomed him as a conquering liberator...By early 1996, (as agreed in the Oslo Accords), hundreds of PLO officials and former Palestinian fighters had begun to return from their exile in Tunis." P. 224

Arafat was welcomed back as a conquering liberator! Why? What had he conquered and what had he liberated? He had been exiled for years, first in Jordan from where he was expelled, he went to Lebanon and was expelled from there, also, and now he had been given permission to return to Israel from Tunisia because he had written a letter to Prime Minister Itzhak Rabin in which he "promised to 'renounce the use of terrorism and other act of violence' and 'discipline violators.'" p. 224

This is a returning "conquering liberator"? Sounds more like Arafat returned only when he was given permission to return, and with his tail between his legs. What was to celebrate?

Several decades later, in 2012, after Israel reluctantly accepted an Egyptian-brokered cease-fire in a war with Gaza, TV would show Gazans again celebrating wildly in the streets, this time for their "victory" over Israel while they dragged suspected Israeli collaborators behind cars over potholed roads that could hardly be called roads to their deaths. (Great way to get rid of someone one owes money to: call him a collaborator.)

And is there no reality amongst the Palestinians? Bashir is still unaware, or unwilling to accept, that it was the Palestinians who started the war in 1948, the *nakba*. And his cousin Ghiath, who married Nuha, the most rational of the Khiaris says," Now, Israel rules America." p. 254.

In August, 2011, Bashir, now in his sixties, again found himself in prison, this time under administrative detention. (See "administrative detention" in "The Miko Peled Talk.") Of course, Bashir would have no idea why he was there, just as he had questioned, in Tunis, why he was exiled, away from his wife and children. Bashir was still the "righteous victim," the one who had been wronged, who knew that his people had no responsibility for their disbursement from their homes.

"The Israelis created this problem," he told Dalia on her visit to his office in Ramallah when she was, again, pleading with him that they should each see the other's point of view. p. 261 Dalia had said, "If you say everything is all Palestine and I say everything is the whole land of Israel, I don't think we'll get anywhere...We share a common destiny, here. I truly believe that we are so deeply and closely related--culturally, historically, religiously, psychologically. And it is so clear to me that you and your people are holding the key to our freedom. And I think I could say, also, Bashir, that we hold the key to your freedom. It's a deep interdependence...We are so deeply connected.

And what connects us? The same thing that separates us. This land." p. 260, 262

In 1998, the fiftieth anniversary of the War of Independence, the "Catastrophe," the lemon tree died…On *Tu B'shvat*, the day the Jewish sages call the holiday of the new year for trees," p. 263 Arab and Jewish children from Open House along with Dalia planted a new lemon tree sapling in the corner of the yard where Ahmed Khairi, sixty-two years before, had built a home for his family, with love.

Critique Summary: How many times had Bashir said, "I love Palestine; I hate the occupation" and then, "I love Palestine more, and I hate the occupation more"?

Well, there didn't have to be an occupation at all. The day the British left, the end of the British Mandate, the new Prime Minister David Ben Gurion declared the State of Israel. Why didn't the Palestinian leaders declare the State of Palestine? The two fledgling nations could have lived together in peace sharing, as the United Nations Declaration had decreed, "railroads and postal service," and why not, also, technology, commerce, and education, learning of all sorts? *Where would the Palestinian people be today if its leaders had accepted the United Nations Partition Plan and established the State of Palestine,* the State Bashir so longs for, instead of gathering its Arab neighbors and invading Israel in a war it lost and caused Ahmed Khairi and tens of thousands of other Palestinians to become refugees kept by their brethren in refugee camps in deplorable, squalid conditions, not like the Jewish refugees who were, as quickly as possible, integrated into Israeli society?

The Palestinian refugees willingly left their homes in 1948 with the promise that they would return in fifteen days. Close to three quarters of a century has passed since then.

But there is progress for those Arabs that are Israeli citizens. The International Edition of *The New York Times*, Jan. 10, 2016, has an article about an all Bedouin tech company, Sadel Tech, a start-up with an Israeli technology investor, the result of "government initiatives aimed at bringing more young Arabs into the technology work force…two organizations, ITT Works and Tsofen,(Stef Wertheimer's Entrepreneurship Incubator), operate the program which helps Arab graduates into tech companies such as Amdocs and Check Point and the Israeli branch of Intel, the multinational chip maker."

Ibrahim Sana, founder and Chief Executive Officer of Sadel, grew up in a Bedouin town in the Negev Desert, son of a feed store operator, graduated from Technion Institute of Technology in Haifa and received a Master's degree at Ben Gurion University of the Negev. "Sadel (Tech), in an industrial park about five miles from a growing technology center in Be'er Sheva, mixes technology with tradition. At lunchtime, the employees take out their prayer mats and perform Muslim midday prayers." A Bedouin woman employee, Rabaa al-Hawasheh, said that "her mother, Hesen, and her husband were proud that they had educated their girls…Ms. Hawasheh said that when she first started working at Sadel, her parents did not tell relatives, assuming that they would disapprove…'Now, they all know.'"

An agreement will never be met until both sides respect the needs of the other, empathize with the other. As introspective, compassionate Dalia, or as Bashir described her, "morality, sensitivity, and sensibility" p. 216 said to Bashir's family, "Everybody will have to do with less than they deserve…must not each of us be willing to compromise?" p. 212, 213 A solution to the Israeli/Palestinian problem has to be an accommodation to both sides' desires, but as long as the Israelis need to thrive in their ancestral homeland in the beautiful, nay, the magnificent country they have built and the Arabs want to drive them into the sea, there can be no accommodation.

However, there have been some moderating voices among the Arabs. Abdul Aziz Al ash-Sheikh, a member of Saudi Arabia's leading religious family and current Grand Mufti of Saudi Arabia pressed the Palestinians in a recent article to accept that the two-state solution is the only practicable route for them to take and that this is supported by most of the world, particularly in view of the current circumstances in the Arab world which is consumed with more urgent crises and is no longer particularly upset about the Palestinian cause.

Al-Sheikh cautioned his Arab brothers in this article that a stubborn insistence on armed resistance will only result in harming the Palestinians themselves, adding that Israel is now a diplomatic powerhouse and has the firm backing of the powerful world powers.

"In light of this, it can be said that relying on armed resistance to confront all of these global powers while making the option of peace, especially the two-state solution, a more remote possibility--as implied by the statements of radical Palestinians nationalists and of those purporting to be devout--constitutes a kind of political suicide that only political ignoramuses [can] condone," Al-Sheikh wrote, according to a translation by MEMRI (Middle East Media Research Institute).

He, also, stressed that the Palestinians have to recognize that the Arabs of today are not the Arabs of yesterday and that the Palestinian cause is not as important to Arabs today as it was in the past. It is not a top priority for them, now, as civil wars are trouncing four Arab countries and because fighting Islamic terrorism is of the upmost concern that all Arabs, without exception, are focusing on at this time. It is foolhardiness to ask someone to sacrifice attention to his own difficulties and national interests in order to help the Palestinians solve their problems, Al-Sheikh stressed.

"All I can say to my Palestinian brethren is that stubbornness, contrariness, and betting on the [support of] the Arab masses are a hopeless effort, and that ultimately you are the only ones who will pay the price of this stubbornness and contrariness," he concluded.

A Palestinian, Badr Madoukh, refuted Al-Sheikh's column in several tweets; for example, "...What would you have said if your country, your land and your home had been taken by force and you and your family had been expelled from them and sent into exile?!" Madoukh is, obviously, like the majority of the Palestinians, not aware that it was the Grand Mufti of Jerusalem, Hajj Amin el-Husseini, and not the Jews of Palestine that demanded that his people flee their homes and that the Jews didn't start a war to take their homes.

On the front page of the New York Times on Feb. 15, 2017, "Awash in Turmoil, Arab World Leaves Two-State Goal Adrift," a Palestinian, Wail al-Galshan, moving his family into a spacious three bedroom, two bath new apartment that he will rent for $40 a month in the new neighborhood being built in Gaza by Qatar was asked what else he would want. "I want…to live without occupation," he answered.

Where has he been living, on Mars?

Certainly, he hasn't been living in Gaza or he would, surely, know that except for a few days during Operation Protective Edge in 2014 when Israeli troops infiltrated in an attempt to clean out Hamas militants who had been firing rockets into Israel for thirteen years, there hasn't been an Israeli on Gazan soil since 2005! Or, is he totally brainwashed by his parents and teachers? Wail Al-Galshan has five children, so even in that culture he has to be at least twenty-five years old. He's been living without occupation for twelve years, probably half his life, and he doesn't know it? So much for ninety-two percent literacy. I guess he can read, but can he think? If this cycle is not broken, what will he be teaching his children?

Omar Abu Bakr tweeted, "Reasonable words [referring to Al-Shiekh's article], especially the claim that Arab attention has been diverted away from the Palestinian cause due to the Arabs' domestic problems and their opposition to the Iranian infiltration [of Arab countries]."

Way back in 1993, Shimon Perez, a negotiator of the 1993 Oslo Peace Accords and of the peace treaty with Jordan and a winner of the Nobel Peace Prize in 1994 along with then-Israeli Prime Minster Yitzak Rabin and Yasser Arafat, who was at the time chairman of the Palestinian Liberation Organization (PLO), published an article in *The*

New Middle East on his vision of a prosperous Palestinian population that would be a good neighbor for Israel. However, both then and now, his hopes have been shattered by Palestinian rejectionism, incitement, and death cultism.

In his January 2, 2017, column in the official Saudi daily *Al-Jazirah*, titled "The Palestinians Have No [Choice] But Peace," journalist Muhammad Aal Al-Sheikh criticized Palestinian factions that advocate armed and violent resistance. Rejecting the option of peace is political suicide, he said.

Change comes, only, with good will on both sides. In a recent radio interview with the common Palestinian on the street, the question was asked as Dalia had asked about her people so many years before to Bashir, "But where would they go?"

"They can go to hell!"

CHAPTER 10

Letter to Sandy Tolan Author of *The Lemon Tree*

April 12, 2011
Mr. Sandy Tolan, Author, *The Lemon Tree*
The USC Annenberg School for Communication and Journalism
Watt Way
Los Angeles, CA 90007

Re: let's talk of Thorns on the Lemon Tree

Dear Mr. Tolan:

"I understand your deep sorrow, Bashir, and I know you are aware of my sympathies for you, for your family, and for all your people who suffer with you, but also, of necessity, of my competing views. Over all these years, we have been able to empathize with each other, each of us with the ardent hope of achieving his own goal with as little discomfort to the other as possible. But we also know that that cannot be, that one of our peoples must suffer to the accommodation of the other.

"But Bashir, never once, I have to say, did you look deeper into the cause of all our many problems, both yours and mine. Not once did you look below the surface of what has happened to you and to your beloved family whose friendship I treasure with all my heart.

"My dear friend, it pains me to confront your deep-seated beliefs, the convictions that have steered the path your life has taken, the path that has led you to so many prisons and to exile separated from your parents, your brothers and sisters, your wife, and your dearly-loved children for years at a time breeding the same hatred in your children's generation. You have one goal in mind and only one, the return that, my dear friend, will never happen; I am sorry to tell you, never.

"You say the Crusaders were expelled after two hundred years. Yes, you are right. They were expelled after two hundred years. So how would that help your family if that were to happen to the Jews, not that I believe, not in a thousand years never mind two hundred, this will happen in this land which we both covet? You have already spent your lifetime battling for a cause which was not attained in your dear father's lifetime, which, apparently, will not be attained in your mother's lifetime, and which, I honestly believe, Bashir, will not be reached in your or your children's lifetimes. So what will you have achieved by all your fight and stress? Should your dream become a reality and your family be able to return to its home, to our home, in two hundred years, who will wake you all from your graves to tell you it's all right to go home?

"How different your life would have been, the lives of all your family would have been, had you looked deeper into the cause of all you have been through since you were a small child of six. Had you done so, you may have made an accommodation to your exile from your home, the beautiful home your father built, with love, for his family, where I grew up and love as my home; but you would have been fighting the correct enemy, the one that did this to you so, perhaps, you and your family could have reached an acceptable way of life, a life without your constant estrangement from all whom you love.

"You say you were the indigenous people in this land. No, you weren't, I'm sorry to tell you. The Indians were the indigenous people in the land now called America. Their culture was a thousand years old in the land they inhabited. They had come from Asia and settled the entire expanse of the Americas before the first glimmer in a European man's eye as he looked toward the new world.

"But Islam is a new religion. How many years old? Mohammed only lived in the sixth century, and in Saudi Arabia, not Palestine. Jesus Christ was born well over a thousand years before that in this land. He was a Jew, born into a land that the Jews had already inhabited in for several thousand years. The Jews dispersed to the diaspora, to lands across the entire globe; but never was there a time when there was not a Jewish presence in this, the Holy Land, not during the time of the Greeks, the Romans, and the occupiers after them. This was, has been, and forever will be, my dear friend, the homeland of the Jews, which they were willing to share with you, *willing to accept less than they aspired to and felt was their right to have because they knew you were here, you were here and had been here for many centuries and had a right to remain.*

"Bashir, did you ever look at a map of the division of this land by the United Nations? Did you see that your beloved al-Ramla was right on the border of the new State of Israel, and that Lydda lay very close by? Within eight hours of the declaration of the State of Israel, five Arab nations in an attempt to help the Palestinians conquer the whole of the land in addition to what was allotted them by the United Nations attacked the new State of Israel which was to abide alongside the State of Palestine which, had your Palestinian leadership wanted, could have been declared a State and co-existed and thrived alongside the new Israel, two fledgling nations sharing, as outlined by the United Nations Declaration, rail and postal services in cooperation with each other, to the benefit of each other.

"The Jews were willing to accept the United Nations' plan, to allow you to live as you had been living for fourteen hundred years; but it was you, Bashir, your Palestinian leaders, who were determined not to allow the Jews to live as they had been living for not fourteen hundred years but for thousands of years, thousands of years before Jesus Christ was born in his Jewish homeland! In all your travels, in your exile, you never heard from your friends in Lebanon and elsewhere that they had attacked in an attempt to conquer the entire land for the Palestinian people by driving the Jews into the sea? Or have you been aware of this, but the true cause of your family losing the house your beloved father had built, with love, for his family was something you were not willing to accept?

"Perhaps your family did not leave its home to make way for the Arab armies to push the Jews into the sea, but other families did. Those families still reside in refugee camps, even in a refugee camp in Jenin and one in East Jerusalem which are within Palestinian territory! 'The Electronic Intifada,' February 28, 2016 reports that Jabaliya refugee camp in Gaza is home to eighty thousand Palestinian refugees and their descendants for the past sixty-eight years! And you speak of their suffering? Where, Bashir, are the Jewish refugee camps? Along the Mediterranean Sea where the refugees arrived? Out in the Negev Desert where there is sufficient land to build camps to dump the refugees? Why do the Arab nations that were so willing to help the Palestinians push the Jews into the sea keep their brethren whom they were willing to die for in battle in refugee camps and not absorb them into their society as the Jews absorbed their refugees into the Israeli society?

"But let's get back to the proximity of al Ramla and Lydda to the UN mandated border between the new States of Israel and Palestine. Did it ever occur to your leaders that the Jews might not, simply, willingly march right into the sea and drown taking their children, parents, all their loved ones with them? What would happen to the Khairi family, to the extended Khairi family with all its cousins and to all the other families of al Ramla and Lydda and to the other Arab villages if the Jews pushed back, determined to claim the land they had lived in for thousands of generations and which was mandated to them by the world organization?

Did your Palestinian leaders think this was even possible? Did they care? Were they concerned? You say that the Jews did some bad things to your people. There were bad things done on both sides *because this was war, a war that your people, your people, Bashir, started. War, which is hell! This was not a rose garden that they planted, the rose garden it could have been with the Khairi family in its lovely home in al-Ramla which your father had built, with love, for his family had your people not started this war which they lost,* with the consequences this inflicted on their innocent Palestinian people, such as your family, your people that your leaders had an obligation to protect.

"Bashir, you told me that your lifetime of struggle and the resultant sacrifices of your family were because the Jews invaded. No, Bashir, my dear friend, you are wrong. The Jews did not invade: they were attacked, invaded upon. You cannot distort history to your convenience. The invasion of the five Arab countries eight hours after the Declaration of the State of Israel is fact recorded in history in a myriad of writings. But the Jews pushed back. They refused to lie down and die, with their children and their parents. They are occupiers? What else should they do? Go back to the UN mandated borders as though nothing had happened, as though the sons and husbands and brothers, yes, daughters, too, they lost in their War of Independence, what you call "the catastrophe," a war they were forced to fight against your aggression for an independence they had already lawfully declared were of no value, that their losses were less than your losses by your inflicted war? Why, so you could re-group, re-arm, again accept help from other Arab nations, and in your stronger condition attack again to drive the Jews into the sea, and then again? And each time the Jews should simply go back as though they had not been attacked and lost more loved ones?

"No. It did not happen and it will not happen. That is why I say, you will never go back to our home, never, because you have not made the adjustment to truth, the truth that it was your leaders who attacked, not the Jews, that your Palestinian leaders are to blame for the Jews fighting back right over what is now known as "the green line," just past our mutual home.

"I read of all the crops you left behind, in abundance. Then why is it called "the green line"? Is that a line of green paint drawn in the desert? No. We Jews made the desert flourish. We grew crops where there had only been sand. Nothing but sand. When we first started to put in irrigation systems so the corn and wheat and vegetables would grow, your people called it "Jewish rain." So how did all your bountiful crops that I read about grow, before the "Jewish rain"? They couldn't. They didn't. Vegetation requires water, water from the irrigation you did not have except for some small amounts from the local well and some springs to water your kitchen gardens and your few, small farms.

"Bashir, every aspect, almost every conversation and certainly each and every occurrence in *The Lemon Tree* is documented in the extensive notes, sixty-five pages of notes with type so small that the notes are hardly readable to support two hundred and sixty-four pages of manuscript in larger type, no doubt more notes than actual copy. Conversations are recalled by specific people, happenings by recollections, often conflicting, and by records either in newspapers, journals, and books written by historians and others who have recorded the events of the war between Arabs and Jews. You remembered that I served you small cups of coffee in the garden on your first visit to our house; I remember that it was lemonade.

"But, Bashir, my friend, missing are any notes, not recollections of your many relatives who were interviewed or writings in journals or books of the small toy that exploded in your hand causing you to lose four fingers and your palm. Why would that be? If the Israelis had booby trapped toys that were left for the Arab children, were you the only child to suffer from an exploding toy? Nowhere was it written, to be documented in the notes to *The Lemon Tree* about these booby trapped toys that you seem to remember that the Israelis gave as gifts to the Arab children? No other child picked up a colorful, Israeli-left toy and suffered from its explosion? Only you? And, Bashir, you are, obviously right handed; but you carried this toy in your left hand, the hand that you claim was disfigured by the exploding toy in the kitchen of the cinder block house your family was living in in Gaza? And all the other children ran away when the water jug crashed to the floor and only you, brave boy of six, stayed in the kitchen?

"The story of is Dier Yassin is part of the Khairi family history "passed down through the generations." Is this a credible source? No verification, no reference to documentation in the multitude of writings by historians of the period that were used to compile this book. There were American journalists in the area at the time, Bilsby of the *Herald Tribune* and Gene Currivan of the *New York Times* and a reporter from *The Chicago Sun Times* who reported on the expulsions from al-Ramla and Lydda, but not a word from them on a massacre and rapes that, according to you, Bashir, took place in neighboring Dier Yassin (at that time, not generations before). Why?

"Bashir, you have lived a life of violence, a life of misdirected hate. Your hand could have been disfigured through any number of violent acts throughout your life, or you could have been born with a deformity which you only became cognizant of when you were six years old. However you lost your fingers and your palm, were it by means of a booby trap, surely this would have been mentioned in the sixty-five pages of notes in very fine print, either through the memory of a family member who was there or in documentation in some writing about the war. No, my dear friend, I believe in this particular case, and perhaps in others in addition to coffee in little cups rather than lemonade, your recollections are, at times, distorted, either by a faulty memory or to accommodate what you fervently believe in, what you believe in because you have not searched below the surface to seek out the truth of the cause of your troubles.

"Ah, Bashir, we could have lived so wonderfully together, sharing not only railroads and postage stamps, but technology, commerce, and education, learning of all sorts, and eventually, possibly, even love. Please, my friend, stop your hate. Let's make some sort of an accommodation. Let's live in the peace we could have and should have been living in all along had your Arabs not started a war, invaded to push the Jews into the sea instead of planting a rose garden."

Dear Mr. Tolan:

As you can see, I could have taken your research, all of which is valid and, I believe, true, and written a different book.

I am a writer, as you could see by checking me out on Amazon.com. I would like to speak with you about our possible collaboration on a sequel to your excellent and most readable *The Lemon Tree.* I believe both Dalia and Bashir are still alive. Perhaps Dalia, today, might respond to Bashir's insistence that her people leave this land other than, "But where would we go?" Their compassionate story can go on.

I can be reached at the above address. I look forward to hearing from you and, perhaps, could contribute valid and attention-grabbing input to a sequel.

Yours sincerely,
Ruth Moss

Sandy Tolan did not answer this letter.

CHAPTER 11

The Hell of Israel Is Better than the Paradise of Arafat

by *Daniel Pipes: Middle East Forum*

In the Palestinian Authority's (PA) elections that took place in January 2005, a significant percentage of Arab Jerusalemites stayed away from the polls. For example, the Associated Press quoted one taxi driver responded with indignation, "Are you kidding? To bring a corrupt [Palestinian] Authority here. This is just what we are missing."

This reluctance—as well as administrative incompetence—helped explain why, in the words of the *Jerusalem Post*, "at several balloting locations in the city [of Jerusalem], there were more foreign election observers, journalists, and police forces out than voters." It also explains why, in the previous PA election in 1996, a mere ten percent of Jerusalem's eligible population voted, far lower than the proportions elsewhere.

At first blush, surprisingly, worry about jeopardizing Israeli residency turns out to be widespread among the Palestinians in Israel. When given a choice of living under Zionist or Palestinian rule, they decidedly prefer the former. More than that, there is a body of pro-Israel sentiments from which to draw. No opinion surveys cover this delicate subject, but a substantial record of statements and actions suggest that despite their anti-Zionist swagger, Israel's most fervid enemies do perceive its political virtues. Even Palestinian leaders, between their fulminations, sometimes let down their guard and acknowledge Israel's virtues. This undercurrent of Palestinian love of Zion has hopeful and potentially significant implications.

Pro-Israel expressions fall into two main categories: preferring to remain under Israel rule and praising Israel as better than Arab regimes.

No Thank You, Palestinian Authority

Palestinians already living in Israel, especially in Jerusalem and the "Galilee Triangle" area, tell, sometimes volubly, how they prefer to remain in Israel.

Jerusalem. In mid-2000, when it appeared that some Arab-majority parts of Jerusalem would be transferred to Palestinian Authority control, Muslim Jerusalemites expressed less than delight at the prospect. Peering over at Arafat's PA, they saw power monopolized by domineering and corrupt autocrats, a thug-like police force, and a stagnant economy. Arafat's bloated, nonsensical claims ("We are the one true democratic oasis in the Arab region") only exacerbated their apprehensions.

'Abd al-Razzaq 'Abid of Jerusalem's Silwan neighborhood pointed dubiously to "what's happening in Ramallah, Hebron, and the Gaza Strip" and asked if the residents there were well off. A doctor applying for Israeli papers explained: the whole world seems to be talking about the future of the Arabs of Jerusalem, but no one has bothered asking us. The international community and the Israeli left seem to take it for granted that we want to live under Mr. Arafat's control. We don't. Most of us despise Mr. Arafat and the cronies around him, and we want to stay in Israel. At least here I can speak my mind freely without being dumped in prison as well as having a chance to earn an honest day's wage.

In the colorful words of one Jerusalem resident, "The hell of Israel is better than the paradise of Arafat. We know Israeli rule stinks, but sometimes we feel like Palestinian rule would be worse."

The director of the Bayt Hanina community council in northern Jerusalem, Husam Watad, found that the prospect of finding themselves living under Arafat's control had people "in a panic. More than fifty percent of east Jerusalem residents live below the poverty line, and you can imagine how the situation would look if residents did not receive [Israeli] National Insurance Institute payments." In the view of Fadal Tahabub, a member of the Palestinian National Council, an estimated seventy percent of the 200,000 Arab residents of Jerusalem preferred to remain under Israeli sovereignty. A social worker living in Ras al-'Amud, one of the areas possibly falling under PA control, said: "If a secret poll was conducted, I am sure an overwhelming majority of Jerusalem Arabs would say they would prefer to stay in Israel."

Indeed, precisely when Palestinian rule seemed most likely in 2000, the Israeli Interior Ministry reported a substantial increase in citizenship applications from Arabs in eastern Jerusalem. A Jerusalem city councilor, Roni Aloni, heard from many Arab residents about their not wanting to live under PA control. "They tell me—we are not like Gaza or the West Bank. We hold Israeli IDs. We are used to a higher standard of living. Even if Israeli rule is not so good, it is still better than that of the PA." Shalom Goldstein, an adviser on Arab affairs to the Jerusalem mayor, found likewise: "People look at what is happening inside the Palestinian-controlled areas today and say to themselves, 'Thank God we have Israeli ID cards.' In fact, most of the Arabs in the city prefer to live under Israeli rule than under a corrupt and tyrannical regime like Yasser Arafat's."

So many Jerusalem Arabs considered taking out Israeli papers in 2000 that the ranking Islamic official in Jerusalem issued an edict prohibiting his flock from holding Israeli citizenship (because this implies recognizing Israeli sovereignty over the holy city). Faysal al-Husayni, the Palestine Liberation Organization's man in charge of Jerusalem affairs, went further, "Taking Israeli citizenship is something that can only be defined as treason," and he threatened such people with exclusion from the Palestinian state. Finding his threat ineffective, Husayni upped the ante, announcing that Jerusalem Arabs who take Israeli citizenship would have their homes confiscated. The PA's radio station confirmed this, calling such persons "traitors" and threatening that they would be "tracked down." Many Palestinians were duly intimidated, fearing the authority's security forces.

But some spoke out. Hisham Gol of the Mount of Olives community council put it simply: "I prefer Israeli control." An affluent West Bank woman called a friend in Gaza to ask about life under the PA. She heard an ear-full, "I can only tell you to pray that the Israelis don't leave your town," because "the Jews are more human" than Palestinians. One individual willing publicly to oppose Arafat was Zohair Hamdan of Sur Bahir, a village in the south of metropolitan Jerusalem; he organized a petition of Jerusalem Arabs demanding that a referendum be held before Israel lets the Palestinian Authority take power in Jerusalem. "For thirty-three years, we have been part of the State of Israel. But now our rights have been forgotten." Over a year and a half, he collected more than 12,000 signatures (out of an estimated Jerusalem Arab population of 200,000). "We won't accept a situation where we are led like sheep to the slaughterhouse." Hamdan also expressed a personal preference that Sur Bahir remain part of Israel and estimated that the majority of Palestinians reject "Arafat's corrupt and tyrannical rule. Look what he's done in Lebanon, Jordan, and now in the West Bank and Gaza Strip. He has brought one disaster after another on his people."

The Galilee Triangle. Nor are such pro-Israeli sentiments limited to residents of Jerusalem. When Prime Minister Ariel Sharon's government released a trial balloon in February 2004 about giving the

Palestinian Authority control over the Galilee Triangle, a predominantly Arab part of Israel, the response came strong and hard. As Mahmoud Mahajnah, 25, told *Agence France-Presse,* "Yasir Arafat runs a dictatorship, not a democracy. No one here would accept to live under that regime. I've done my [Israeli] national service; I am a student here and a member of the Israeli Football Association. Why would they transfer me? Is that logical or legitimate?" One resident quoted what he called a local saying, that "the 'evil' of Israel is better than the 'heaven' of the West Bank." Shu'a Sa'd, 22, explained why, "Here you can say whatever you like and do whatever you want—so long as you don't touch the security of Israel. Over there, if you talk about Arafat, they can arrest you and beat you up." Another young man, 'Isam Abu 'Alu, 29, put it differently, "Mr. Sharon seems to want us to join an unknown state that doesn't have a parliament, or a democracy, or even decent universities. We have close family ties in the West Bank, but we prefer to demand our full rights inside Israel."

The entrance to Umm al-Fahm, the largest Muslim town in Israel, sports the green flags of the Islamic Movement Party that rules the town, along with a billboard denouncing Israel's rule over Jerusalem. That said, Hashim 'Abd ar-Rahman, mayor and local leader of the Islamic Movement, has no time for Sharon's suggestion, "Despite the discrimination and injustice faced by Arab citizens, the democracy and justice in Israel is better than the democracy and justice in Arab and Islamic countries." Nor does Ahmed Tibi, an Israeli Arab member of parliament and advisor to Arafat, care for the idea of PA control, which he calls "a dangerous, antidemocratic suggestion."

Just thirty percent of Israel's Arab population, a May 2001 survey found, agree to the Galilee Triangle being annexed to a future Palestinian state, meaning that a large majority prefers to remain in Israel. By February 2004, according to the Haifa-based Arab Center for Applied Social Research, that number had jumped to ninety percent preferring to remain in Israel. No less startling, seventy-three percent of Triangle Arabs said they would resort to violence to prevent changes in the border. Their reasons divided fairly evenly between those claiming Israel as their homeland (forty-three percent) and those cherishing Israel's higher standard of living (thirty-three percent). So intense was the Arab opposition to ceding the Galilee Triangle to the Palestinian Authority that Sharon quickly gave the idea up.

The issue arose a bit later in 2004 as Israel built its security fence. Some Palestinians, like Umm al-Fahm's Ahmed Jabrin, 67, faced a choice on which side of the fence to live. He had no doubts. "We fought [the Israeli authorities] so as to be inside of the fence, and they moved it so we are still in Israel. We have many links to Israel. What have we to do with the Palestinian Authority?" His relative, Hisham Jabrin, 31, added: "We are an integral part of Israel and will never be part of a Palestinian state. We have always lived in Israel and there is absolutely no chance that that will change."

Preferring Israel to the Arab Regimes

Palestinians—from the lowest level to the highest ranking—sometimes acknowledge how they prefer Israel to Arab countries. As one PLO official observed, "We no longer fear the Israelis or the Americans, regardless of their hostility, but we now fear our Arab 'brothers.'" Or, in the general observation of a Gazan, "The Arabs say they're our friends, and treat us worse than the Israelis do." Here are examples of attitudes toward three states:

- *Syria.* Salah Khalaf (a.k.a. Abu Iyad), one of the PLO's top figures, declared in 1983 that crimes committed by the Hafiz al-Assad regime against the Palestinian people "surpassed those of the Israeli enemy." In like spirit, Yasir Arafat addressed a PLO figure murdered at Syrian instigation at his funeral, "The Zionists in the occupied territories tried to kill you, and when they failed, they deported you. However, the Arab Zionists represented by the rulers of Damascus thought this was insufficient, so you fell as a martyr."
- *Jordan.* Victor, a Jordanian who once worked as advance man for a senior Saudi government minister, observed in 1994 that Israel was the only Middle Eastern country he admires. "I wish Israel would just take over Jordan," he said, his brother

nodding in vigorous agreement. "The Israelis are the only people around here who are organized, who know how to get things done. And they're not bad people. They're straight. They keep their word. The Arabs can't do anything right. Look at this so-called democracy in Jordan. It's a complete joke."

- *Kuwait.* Palestinians collaborated with Iraqi forces occupying Kuwait in 1990, so when the country was liberated, they came in for some rough treatment. One Palestinian newspaper found that in Kuwait, "Palestinians are receiving treatment even worse than they have had at the hands of their enemies, the Israelis." After surviving the Kuwaiti experience, another Palestinian minced no words, "Now I feel Israel is paradise. I love the Israelis now. I know they treat us like humans. The West Bank [still then under Israeli control] is better [than Kuwait]. At least before the Israelis arrest you, they bring you a paper." With less exuberance, Arafat himself concurred: "What Kuwait did to the Palestinian people is worse than what has been done by Israel to Palestinians in the occupied territories."

Many Palestinians already understood the virtues of Israeli political life decades ago. As one man from Ramallah explained, "I'll never forget that day during the Lebanon war [of 1982], when an Arab Knesset member got up and called [Prime Minister Menachem] Begin a murderer. Begin didn't do a thing [in response]. If you did that to Arafat, I don't think you'd make it home that night." Before the Palestinian Authority came into existence in 1994, most Palestinians dreamt of autonomy without worrying much about the details. After Arafat's return to Gaza, they could make a direct comparison between his rule and Israel's, something they frequently do. They have many reasons for preferring life in Israel:

Restraints on violence. After the PA police raided the house of a Hamas supporter in an after-midnight operation and roughed up both him and his 70-year-old father, the father yelled at the police, "Even the Jews did not behave like you cowards." And the son, when he came out of the PA prison, declared his experience there much worse than in the Israeli jails. An opponent of Arafat's pointed out how Israeli soldiers "would first fire tear gas, and then fire rubber bullets, and only then shoot live ammunition. They never shot at us without a direct order to shoot, and then they only shot a few bullets. But these Palestinian police started shooting immediately, and they shot everywhere."

Freedom of expression. 'Adnan Khatib, owner and editor of *Al-Umma*, a Jerusalem weekly whose printing plant was burned down by PA police in 1995, bemoaned the troubles he'd had since the Palestinian Authority's heavy-handed leaders got power over him, "The measures they are taking against the Palestinian media, including the arrest of journalists and the closure of newspapers, are much worse than those taken by the Israelis against the Palestinian press." In an ironic turn of events, Na'im Salama, a lawyer living in Gaza, was arrested by the PA on charges he slandered it by writing that Palestinians should adopt Israeli standards of democracy. Specifically, he referred to charges of fraud and breach of trust against then-prime minister Binyamin Netanyahu. Salama noted how the system in Israel allowed police to investigate a sitting prime minister and wondered when the same might apply to the PA chieftain. For this audacity, he spent time in jail. Hanan Ashrawi, an obsessive anti-Israel critic, acknowledged (reluctantly) that the Jewish state has something to teach the nascent Palestinian polity, "Freedom would have to be mentioned although it has only been implemented in a selective way, for example, the freedom of speech." 'Iyad as-Sarraj, a prominent psychiatrist and director of the Gaza Community Mental Health Program, confesses that "during the Israeli occupation, I was 100 times freer [than under the Palestinian Authority]."

Democracy. Israel's May 1999 elections, which Netanyahu lost, impressed many Palestinian observers. Columnists cited in a Middle East Media and Research Institute (MEMRI) study remarked on the smooth transition in Israel and wanted the same for themselves; as one put it, he envies the Israelis and wants "a similar regime in my future state." Even one of Arafat's employees, Hasan al-Kashif, director-general of the PA's

Information Ministry, contrasted Netanyahu's immediate and graceful exit from office with the perpetual power of "several names in our leadership" who go on ruling in perpetuity. Nayif Hawatma, leader of the terrorist Democratic Front for the Liberation of Palestine, wished the Palestinian Authority made decisions more like Israel:

We want the PNC [Palestine National Council] to discuss the developments since 1991, particularly the Oslo Accords which were concluded behind the back of the PNC contrary to what happened in Israel, for example, where the accords were presented to the Knesset and public opinion for voting.

His facts might not be completely accurate, but they do make his point.

Rule of law. As the *intifada* of 1987 degenerated into fratricidal murder and became known as the "intrafada," PLO leaders increasingly appreciated Israeli fairness. Haydar 'Abd ash-Shafi', head of the Palestinian delegation to the Washington peace talks, made a remarkable observation in 1992 according to a transcript published in a Beirut newspaper, "Can anyone imagine that a family would be happy to hear a knock at the door in the middle of the night from the Israeli army?" He continued: "When the infighting began in Gaza, the people were happy because the Israeli army imposed a curfew." Likewise, Musa Abu Marzouk, a high-ranking Hamas official, scored points against Arafat in 2000 by comparing him unfavorably with the Jewish state. "We saw representatives of the Israeli opposition criticize [Israeli Prime Minister Ehud] Barak and they were not arrested …but in our case, the Palestinian Authority arrests people as the first order of business."

Protection of minorities. Christians and secular Muslims particularly appreciate Israel's protection at a time when Palestinian politics has taken an increasingly Islamist cast. The French weekly *L'Express* quotes a Christian Palestinian to the effect that when the Palestinian state comes into existence, "the sacred union against the Zionist enemy will die. It will be time to settle accounts. We will undergo the same as our Lebanese brothers or the Copts in Egypt. It saddens me to say so, but Israeli laws protect us." His fear is in many ways too late, as the Palestinian Christian population has precipitously declined in recent decades, to the point that one analyst asks if Christian life is "to be reduced to empty church buildings and a congregation-less hierarchy with no flock in the birthplace of Christianity?"

Economic benefits. Palestinians who live in Israel (including Jerusalem) appreciate Israel's economic success, social services, and many benefits. Salaries in Israel are about five times higher than in the West Bank and Gaza Strip, and Israel's social security system has no parallel on the Palestinian side. Palestinians living outside of Israel want economically in; when the Israeli government announced the completion of an 85-mile-long section of a security fence to protect the country from Palestinian terrorists, one resident of Qalqiliya, a West Bank border town, reacted with a revealing outrage, "We are living in a big prison."

Tolerance of homosexuals. In the West Bank and Gaza, conviction for sodomy brings a three-to ten-year jail term, and gay men tell of being tortured by the PA police. Some of them head for Israel where one estimate finds 300 mostly male gay Palestinians living. Donatella Rovera of Amnesty International comments, "Going to Israel is a one-way ticket, and once there their biggest problem is possibly being sent back."

Palestinians living in the West who visit the Palestinian Authority are vividly aware of its drawbacks compared to Israel. "There is a difference between the Israeli and the PA occupation," wrote Daoud Abu Naim, a medical researcher in Philadelphia while visiting family in Shuafat, "The Israelis whom I met with over the years have been diverse. Some have been insensitive to our needs, and some have not been. On the other hand, the Arafat/Rajoub regime is more than simply 'corrupt.' It is exclusively interested in setting up a dictatorship in which Palestinian citizens will have no civil liberties whatsoever."

Rewadah Edais, a high school student who lives most of the year in San Francisco and visits Jerusalem regularly, added, "The Israelis took our land, but when it comes to governing, they know what they're doing."

Conclusion

Several themes emerge from this history. First, for all the overheated rhetoric about Israel's "vicious" and "brutal" occupation, Palestinians are alive to the benefits of its liberal democracy. They appreciate the elections, rule of law, freedom of speech and religion, minority rights, orderly political structures, and the other benefits of a decent polity. There is, in short, a constituency for normality among the Palestinians, difficult as that may be to perceive in the hate-filled crowds that so dominate news coverage. Second, many of those who have tasted Israel's economic benefits are loathe to forego them; however impervious Palestinians may seem to economics, they know a good deal when they have one. Third, the percentage of Palestinians who would prefer to live under Israeli control cited in the estimates noted above—an overwhelming majority of seventy to ninety percent—point to this being more than a rarity among Palestinians. This has obvious implications for Israeli concessions on the "right to return" suggesting that Palestinians will move to Israel in large numbers. Fourth, it implies that some of the more imaginative final status solutions that involve the redrawing of borders will be hard to implement; Palestinians appear no more eager to live under Palestinian Authority rule than are Israelis.

In word and deed, then, even Palestinians acknowledge Israel as the most civilized state in the Middle East. Amid the gloom of today's political extremism and terrorism, this fact offers wisps of hope.

CHAPTER 12

Boycott Israel:

Don't Use Any Israeli Products

Those awful Israelis! Let's show them what our economic sanctions can do to them. We won't buy the products they sell on the world market, which will, certainly, hurt their economy; but being true to the genuine spirit of "boycott," let's, also, stop using items that Israel developed and sold in the past, even if Israel no longer receives payment for these products. We'll show them.

(Or us?)

The State of Israel has faced ostensibly insurmountable odds during the course of its entire history. Hostile neighbors, a vast desert terrain, and its unique demographic make-up have caused the Jewish state to surmount a myriad of impediments. Still, it has come forward as "a light unto the nations." The Jewish state is today a member of the elite Organization for Economic Cooperation and Development (OECD), has hundreds of companies listed on Nasdaq and its expertise, technology, humanitarian assistance, and defense strategies are used by countries on all continents.

There are, also, less glamorous Israeli expertise such as the irrigation, desalinization, and dry land farming technologies that water-poor Israel has developed over the decades. Because Israel is sixty percent desert, its farmers and agricultural scientists have, since even before the establishment of the State, focused on increasing both the yield and Quality of crops, along with making agriculture more efficient, in general, by advancing vital agricultural techniques. Israel has developed flourishing agriculture on arid land, the basis of the "green line," and gives these agricultural and irrigation technologies, developed at great cost, gratis to developing countries.

A particular Israeli invention out of the myriad of discoveries that continuously come out of Israel deserves special recognition because of its value to the world in food production and water conservation. This is the drip irrigation system developed on an Israeli kibbutz and is, currently, employed globally in one hundred and twelve countries with thirteen factories all over the world. The drip irrigation system makes it possible to get larger, high quality yields of agricultural products with significantly smaller amounts of water than just a few decades ago. With this system in position, not only are farmers getting significantly greater crop yields but by managing the water resource more adeptly, drip irrigation means the use of a decreased quantity of fertilizer. The manufacture of fertilizers is a significant source of greenhouse gas production.

Drip irrigation has turned out to be well-liked by fruit and vegetable growers in dry weather regions from the desert areas of sub-Sudan Africa to Southern California to the Middle East to India. Israeli experts gave a course on drip irrigation and crop management in Swaziland after a severe draught caused by the effects of El Nino almost crippled Swaziland last year leaving thousand without food. The Israeli experts trained nineteen agronomists in techniques to train farmers to irrigate and manage crops correctly to yield considerably more from their plantings.

The world's first surface drip irrigation system was developed in the 1960s at Kibbutz Hatzerim near Be'er Sheva. Also, Israeli scientists have advanced genetically modified, disease-resistant bananas, peppers, and other crops that are increasing the world's food supply and facilitating keeping prices down at grocery stores all over the world. Dr. Clive Lipchin, Dir. Center for Transboundry Water Management at Israel's Arava Institute for Environmental Studies speaks on how Israel has turned from a water poor country to a water rich country through efficient water management, centralized water planning, effective conservation, use of drip irrigation and brackish water, recycling, and desalination.

So, shall we refuse to buy high quality, lower priced food because the food was grown using drip irrigation technology developed in Israel? Let's hold that in abeyance. Perhaps we can find enough other products to boycott Israel with.

Israel used to export Jaffa Oranges. Now, Jaffa oranges are grown under license in Spain. The Sharon Valley along Israel's Mediterranean coast where Jaffa oranges were grown and which, in the spring for many, many miles gave off the sweet, fragrant aroma of citrus blossoms is now dotted with beautiful, glass, high rise buildings housing America's premier computer companies which employ thousands of Israeli workers, both Arabs and Jews. The land, today, is much too valuable to grow oranges on so, if we boycott Jaffa oranges, will we be hurting Israel or Spain? A conundrum.

Besides for computer technology and drip irrigation, among Israel's major exports, today, are packaged medications which include antibiotics, insulin, hormones, and alkaloids. Well, we could use these, but if it's a question of using a different cough drop--and who even knows what an alkaloid is--we can avoid Israeli products without any discomfort to ourselves.

Israel has a tremendous diamond cutting industry, amongst the world's largest, but I can, in all good conscience, avoid buying Israeli-cut diamonds, today. It's not like I'm avoiding using my cell phone. I resolve not to buy a fistful of diamonds, today.

(We'll show them!)

Israel, also, exports flowers; but I can live without Israeli flowers, especially since I don't know if these perishable flowers are exported as far as the United States and besides, I can go onto my computer and have fresh flowers delivered to my beloveds. No need to look for Israeli flowers.

Another major Israeli export is medical technology. Israeli doctors, scientists and researchers have turned out innumerable medical advances throughout Israel's history. Whether attained through independent research or through joint projects with the United States, the medical breakthroughs made by the Jewish state are enhancing the lives of millions around the world.

But most Americans are healthy. They keep a good diet and work out; we're not concerned about medical technology, especially since we don't purchase this directly like we would Jaffa oranges or cough drops. When we go into the hospital, we're treated. We don't know where the machinery that takes images of us or keeps us alive during operations came from, or where the machines were developed.

Besides, we hear of people with all kinds of physical and medical problems, but how often are we, really, affected by a serious physical problem or a disease? Watch your diet, work out, and don't smoke like an Israeli, and don't worry about getting sick. Much more important to us are our everyday lives and the things we need and use every day. So, we'll look at what Israel has come up with lately in medical technology, but that hardly affects us like our computers and cell phones do.

In *Uncovering Israel21c,* April 15, 2016, "Israel has developed ApiFix a less expensive and more efficient system to correct acute spinal curvature (scoliosis)" which "minimizes risks, scar size, complications, and recovery time." Mazor Robotic's Spine Assist and other surgical robots are transforming spine surgery from freehand procedures to highly accurate, state-of-the-art operations with less need for radiation "and Rewalk, a robotic exoskeleton that was showcased on the popular TV show 'Glee' which allows runners to participate in marathons." Rewalk enables otherwise debilitated persons to sit, stand, walk, turn, and climb and descend stairs by operating the system single-handedly.

An innovation called IceSense3 has been employed in the US since 2011 to eradicate non-malignant breast lumps in a ten minute procedure that perforates the tumor and surrounds it with ice. And for women who undergo hysterectomies every year to treat uterine fibroids, ExAblate 2000 System is a system of using MRI ultrasound technology to obliterate tumors and uterine fibroid cysts without surgery.

Surgical incisions using cold plasma instead of painful stitches, staples, or glue within minutes, seals and disinfects the wound with minimal scarring and recovery time are being bonded by BioWeld1.

"MicronJet is a single-use needle for painless delivery of vaccines into the skin. The product has been proven to generate superior immune response with less vaccine because it does not go past the skin level." Less serums in our bodies, especially the yearly flu shot which is a guess of which strains of flu *might* be prevalent the following year.

A new invention is WatchPAT which one can use to diagnose sleep disorders at home and EndoPat, a cutting-edge test for the early onset of arteriosclerosis.

Newly developed in Israel is ExAblte OR which uses MRI-guided focused ultrasound to destroy tumors and uterine fibroid cysts without surgery and the US Food and Drug Administration (FDA) has just, in July, 2016, approved its sister, ExAblate Neuro, which can alleviate essential tremor, a common movement disorder, using the same non-invasive technology to appreciably lower risk of infection, hemorrhage, brain damage, and heart disease.

Another Israeli invention, the GI View Aer-O-Scope is a one-time use colorectal cancer diagnosis apparatus which will render lifesaving colonoscopy screenings less expensive, more secure, and more available worldwide. The self-navigating, malleable Aer-O-Scope eliminates the danger of puncturing the colon. The Aer-O-Scope

Colonoscope is devised to profoundly transform the manner in which colorectal cancer assessment will be done. It is fabricated to assist GI practices and hospital outpatient departments encountering mounting requests for colorectal screening with a dependable, easy-to-use, and economical throwaway colonoscope. Pre-clinical and clinical tests were performed in Israel to validate the Aer-O-Scope system's three hundred and sixty degree imagining proficiencies as well as safety and intubation rate targets.

Uncovering Israel21c reported on NBM-200, "A non-invasive monitor is relied upon by blood donation centers in forty countries for measuring of potential donors' hemoglobin level (to check for anemia) and other blood constraints. This device eliminates the need for finger pricking as well as biologically hazardous equipment and waste."

(Ouch, colonoscopies and exoskeletons are fine, but I hate to have my finger pricked!)

Uncovering Israel, also, reports on "NeuroEndoGraft flow diverters redirect blood flow from a brain aneurysm (a bulge in a weak artery wall), so that a stable clot can form and the potentially fatal aneurysm no longer is in danger of rupturing."

And anyone who has ever tended to an elderly family member or young, bedbound competitor and any nurse can connect with "Total Lift Bed [which] is the world's only hospital-grade bed that can elevate a patient from a lying to a fully standing position with no lifting required of the caregiver."

Too much gibberish. All these things are important, but it's a matter of prerogatives. Would I give up my cell phone or my computer in the expectation that I might, someday, need to lift someone out of a bed? You bet I wouldn't.

Israel is progressing in the development of products to cure blood cancers, dense tumors, blood disorders like sickle-cell anemia, autoimmune diseases, and genetic diseases. The first patient has been successfully transplanted at Duke University Medical Center.

Additional medical technical discoveries can be found in "The Jewish Virtual Library" "Weizmann University Professor Zelig Eshhar pioneered the innovative adaptive immunotherapy technique which is now being hailed as a "potentially extraordinary development" in cancer treatment. An article published in *Science Translational Medicine*, University of Pennsylvania's Abramson Cancer Center and the Perelman School of Medicine reported that twenty-seven out of twenty-nine patients suffering from advanced blood cancer saw their disease *go into remission or disappear completely* when treated with adaptive immunotherapy. The documentation is from "The Jewish Virtual Library," but authenticated by the two publications mentioned.

Hadassah Hospital can, now, identify disease through acid levels in the body's tissues. With this ground-breaking diagnostic tool, a non-invasive method of imaging the pH levels in the body's tissues, malignant cells can be identified with greater certainty, a more precise identification of tumor as benign or malignant.

For the first time ever, live human bone tissue grown outside the body has been successfully transplanted into a person's arm. This sets a new standard of hope for rapid healing and was the only solution for a patient when nothing else helped. The success of this experiment may lead to a new era in which it will be possible to achieve full recovery, otherwise non-achievable.

"Electro-optic medical devices for non-invasive treatment of skin cancer, benign lesions, varicose veins, skin rejuvenation, and hair removal have been developed."

(So far, several different cancer treatment devices.)

"A catheter-delivered ultrasound for thrombolysis, a non-invasive therapeutic ultrasound in the heart which early studies have shown could break up clots in peripheral vessels" has, also, been developed, as has "T-Scan devices which significantly improve mammography diagnostic accuracy with no additional radiation; kits for detecting mental illnesses; sonometers which detect subtle changes in bone quality, as in osteoporosis and other bone diseases; Sure-Closure Skin-Stretching system, replacing costly skin grafts or flaps to close large wounds and avoid disfiguring scars; and Silicone sheeting which eases intense pain after scar-tissue removal operations."

A device which sends out an alarm if a baby stops breathing while asleep, as happens in SIDS (sudden infant death syndrome) is called Babysense; and, also, to prevent SIDS, there is, now, an early warning monitor which senses lowered breathing and pulse levels.

(You can tell anxious parents who are aware of SIDS to just let their babies die in their sleep because you want them to boycott Israeli products.)

Young children with breathing problems will soon be sleeping more soundly thanks to a new Israeli device called the Child Hood. This innovation replaces the inhalation mask with an improved drug delivery system that provides relief for the children and parents who choose not to go along with our boycott.

Israeli researchers have come up with a non-invasive fetal ECG and a fetal heart rate monitoring system which prevents unnecessary C-section deliveries, and the Tissue Vitality Analyzer (TVA), which is expected to save lives and millions of dollars by detecting failed organs before implantation.

(How would you like to get an organ transplant and then find out that the organ was no good!)

Israeli researchers have, also, come up with compact, pocket-sized, battery-powered Transcutanous Electronic Nerve Stimulation (TENS) stimulator to relieve menstrual pain."

(If the reader is a woman, she can, certainly, relate to this.)

Anyone interested in devices for treating kidney stones, gallstones, or a device to treat urinary incontinence and various prostate disorders?

(Prostate disorders? Now, male readers could be interested, too. Not so boring, is it?)

All nations should be interested in the newly discovered anti-radiation therapy, able to cure almost all patients exposed to nonconventional radiological incidents, such as dirty bombs or attacks on nuclear power plants.

And I'll stop with "a thermal imaging system for real-time images of blood flow through exposed coronary arteries without ingesting toxic contrast materials or exposure to radiation."

Another source listing Israel's medical advances is "Take a Pen Global." Here are some additional recent medical discoveries in Israel the "Take a Pen" lists.

(Don't they do anything else in Israel like play soccer, dodge rockets from Gaza, or eat falaful?)

"An Israeli company has developed a simple blood test that distinguishes between mild and more severe cases of Multiple Sclerosis."

(So, if you know anyone suffering from MS, tell them to ignore this discovery that could more accurately diagnose their symptoms.)

"Take a Pen" lists an Israeli-made device that helps restore the use of paralyzed hands." This device electrically invigorates the hand muscles, offering hopefulness to millions of stroke victims and sufferers of spinal, or other, injuries"

The Baltimore Sun on Dec. 20, 2017 reported that an "Israeli company's technology lets quadriplegics use the phone without physical assistance" and that video game technology has allowed payers to control their games by moving their heads. This led to the creation of "Open Sesame, later called Sesame Enable," an app that allows control of a touch screen smartphone or tablet by a small head movement or voice commands.

"Take a Pen" tells of the discovery of human monoclonal antibodies which can deactivate the extremely transmittable smallpox virus without generating the perilous side effects of the present current vaccine has been created by a researcher at Israel's Ben Gurion University of the Negev.

Frank's Sign: a team of Israeli researchers has recommended that doctors add Frank's Sign, a diagonal earlobe crease, to the list of key indicators that patients are susceptible to strokes. Published in the *American Journal of Medicine* (AJM), their study found that seventy-eight of eighty-eight patients (eighty-eight per cent) who had suffered a full-blown stroke had the diagonal lobe creases. Additionally, sixty-six of the patients who suffered the most common type of stroke, acute ischemic (where a blockage cuts off blood supply to the brain), had previously experienced a heart attack. In this group, almost nine out of ten had the Frank's sign marker.

From these findings, researchers concluded that Frank's sign could predict ischemic cerebrovascular events (strokes) and that patients with classical cardiovascular risk factors had the ear crease in higher numbers. The crease may signal poor blood supply to the earlobes, or could be a symptom of weakening in the blood vessels. It could also be related to aging.

A new research center in Israel hopes to discredit demystify brain disorders such as depression and Alzheimer's disease.

Israeli scientists may have found a cure for some of the worst inflammatory diseases, affecting millions worldwide with a single drug. Prof. David Naor of the Hebrew University-Hadassah Medical School in Jerusalem says he may have discovered a new game-changing treatment with just one drug that targets several chronic inflammatory and neurodegenerative diseases, including multiple sclerosis, Alzheimer's, rheumatoid arthritis, Crohn's and colitis.

For their discovery of one of the human cell's most essential cyclical progressions which will blaze the way to DNA and immune defense systems overhaul two Israelis have received Nobel Prizes in Chemistry.

The elimination of the physical manifestations of Parkinson's disease has been achieved by Israel's Movement Disorder Surgery Program. A Hebrew University doctoral student has developed a tool to diagnose Parkinson's Disease in an earlier stage than it previously could be detected. This could lead to a minimally invasive and cost effective method to improve the lives of those afflicted with the disease.

Israel is developing a nose drop that will provide a five-year flu vaccine.

Israel's Given Imaging has come up with PillCam, a minute camera encapsulated in a pill. With PillCam, physicians can investigate the small bowel, esophagus, and colon with this small, disposable capsule and monitor and diagnose disorders of the gastrointestinal tract without sedation or invasive endoscopic. Patients, simply, swallow the pill that contains the camera. For this, Given Imaging was awarded The 2004 Wall Street Journal Technology Innovation Award.

Researchers at Hebrew University, working with scientists at the Massachusetts Institute of Technology, have developed a special protein designed to attack cancer cells. The major challenge in treating cancer has been to minimize damage to healthy cells while eliminating cancer cells. Indeed, cancer patients are all too familiar with the debilitating effects on the body resulting from toxic chemicals and radiation. This international consortium of researchers from Boston's MIT and Israel's Hebrew University have succeeded in using the portion of human DNA that identifies disease to develop a protein that naturally targets cancer cells, while avoiding healthy ones.

Enough about cancer, the flu, all kinds of operations, cures for various disorders, what about our eyes? Are Israeli researchers going to ignore our eyes? We all know the answer to that. They have come up with Bio-Retina, a tiny implantable device inserted into the retina in a thirty minute procedure that turns into an artificial retina that merges to the neurons in the eye. Activated by special eyeglasses, the device transforms natural light into an electrical impulse that arouses neurons and inspires them to send pictures to the brain.

EarlySense is a monitoring system that enables hospital nurses to monitor and document patients' heart rate, respiration, and movement remotely including patient falls.

Israeli-invented surgical robots are converting spine surgery from by hand-techniques to precise, state-of-the-art operations with less necessity for radiation.

These are some of the medical advances and ongoing research you can help eliminate by boycotting anything developed or produced in Israel. But have you, really, made a sacrifice? Can you count on the fingers of your left hand those whom you, personally, know who have benefited from these medical advances as you go on with your daily life without disruption? And do you, really, know where the diagnostic apparatus you have been subjected to in tests or treatments came from? Even if you would be willing to forgo treatment because the piece of equipment came from or was invented in Israel, would you deny your child, your spouse, or your parent these life-saving procedures?

All of the innovations listed here are of importance to society in general and of vital importance to those suffering from the specific ailments that can be alleviated by these discoveries. However, one particular medical advance deserves special acclaim for anyone serving in his country's military and any family member of a combat serviceperson. An advanced new bandage developed in Israel that saves lives by stopping traumatic hemorrhaging wounds is, now, being used by American forces. Before this innovative bandage, the same dressings as those used in World War II were still being used to patch up wounds.

A foremost cause of death for wounded soldiers was not the wound itself, but the loss of blood on the battleground. In the Vietnam War, twenty-five percent of wounded soldiers died from hemorrhage bleeding or wounds to their extremities. Now, only ten percent of the deaths are attributable to loss of blood on the battlefield. Before the invention of this, new emergency bandage, soldiers were taken off the battlefield to a medical facility to be treated for their injuries. Today, they are treated immediately, which greatly improves their odds of survival. This new Israeli bandage can stop what was once thought to be uncontrollable bleeding. The new technology is hailed as a life-saving bandage that can succeed where conventional treatment procedures might fail to stop a deadly hemorrhage.

At Ben Gurion University of the Negev, Shani Eliyahu-Gross developed WoundClot, a gauze that absorbs twenty-five times its own weight of blood and forms a coagulating gel membrane on the open wound. WoundClot, not only stops severe bleedings within minutes without the need to apply pressure on the wound but also enhances the blood's natural process of clotting.

In 2001, the Army Rangers began to use these emergency bandages followed by the mainstream US army and marines. Today, all the US Special forces including the Navy Seals and, also, the CIA, the FBI, and other special units use the Emergency Bandages.

We won't go into detail as we did with medical technology, but Israel has come up with security capability to aid in the battle against terror and has offered this technology to the US for its homeland security, including a phone that can activate a bomb from a distance or be utilized for strategic interactions with terrorists, bank robbers, or hostage-takers as well as cellular jamming and detection results that security and law enforcement authorities have entrée to. *Yahoo!* tech columnist Rob Pegoraro wrote earlier this year that the United States could learn a lot from Israel's approach to cybersecurity.

Israel is furthering a cleaner world. Israel is the forerunner in the world in such decisive disciplines as solar power generation and seawater desalination in this era of expanding populations, decreasing resources, and environmental deterioration. As nations strive to utilize their resources as economically as possible, Israel's avant-garde technologies have the capability to advance the health and living standards of hundreds of millions throughout the world while making industry more proficient and diminishing the environmental effect of human activities.

Israel's plan to break away from gasoline dependence is making available structure and predictability to the marketplace, merging lasting public sector guarantees with regulatory constancy to send a strong message that transformation will take place in Israel. Through investments in basic science and industrial R&D and the opening of pilot programs and full scale-ups for promising technology, Israel is taking the lead in challenging one of the most urgent security matters of our time. A country of under eight million people, Israel single-handedly cannot terminate gasoline's global monopoly nor stop the West's dependency on hostile petro-regimes. But jointly with international partners, Israel can function as an initiator of intellectual property and a test-bed for inventive resolutions, contesting the economic and security exposure that the United States and Israel, and much of the rest of the industrialized world, face owing to gasoline dependence.

Israel has established a national objective in accordance with the Copenhagen Accord to amplify its share of renewable energy in electricity generation to ten percent by 2020. In that same time frame, Israel intends to cut down its electricity usage by twenty percent.

We mentioned, briefly, that the computer industry is very prevalent in Israel, and we won't dwell on Israeli achievements in this area, either, to the extent that we did with medical technology, but—Oh! My goodness!—most of Windows was developed in Israel, as was the Pentium MMX chip and the Pentium 4 microprocessor and the Centrino processor!

I can't use my computer! Not if I'm going to truly boycott Israel! But I'm saved; I can get everything I am used to getting on my computer on my phone and fool myself into thinking that I'm still boycotting Israel, or I can switch to a Mac. Whew! I won't even concern myself that voice mail and the AOL Instant Messenger ICQ were, also, developed in Israel or I'll, simply, go into denial.

What more can happen to my quiet, secure life? I'm glad I'm through with what these horrible, narcissistic Israelis have invented while they're dodging the rockets from Gaza in the south and from Hezbollah in the north. At least they can let me live in peace with my mobile phone. Wait a minute! The phone technology "that can activate a bomb or be programed to jam for security reasons." Not my phone! My precious phone! I can't live without my phone! *It was developed in Israel*, as well as the latest phone technology!

Many offices now have computerized phones that plug into the Internet, taking advantage of Voice over Internet Protocol, or VoIP. VocalTec Communications of Herzliya, Israel, developed the first practical Internet phone software. Likewise, those who love talking with acquaintances over the Internet may be interested to realize that this online marvel started in Israel. Even though the technology now belongs to AOL, Israel's Mirabilis developed the first popular Internet chat program, ICQ.

Know what else you can get on your phone, WAZE, developed in Israel to get you where you're going.

Millions of Americans watch online streaming video for entertainment or educational purposes on a daily basis. Metacafe, the world's third-most-popular video sharing website, was founded in Israel. Tech-savvy Americans over the age of thirty can recall the original IBM Personal Computer of the early 1980s. What they may not know is that its brain, the Intel 8088 processor, was developed by Intel's Israel division. More recently, the Pentium M series of processors for laptop computers using the Intel Centrino platform, as well as some of Intel's latest processors (Yonah, Merom, Woodcrest), were also devised by Intel Israel. Furthermore, Amazon.com's Kindle e-reader is indebted for much of its success to technology developed in Israel.

For the iPhone X, although Apple is located in CA, it uses hundreds of suppliers, and many of the components inside the iPhone are built and assembled in Israel. Apple CEO Tim Cook recently visited Apple's second largest research and development facility which is located in Herziliya, Israel; and earlier this year, Apple acquired RealFace, an Israeli company that specializes in cybersecurity and which developed facial recognition software for users to log in.

Vishay is a major manufacturer of Smartphone components with factories located in the Negev Desert cities of Be'er Sheva and Dimona and in the Galilee town of Migdal Ha'emek.

Orbotech is another Israeli company that has helped develop iPhone models. Another Apple-acquired company, PrimeSense, specializes in the development of motion sensors and 3D sensing cameras.

The Palestinians haven't given up harassing and murdering the Israelis, but I give up. I'll give up my boycott and admit it to myself. The Palestinians have started wars, including the two major ones in 1948 and 1967 with the expressed desire of exterminating Israel and its Jewish population and have, since then, bombarded Israeli cities with rockets that have no precision like the old B 52 bombers that dispensed packs of bombs, the theory being that at least some would hit a target while the Palestinian leaders keep their pitiable subjects in purposefully despicable conditions so they can blame the Israelis and indoctrinate the children with make-believe atrocities so they can grow up to be suicide bombers.

And all the while, Israeli inventiveness has contributed more in the way of in science, medicine, agriculture, communications, and security to the wellbeing of the world than any other nation in history, and to the welfare of the Palestinians as well, many of whom receive excellent medical care in Israeli medical facilities as well as electricity and pure water from Israel.

I changed my mind: let's not boycott Israel.

Recently, in America, there has been a backlash against the BDS (Boycott, Divestment and Sanctions) movement.

Florida and California have taken legislative measures against the BDS movement and other anti-Israel groups and businesses. The original anti BDS legislation was passed by the Tennessee Senate for its anti-Israel activity and the damage it inflicts on the cause of peace in the Middle East. California and Florida have introduced the Israel Commerce Protection Acts which will require these States to divest themselves from all companies that participate in boycotts of Israel. Illinois has signed into law a bill will set up a blacklist of companies that boycott Israel and require the state's pension funds to divest from those companies.

The latest is New York. The *Israel Times,* June 10, 2016, reported that just prior to the New York Israel Day parade, Gov. Andrew Cuomo addressed the crowd saying, "We want to take immediate action because we want the world to know, we want Israel to know, we're on its side. If you boycott Israel, New York will boycott you. If you divert revenues from Israel, New York will divert revenues from you. If you sanction Israel, New York will sanction you."

Like anti-BDS measures passed in other states, Cuomo's order bans New York state agencies and departments from investing in companies or groups that, as a policy, promote or engage in boycotts, divestment or sanctions against Israel. The order also requires the state to draw up a public list of companies that engage in or promote BDS.

Christians United for Israel sums up Israel's contributions to the world, "The Jewish contribution to humanity is immense, and Israel is a world leader in developing innovative life-enhancing and life-saving technologies.

"By contrast, the only major innovations for which the Palestinians are known are the Qassam rocket and the suicide bomb vest."

Addendum:

Soda Stream: The Christian Science Monitor, Jan 30, 2016

"The boycott campaign resulted in the closing of the SodaStream West Bank factory in Ma'ale Adumim in October 2015, with more than nine hundred Palestinian workers losing their jobs."

SodaStream employed thirteen hundred workers, including nine hundred and fifteen Arabs in its West Bank factory. The Israeli government agreed to a grant for SodaStream to build a plant near the predominantly Bedouin city of Rahat in the northern Negev Desert. The plant is operational and provides employment for around a thousand workers. Since this is a new plant, more automation was introduced reducing the number of workers needed to produce the same amount of product. It might be noted that the Israeli government approved the grant for a plant to be built in the vicinity of Rahat, an Israeli Arab city. This plant could have been built anywhere in Israel.

Actress Scarlett Johansson, spokesperson for SodaStream, described SodaStream as "not only committed to the environment but to building a bridge to peace between Israel and Palestine, supporting neighbours working alongside each other, *receiving equal pay, equal benefits and equal rights."*

SodaStream is not only building bridges between Israelis and the Palestinians, it provides Palestinians with respectable employment opportunities at appropriate salaries, the same salaries that SodaStream's Jewish workers receive.

"Supporters of the factory cite the West Bank's high unemployment rate and low GDP as evidence the jobs are badly needed. Workers' incomes at the SodaStream factory were substantially above the 1,450 shekels/month Palestinian Authority minimum wage."

On August 2, 2016, a little less than a year after the closing of the West Bank plant, SodaStream reported its earnings for the second quarter of 2016: revenues of $119 million, up seventeen point two percent from the same period in 2015. Most of the increased revenue was from sales in Germany, Canada, Japan, France, and South Korea. Sales in the U S rose only twelve percent above the prior year so, perhaps, the boycott in the US was having some effect. However, SodaStream's net income increased one hundred twenty point eight percent for this quarter. In July, 2017, Soda Stream announced that its stock rose three hundred percent in the last eighteen months. And the company was projecting an additional ten percent revenue growth for fiscal 2017.

Victoria's Secret has a shop in Ma'ale Adumim, the site of the, now, closed SodaStream plant. In the impoverished West Bank, there was, obviously, enough disposable income to support this luxury-item store, perhaps due to the wages earned by Palestinians at SodaStream and also, conceivably, at Delta Galil, a textile factory in the West Bank from which Victoria's Secret buys fabrics. We could boycott Victoria's Secret, also, and if we are successful in reducing its need for fabric, put the Palestinian workers of Delta Galil out of work, too.

CHAPTER 13

The Middle East Problem: One Side Wants the Other Side Dead

by *Dennis Prager*

The Middle East conflict is framed as one of the most complex problems in the world. But in reality, it's very simple. Israelis want to live in peace and are willing to accept a neighboring Palestinian state. And most Palestinians don't want Israel to exist. As Dennis Prager explains, this is all you need to know. In five minutes, understand how Israel was founded, and how, since that auspicious day in 1948, its neighbors have tried to destroy her, again and again.

When I did my graduate studies at the Middle East Institute at Columbia University's School of International Affairs, I took many courses on the question of the Middle East Conflict.

Semester after semester, we studied the Middle East conflict as if it was the most complex conflict in the world—when in fact it is probably the easiest conflict in the world to explain. It may be the hardest to solve, but it is the easiest to explain.

In a nutshell, it's this: one side wants the other side dead.

Israel wants to exits as a Jewish state and to live in peace. Israel, also, recognizes the right of the Palestinians to have their own state and to live in peace. The problem, however, is that most Palestinians and many other Muslims and Arabs do not recognize the right of the Jewish state of Israel to exist.

This has been true since 1947 when the United Nations voted to divide the land called Palestine into a Jewish state an a Arab state.

The Jews accepted the United Nations partition but no Arab or any other Muslim country accepted it.

When British rule ended on May 15, 1948, the armies of all the neighboring Arab states—Lebanon, Syria, Iraq, Transjordan, and Egypt—attacked the one-day-old state of Israel in order to destroy it.

But, to the world's surprise, the little Jewish state survived.

Then it happened, again. In 1967, the dictator of Egypt, Gamal Abdel Nasser, announced his plan, in his words, "to destroy Israel." He placed Egyptian troops on Israel's border, and armies of surrounding Arab countries were, also, mobilized to attack. However, Israel preemptively attacked Egypt and Syria. Israel did not attack Jordan and begged Jordan's king not to join the war. But he did. And only because of that did Israel take control of Jordanian land, specifically the "West Bank" of the Jordan River.

Shortly after the war, the Arab states went to Khartoum, Sudan, and announced their famous three "No's: no recognition, no peace, and no negotiations."

What was Israel supposed to do?

Well, one thing Israel did, a little more than a decade later, in 1978, was to give the entire Sinai Peninsula—an area of land bigger than

Israel itself, *and with oil*—back to Egypt because Egypt, under new leadership, signed a peace agreement with Israel.

So, Israel gave land for the promise of peace with Egypt, and it has, always, been willing to do the same thing with the Palestinians. All the Palestinians have ever had to do is recognize Israel as a Jewish state and promise to live in peace with it.

But when Israel proposed trading land for peace—as it did in 2000 when it agreed to give the Palestinians a sovereign state in more than 95% of the West Bank and all of Gaza—the Palestinian leadership rejected the offer and instead responded by sending waves of suicide terrorists into Israel.

Meanwhile, Palestinian radio, television, and school curricula remain filled with glorification of terrorists, demonization of Jews, and the daily repeated message that Israel should cease to exist.

So, it's not hard to explain the Middle East dispute. One side wants the other dead. The motto of Hamas, the Palestinian rulers of Gaza, is "We love death as much as the Jews love life."

There are twenty-two Arab states in the world stretching from the Atlantic Ocean to the Indian Ocean. There is one "Jewish State" in the world. And it is about the size of New Jersey. In fact, tiny El Salvador is larger than Israel.

Finally, think about these two questions: if tomorrow, Israel laid down its arms and announced, "We will fight no more," what would happen? And if the Arab countries around Israel laid down their arms and announced, "We will fight no more, "What would happen?

In the first case, there would be an immediate destruction of the State of Israel and the mass murder of its Jewish population. In the second case, there would be peace the next day.

As I said at the outset, it is a simple problem to describe: one side wants the other dead—and if it didn't, there would be peace.

Please, remember this: there has never been a state in the geographic area known as Palestine that was not Jewish. Israel is the third Jewish state to exist in that area. There was never an Arab state, never a Palestinian state, never a Muslim or any other state.

That's the issue: why can't the one Jewish state the size of El Salvador be allowed to exist?

That is the Middle East problem.

CHAPTER 14

Where Would You Rather Live, Mohammed, in Israel or an Arab Country of Your Choice?

News! Breaking news! An Israeli soldier stopped a Palestinian for a security check! The world yells, "Harassment! Persecution! Apartheid!" This Palestinian lives in Israel, a country where he has schooling, medical insurance, and his Arab representation in the *Knesset* (Parliament) is looking out for him. He is eligible to receive social security benefits, health care, and free schooling for his children. He can own a home and work in any job or profession he is qualified for and wants to work in, just like the Israelis, and he receives equal pay and benefits.

He is unhappy because he has been taught that the Jews should be driven into the sea so they, his Palestinian people, can have all of this land to live a better life than they are now living under the Israeli government. Then they will be free.

Well, let's see how "free" the Palestinians are in the neighboring Arab countries, and how much better those lives are. Let's examine their quality of life and compare theirs to his under Israeli rule.

Gatestone Institute published Khaled Abu Toameh's "Palestinians in the Arab World: Why the Silence?" on July 20, 2010 in which he questions why the United Nations Security Council hasn't condemned Arab governments for their mistreatment of Palestinians. The Security Council, certainly, never hesitates to condemn Israel for her transgressions against the Palestinians, real or imagined, like when a Palestinian youth is killed running towards an Israeli wielding a knife. It would be a major step toward peace in the Middle East if the international community would recognize the need *to end the system of apartheid in the Arab countries.*

Which of the experts on apartheid, Desmond Tutu, Scott Walker, or Jimmy Carter is willing or likely to take that initial step?

Let's look, first, at Lebanon. Palestinian refugees live in Lebanon in what *Human Rights Watch* calls "appalling social and economic conditions." Not only are Palestinians' travel rights restricted--they are classified as foreigners and are, often, issued only one-way travel documents, to leave the country--but their right to medical care, social security, and the right to own property or even to repair the homes they are living in are, also, restricted, or forbidden.

Martial law is imposed on the refugee camps where they are forced to live. The Lebanese army stops people from entering and exiting. Palestinians are not only not allowed to live outside the refugee camps, the camps are not allowed to grow and are, with the birth rate of the Palestinians, far beyond the capacity that can be housed in them; and there are limitations in the camps on schools for Palestinian "foreigners."

The Redditor quotes British member of Parliament Gerald Kaufman on his 2010 visit to the refugee camps in Lebanon, "When I went to Gaza in 2010, I thought I had seen the worst that could be seen of the appalling predicament of Palestinians living in conditions which no human being should be expected to endure. But what I saw in the camps in Lebanon is far worse and far more hopeless. The conditions are unspeakable; but for these, our fellow human beings, this is their life today, tomorrow, and for a future that cannot even be foreseen. At least in Gaza, frightful though the situation is, the people are free within the confines of their blockaded prison. In the camps of Lebanon they are not free."

In Lebanon, Palestinians are prohibited from working in many jobs and professions. The number of jobs they are blocked from has been reduced to about fifty, but they are still not allowed to work as physicians, journalists, pharmacists, or lawyers. Palestinians in Lebanon suffer from a large number of humiliating restrictions.

From 1995 until 1999, Lebanon had a law prohibiting Palestinians from entering the country without a visa, and visas weren't being issued. Those Palestinians expelled from the Gulf States could not join their families in Lebanon.

In 2007, thirty-one thousand Palestinians became homeless because the Lebanese Army destroyed the Nahr el Bared refugee camp.

Lebanon turns many Palestinian refugees from Syria away at the border and restrictions are placed on the ability of Palestinians from Syria to legally renew their residency papers.

Rami Khouri, a prominent Lebanese journalist, wrote in *The Daily Star*, "All Arab countries mistreat millions of Arab, Asian, and African foreign guest workers who often are treated little better than chattel or indentured laborers...The mistreatment, abysmal living conditions and limited work, social security, and property rights of the Palestinians are a lingering moral black mark.."

In Israel, there are a multitude of Arab doctors and lawyers. Can one imagine the outcry if Israel decided to, like Lebanon, ban Arabs from working in these professions, or from being computer specialists, teachers, taxi drivers or waiters? Go to any Israeli university and view the student body and you will see a huge number of Arab students, the young women more visible than the young men because of their dress whereas it's difficult to tell the male Arab students from the Jewish Israeli students, especially those of Sephardi decent.

The Arab *Elder of Ziyon* reports on Arab discrimination and abuse against Palestinians. Palestinians are not allowed to become citizens of Arab countries in accordance with Arab League Decree 1547 passed in 1959, except in a few special circumstances.

Palestinians face severe travel restrictions not only in Lebanon but throughout the entire Arab world. Since they cannot become citizens, they do not receive passports and cannot vote or run for office in national elections. Children born to Palestinians do not get citizenship in their host Arab countries.

The situation is somewhat better for the Palestinians in Jordan than in Lebanon; however, those Palestinians who went to Jordan, mostly from the West Bank after the Six Day War when Jordan lost the West Bank to Israel, are not allowed to become Jordanian citizens and so they get no government services; and in 1988, Jordan revoked citizenship for millions of Jordanians who remained in the West Bank. Although Palestinians in Jordan who are Jordanian citizens can serve in the Parliament, Palestinian members of Parliament are limited to less than ten.

Jordan places the limited number of refugees from Syria that it accepts in camps separate from other refugees and turns hundreds of thousands away.

Palestinians who are Jordanian citizens do not have equal rights in the military or in getting college scholarships and being admitted to some public universities.

And how has Egypt treated their Palestinian brethren? Any better than the Jordanians and Lebanese? Let's see. Palestinians fled to Egypt in 1948 during the war that the Arabs started against the new nation of Israel. The women and children were put into camps, but the men were forced to go back to fight; and within a year, Egypt expelled the Palestinian women and children from these camps. They were sent to Gaza. Some few Palestinians managed to remain in Egypt but were barred from schooling and from employment.

At the start of the Syrian civil war, those Palestinians who fled from Syria were put into jail as they attempted to enter Egypt. Those who managed to stay are not given residency permits, nor can they get any government services.

Egypt has closed the Rafah border with Gaza, even limiting hospital patients from traveling, and since the only other border Gaza has is its closed border with Israel, this effectively imprisons one point seven million Gazans.

"It makes no sense to travel all over the world, then Egypt, an Arab country, treats you like an animal," Youssef Ramadan, a thirty-six year old merchant from Gaza traveling to China through Egypt, told Al Jazeera.

In 1991 in Kuwait, close to half a million Palestinians were harassed and forced to leave the country.

In 1994 and 1995, Libya dismissed Palestinians from their jobs, confiscated their houses, and expelled thirty thousand. Arab countries refused to take in the new refugees and hundreds were stranded in the desert or at sea. Eventually, Libya allowed some to return but kept threatening to expel them again. Palestinians were forced to pay a special tax of $1,550.

Life for Iraq's Palestinians deteriorated after the fall of Saddam Hussein, who had encouraged the migration of thousands of Palestinians to Iraq in the early 1990s. Baghdad became home to thirty thousand Palestinians. After he was deposed, Shiite militias began attacking Palestinians. In 2005 after Hussein lost power, Palestinians were subjected to abduction, hostage-taking, killings, and torture from armed groups.

(Where was the United Nations outcry? No outcry, only silence.)

About fifteen thousand Palestinians were forced to leave Iraq. Thousands were stranded in camps in the desert between Iraq and Syria because no Arab country would allow them to enter. UNHCR (United Nations High Commissioner for Refugees) finally closed this refugee camp on the Iraq-Syria border where Palestinians had been stranded for years.

The Palestinian refugees from Iraq appealed to Mahmoud Abbas, the Palestinian Authority President, saying that they had been denied medical care and had to use fake ID cards to receive treatment.

"After the 2003 war, [Palestinians] were severely targeted (in Iraq) with discrimination or killings and the majority fled the country," *throwaway 874832749* wrote. "If a non-Palestinian Arab speaks of the maltreatment of Palestinians by Israelis, tell them to...demand rights for Palestinians in their [own] countries." Judging from the number of supportive comments he's received, it seems he may have struck a chord.

Qatar refuses to grant Palestinians work visas.

In Syria, Palestinians cannot own farmland or more than one property. From 2005 to 2008, Syria did not allow thousands of Palestinian refugees fleeing from Iraq to enter the country.

The Commentator lists some specifics which should help remind Tutu, Walker, Carter, and others of the "crimes" of Israel that keep its Arab population down. How far "down" are the following: an Israeli Arab judge sits on Israel's High Court; an Arab judge presided over the trial at which a former president of Israel was convicted; an Arab is the captain of the Hapoel Tel Aviv soccer team; another Arab is a member of the Israeli national football team; the deputy mayor of Tel Aviv is an Arab; the former Miss Israel is an Arab woman named Yityish Aynaur; a Druze historian and poet was Israel's ambassador to Ecuador; an Arab is the director of the Emergency Medicine Hadassah Medical Center in Ein Kerem, a section of Jerusalem; a popular Bedouin pop singer is at the top of the charts; the Miss Israel Universe contestant was a half-Arab, half-Russian Christian; the top model, Niral Karantinji, is an Arab; a Druze is a major-general in the IDF (the Israel Defense Force, Israel's army); an Arab Christian woman is the "Voice of Israel" competition winner; an Arab Muslim female was runner-up in the Master Chef competition last year; and a trio composed of an Arab Israeli woman, a male German convert to Judaism, and a Jewish Orthodox woman competed in 2014 to be Master Chef.

Could any of these "crimes" be committed against (or should we say, "for") Palestinians in Arab countries?

The Commentator states that "it is regrettable that John Kerry has not met with Simon Deng, the human rights activist who was raised as a Christian and who at the age of nine became a domestic slave for a number of years in southern Sudan, a Moslem country. Deng defied the anti-Israeli bigots at the third United Nations Durban Conference that was held in New York in September 2011. He praised Israel as a state of people who are 'the colors of the rainbow.' By contrast, he held that Africans are the 'victims of Arab/Islamic apartheid.' The Arab response to events in Darfur was genocide, and 'nobody at the U.N. tells the truth about Darfur.'"

The dirty little secret is out. It is the Arab countries, not Israel, that are apartheid states. Their policies and practices include depriving or limiting people of civil, religious, and political rights; practicing discrimination; infringing on the freedom and dignity of people; subjecting them to arbitrary arrest and illegal imprisonment and prevention from participating in the political, social, economic, and cultural life of their countries.

It is easy to illustrate the general behavior of denial of rights by Arabs by specific reference to racial, ethnic, religious, and gender discrimination against black Africans, the Kurds, Christians and Jews, and women. It is more potent to illustrate it by actions or non-actions regarding the Palestinians, the very people regarded as being "oppressed" by Israel.

One telling feature is the frequent refusal of Arab hospitals to provide medical treatment for Palestinians compared with the hospitality of Israeli hospitals that treat thousands and thousands of Palestinians every year, even wounded would-be suicide bombers from the West Bank and Gaza.

The policy of Arab apartheid was made clear by the Arab League's Resolution 1457 in 1959: Arab countries would not grant citizenship to applicants of Palestinian origin deliberately in order to prevent their assimilation into the host countries.

A statement by Mahmoud Abbas published in the official PLO journal in March, 1976, complains of this policy. "The Arab armies that invaded Israel forced [the Palestinians] to leave their homeland, imposed on them a political and ideological blockade, and threw them into prisons similar to the ghettos in which the Jews used to live in Eastern Europe."

The claim that Israel is an apartheid state has always been a malicious falsehood. It was deliberately manufactured in the 1970s by the then-combination of the Soviet Union, the Arab states, and the non-aligned countries. Its objective was to make Israel a pariah state, a condition that was supposed to lead to Israel's elimination. What it has really done is hinder and prevent advancement of peace talks to end the Arab conflict with, and aggression against, the Jewish state.

Following are letters about the Yarmouk refugee camp in Syria: Friday 17 April 2015 "I wish to stress the sheer despair experienced by Palestinians trapped in the hellhole of Yarmouk in Syria, abandoned by the world at large. That the neighbouring countries around them do not react is hardly surprising: the treatment of Palestinians across the Arab world has been and continues to be appalling. In Lebanon, they have no access to health care or education, are barred from at least twenty-five professions, have no rights to buy property or even circulate freely within the country. This is true apartheid. A milder version of this is practiced in Jordan."

Peter McKenna

"However humiliating and despicable, the level of existence even in the occupied territories is vastly superior to that of Palestinians anywhere in the Arab world with the exception, until recently, of Syria and Iraq before the United Nations sanctions in 1990. This callous indifference to Yarmouk (and to every horrific camp in Lebanon, Jordan, or Syria where Palestinians continue to suffer) can only serve to bolster and encourage the Islamic State in its bloody war of expansion in the Middle East."

Carol Mann
Director of Women in War, Paris

Where are the vocal, chest-thumping supporters of Palestine? How can they march, protest, and boycott when it comes to Israel and keep quiet about what the Arab world is doing to its own, to their own, people?

*****

There is only one country in the Middle East where minorities feel free, comfortable, and that country is Israel. As a religious minority in every country they live in except Israel, the Druze have frequently experienced persecution. One of the larger Israeli minority communities, the Druze is a separate religious entity with its own courts which have jurisdiction in matters of marriage, divorce, adoption, and spiritual leadership. In addition to Druze judges in Israel, there are, also, parliamentarians, diplomats, and professionals such as physicians and university professors who occupy the highest echelons of society. Their culture is Arab and their language Arabic but they opted against mainstream Arab nationalism in 1948 and have since serve in the Israeli army and the Border Police.

In July 2017, ground was broken on a twenty-five thousand square foot heritage center dedicated to telling the story of the Druze contributions to the IDF and the State of Israel. Atta Farhat, chairman of the Druze Zionist Council, says he's proud to sing the Israeli national anthem, *Hatikvah.*

There is, also, a little known small Islamic sect, the Ahmadiyya, a persecuted minority across the Middle East, which enjoys full religious and cultural freedom in Israel, as do all minorities in Israel, and which prays in the only Ahmadi mosque in the Middle East which was opened in 1934 and redone in 1979. The safe haven they have found in the Jewish State mirrors that of the Druze, Bahá'í (visit the beautiful Bahá'í gardens in Haifa), Christians, Armenians, and others.

According to Israeli Ahmadiyya community leader Muhammad Sharif Odeh, the Ahmadis have complete religious freedom in Israel, contrasted to their brethren in the rest of the Middle East and in Pakistan where Ahmadis cannot use any religious symbols or even greet each other with a traditional Arabic salutation.

"Ahmadis in Arab countries in the Middle East suffer a lot," Odeh said. "They are not allowed to have mosques or minarets, and they go to jail for their beliefs and are persecuted."

CHAPTER 15

Response to *NY Times* Apr. 19, 2016 "Bernie's Israel Heresy" by *Roger Cohen*

During the 2016 United States presidential primary, Sen. Bernie Sanders, a Jew who constantly says he is the son of Polish immigrants—true, but not once has he been heard to say "Jewish immigrants," or even "Polish Jewish immigrants"--running against former Secretary of State Hillary Clinton for the Democratic Party nomination repeatedly referred to Israel's mistreatment of the Palestinians. On April 18, 2016, the *New York Times* columnist, Roger Cohen, wrote an op-ed piece entitled "Bernie's Israel Heresy" in which he quotes Sanders telling a New York audience that Israel used "disproportionate" force in Gaza in 2014, that "we are going to have to treat the Palestinian people with respect and dignity," and that the United States has to play "an evenhanded role." Sanders spoke of the Palestinian houses and schools "decimated" by Israeli force in Gaza and "the fact that there are two sides to the issue."

Roger Cohen wrote in this op-ed of "an Israeli government driving the country rightward toward intolerance, permanent dominion over another people and their (the Palestinians') perennial humiliation."

(*What, on earth, is columnist Cohen talking about!* Doesn't he know that something called newspapers exists? Perhaps, he should start to read them. The height of prejudice, which is ignorance, is to never let facts stand in the way of what one wants to believe!)

Following is a response to Mr. Cohen's column, to the lack of knowledge displayed by both Sanders and Cohen. What is written here has, already, been stated; however, to expand on John F. Kennedy's, "The great enemy of truth is very often not the lie—deliberate, contrived and dishonest—but the myth—persistent, persuasive and repeated."

Perhaps, just perhaps, if the truth is repeated often enough, it just might, also, have a "persistent, persuasive and repeated" result.

As a recent, now former, Bernie Sanders fan I must say, he doesn't know what he is talking about, but he doesn't hesitate to talk and to place blame far from where it should lay.

Sanders says Israelis should treat the Palestinians with dignity? Why not propose that Palestinian leaders treat the Palestinians with some dignity? These people have not only been used by their leaders as human shields, as pawns for the successful propaganda war (successful at least as far as Bernie Sanders and Roger Cohen are concerned) against an Israel that is unduly benevolent to them. Yes, I said "unduly benevolent."

So listen up.

First, let's focus on what their leadership has done to them, unremittingly, since well before the UN Partition Plan which created Israel. Led by their leaders in 1948 when the Jews were willing to accept less than they desired and felt they were entitled to of their ancestral homeland, within eight hours of the Declaration of the State of Israel, five Arab nations attacked the fledgling nation. In a call from the Grand Mufti of Jerusalem, Haj Amin al-Huesseni, in order to drive the Jews into the sea, the Palestinians were ordered to leave so they could return in fifteen days and reap all that the Jews had left behind. Now, sixty-nine years later, they are still being held in squalled conditions in decrepit refugee camps while the Jewish refugees who came to Israel were quickly integrated into Israeli society, physicians and university professors initially put to work building roads, and as farmers.

Why did not the Palestinians instead of invading to seize all the land declare the State of Palestine and, as the UN Partition Plan stipulated, "share railroad and postal services" and why not, also, technology, commerce, and education, learning of all sorts? *Where would the Palestinian people be today if its leaders had accepted the United Nations Partition Plan and established the State of Palestine?*

In fact, where would the Palestinian people be, today, if they had won what the Israelis call the War of Independence and the Palestinians call the *Nakba,* the "catastrophe"? Judging from the condition of the Arabs in the neighboring Arab nations, not well off at all, certainly far worse off than the Arab Israelis who cringe at the possibility of, and loudly demonstrate against, as the result of negotiations being subjected to Palestinian authority.

Never mind that there would have been a genocide against the Jewish population; does anyone think that the Arab nations that came to aid the Palestinians would, simply, walk away leaving all they had fought for for the benefit of the Palestinians and take nothing for themselves? Fantasy! Had The eight-hour-old Jewish State not been able to defend itself with its little militia, the *Hagana*, and had, instead, been demolished, isn't it more than likely that Egypt, Jordan, Libya, Syria, and Iraq would have each extorted its pound of flesh by carving up the tiny area and dividing it amongst themselves and kept the Palestinians in dismal, decrepit refugee camps until this day?

Twenty-two Arab nations exist, today, and the Palestinian refugees are held in these squalid refugee camps, their Arab brothers refusing to welcome them into their societies as the Israelis welcomed the remaining Jews of Europe who made their way to Israel into their society.

Arab Israelis are aware of the conditions their brethren are subjected to under Palestinian rule and are very vocal about their wish to remain under Zionist rule.

Before the Grand Mufti ordered the Arabs to clear the way for the invading armies, Azzam Pasha, Secretary-General of the Arab League announced in a cablegram dated 15 May 1948 to the Secretary-General of the United Nations, "It will be a war of extermination. It will be a war of annihilation. It will be a momentous massacre in history that will be talked about like the massacres of the Mongols or the Crusades." (Sounds like Sadam Hussein's "Mother of all Wars," doesn't it?)

Jamal Husseini, a member of the Arab Higher Committee in Palestine, in response to British High Commissioner Sir Alan Cunningham's expressed concern for the welfare of the ordinary Palestinian people threatened *jihad* stating that not only was he prepared to die, but the ordinary Arab population was prepared to die, too. Really? Had Husseini, conferred with the average Palestinian about sacrificing his family in *jihad,* like the Palestinian leaders were running a democracy where the majority ruled instead of those in power?

Dr. Hussein Khalidi, a prominent Palestinian Arab leader, fabricated claims of atrocities at the village of Dier Yassin to encourage Arab regimes to invade the imminent Jewish state. Instead, Palestinians took their families and ran away from their homes "so their daughters wouldn't be raped." (Check out "Best Hoaxes and Pranks.") They lost the war, hence, the "*nakba*," the "catastrophe."

1967: the Six Day War. After three weeks of buildups from nine Arab countries, Israel was surrounded by five hundred thousand troops, more than five thousand tanks, and almost a thousand fighter planes; and Nasser blockaded the Straits of Tiran to Israeli shipping, an act of war under international law. The Israel Defense Forces (IDF) at that time consisted of approximately half that number of troops, two hundred and seventy-five thousand, and Israel had less than half the amount of tanks and a quarter of the combat aircraft that the united Arab forces had amassed against her. However, even with this "disproportionate" buildup surrounding Israel (which Mr. Sanders has not voiced objection to), by midafternoon of the first day, the air forces of Jordan, Syria, Iraq, and Egypt had been demolished. The Six Day War was, essentially, decided in six hours.

But these are not all the causes of the horrendous conditions the Palestinians find themselves in and blame the Israelis for, as does columnist Roger Cohen and Presidential candidate Bernie Sanders in their lack of knowledge of the true situation in the Middle East. Bernie Sanders claims that he knows Israel based on his having spent several months on a Kibbutz picking apples and pears half a century ago. That's like saying one understands US foreign policy because, also close to half a century ago, he spent time at Woodstock listening to jazz and smoking marijuana.

Leslie Stahl hosted a segment on "60 Minutes: Arafat's Billions" on November 7, 2003, on the billions of dollars Yasser Arafat stole from the Palestinian treasury and on how he created monopolies in food commodities, cement, and gasoline which he put under the control of his cohorts and from which he got hefty kickbacks causing his impoverished Palestinians to pay exorbitant prices for food basics and for gasoline. This, of course, contributed greatly to their despicable living conditions. And does the American public, or the world, blame Arafat or Israel for this increased impoverishment?

Take a look at the Palestinians' terrible condition today and contrast that with the high standard of living of the Israeli Arabs, Arabs who cringe at the thought of, and loudly demonstrate against, lands that they live on, possibly, going back to Palestinian authority. A recent Harvard University study found that seventy-seven percent of Arab Israelis would rather live in Israel than in any other country *in the world*! Arabs have also stated that they would much rather live in Israel under Zionist rule than under Palestinian rule.

A previous survey conducted by Pechter Middle East Polls in partnership with the Council on Foreign Relations, Washington, DC, asked a simple question that the leaders both in Israel and the Palestinian authority seem to ignore all too often: what do the people, themselves, want? Here is what the pollsters found:

Thirty-seven percent of the Arab respondents want their children to attend Jewish schools.

Forty-two percent want to live in Jewish neighborhoods.

Fifty-eight percent of the Arabs do not trust Arab leaders in Israel.

Asked if they preferred to become citizens of Palestine with all of the rights and privileges of other citizens of Palestine or citizens of Israel with the rights and privileges of other citizens of Israel, sixty-eight percent chose Israeli citizenship. A follow up question asked respondents if most people in their neighborhood would prefer to become citizens of Palestine or of Israel: sixty-nine percent thought that most people prefer Israeli citizenship.

Asked if they would move to a different location inside Israel, if their neighborhood became part of Palestine, forty percent said they were likely to move to Israel.

When asked to provide the top reasons they chose one citizenship over the other, those who chose Israeli citizenship stressed freedom of movement in Israel, higher income, better job opportunities and government-provided Israeli health insurance, unemployment and disability benefits, and municipal services. The small minority of respondents who chose Palestinian citizenship referred to nationalism and patriotism.

"I assume the Palestinian leadership wouldn't be too happy about the results," said Dr. David Pollock, a senior fellow at The Washington Institute who supervised the survey and analyzed it. "But I think the results are very credible and solid. I was there supervising the survey in Jerusalem in November and I am very confident in the results,"

Pollock said. "The Palestinian leadership might have been nervous because they understood these Palestinians have special benefits and interests not to lose these benefits," Pollock added

"A Palestinian expert and colleague of mine suggested to me that he accepts the results."

The benefits stated by the respondents to this survey were, it appears, from working Israeli Arabs. The survey did not go into benefits such as welfare payments, especially to large families, depending on (reported) family income and number of members in the household.

Also, there are hidden, or not spoken of, benefits from the Israeli government to certain segments of its Arab population. Example: the majority of Israeli military bases have been located in the center of the country, for obvious reasons. This was where the population, then much smaller, was under the British Mandate, and it was the British who built the military bases. The sparsely populated region easily accommodated the military bases. Today, land in the center of the country is extremely valuable. One tends to spend more for an apartment in Tel Aviv or Jerusalem than in Paris or New York. So the government decided to move most of the centrally located army bases to a vast, underpopulated area in the Negev Desert south of Be'er Sheva.

Populations, both Arab and Jewish, had to be displaced by *eminent domain* in order to make room for the relocated bases. Landowners whose property was taken for this new, huge multi-base that would be built were compensated by the Israeli government. The difference is that land available to the Arab displaced persons in or near Arab towns or villages where they would want to settle could be acquired for as little as $2,000 to $4,000 for a lot while the Jewish displaced persons could be paying $50,000 and more for a lot, such as was paid for lots in the neighboring village, grown into a small town, of Ashalim where many army personnel as well as some of those displaced by the government takeover of land for the bases preferred to settle, and were lucky enough to obtain a plot to build on bought.

But true to human nature, many Arabs are angry at the change this is forcing on their way of life. (Many don't realize that this is coming at a most advantageous time for them.) Traveling south on the main road that now will be within the new bases, one used to see young Bedouin girls tending sheep. Well, these young Bedouin girls no longer want to tend the sheep as their mothers, grandmothers, and forbears for multitudes of generations did. These young girls, by Israeli law, must attend school, unlike their forbears. The have smart phones, some wear jeans, and many have aspirations to obtain a higher education after high school, and they go home to their mothers who can neither read nor write although the Israeli government is, now, offering literacy courses in some Arab locals.

So who will tend the sheep and the fields that the Arab men are so despondent about being compensated to give up? Not long ago, there was an article by a Bedouin candidate for a Masters' degree at George Washington University in Washington, DC, against the Israeli government forcing his people to give up the mode in which they have, traditionally, lived referencing, specifically, the grazing of animals on the now to be army base land. I reiterate where this young, angry man was, in Washington, DC, obtaining a Masters' degree not out in the fields that he laments his father having to give up under *eminent domain* and for which his father was duly compensated. Probably, this Masters' degree candidate assumes that it is his sisters' rightful duty to attend the sheep. Did he ask his sisters, now educated, if that is what they aspire to?

Also, in Israel, Arabs tend to have many more rights than Arabs who live in Europe, such as the right to wear *hajab* and the right to live a homosexual lifestyle, if one so desires, without fear of punishment, or death.

Mr. Sanders speaks of the necessity of Israel sharing water with the Palestinians. Does he even know that Israel supplies pure water and electricity to Gaza while southern Israel dodges rockets fired from Gaza, mostly during hours when school children are in the streets? During Operation Protective Edge, the war in 2014, because Gaza has only one, small generating plant most insufficient to meet its needs, Israel was still supplying one hundred and twenty-five megawatts of electricity to Gaza from the power station in Ashkelon despite the rocket attacks on southern Israel, *and on Ashkelon itself.* According to "The Electronic Intifada," Israel, now, supplies sixty-two percent of Gaza's electricity needs. The *Japan Times*, Mar. 15, 2015: Israel will increase the drinking-quality water it supplies to Gaza from five million cubic meters to ten million cubic meters (one point three billion gallons to two point six billion gallons) per year. Neither the water nor the electricity has been paid for, violating the agreement.

Mr. Sanders, if you don't pay your water or electricity bill, what happens?

Gaza is not experiencing food scarcity as Israel is not blocking the entrance of goods into Gaza except for weaponry and dual-use materials.

What else is the Palestinian leadership doing to its population, today? Even you know, Bernie, that weapons caches are stored in populated areas and near or in schools and hospitals so Israel will be blamed when civilians are hurt when the weapons are destroyed. So much for your "Palestinian houses and schools 'decimated' by Israeli force in Gaza," as if you didn't know that this is the case.

But do you know that Hamas sends agents to rent spare rooms in apartments stating that the room will only be used for storage, not mentioning that the storage will be munitions; and when Israel takes these caches out, immediately, the agent who obtained the rental will be there photographing the burned children who were sleeping in the adjacent apartment with a common wall to the storage room so Israel, not Hamas who set up the rouse, can be blamed? Who are you to state that Israel used "disproportionate force" in 2014 in the war Israel was forced into to put a stop to thirteen years of a thousand rockets a year descending on children going to and from school when you're ignorant of the situation there?

It's easy for you, Mr. Sanders, to use the cliché, "...there are two sides to the issue." Dennis Prager simplified all the rhetoric he was subjected in his courses on the Middle East conflict during his graduate studies at the Middle East Institute at Columbia University's School of International Affairs to the following: "One side wants the other side dead." Is that so difficult to understand juxtaposed on the wars the Palestinians have started to drive the Jews into the sea, and on a thousand rockets a year for thirteen years raining down on southern Israel, especially when school children are on the streets? Are you a war monger that is on the side of those perpetrating these crimes instead of those defending themselves?

How do you treat people with "respect and dignity" whose expressed objective is to kill you and, actually, do so at every opportunity they can using children in explosive gear or, simply, kitchen knives? Stephen Rosenberg in his "Let Gaza City West be Palestine" eloquently explains how the Palestinian people can be restored to a people deserving of "respect and dignity." Make West Gaza in the Sinai the new Palestinian homeland (see "A Beautiful, Affluent Gaza in the Sinai).

On March 21, 2016, Mr. Sanders outlined his "Middle East Policy" in which he didn't mention the "disproportionate" number of rockets barraging Israel, a thousand a year for thirteen years compared to a total of zero from Israel into Gaza. Nor did he speak of the equally disproportionate number of suicide bombers and knife wielders, one hundred percent Palestinians, zero Israelis.

He did mention Gaza's extremely high poverty rate and its forty-four percent unemployment rate implying that this was Israel's fault. Mr. Sanders must know that the Palestinians of Gaza looted and then burned down the eight hundred technically advanced, computer-run hothouses that the World Bank and the International Finance Corporation bought from Israel when Israel left Gaza so the four thousand Palestinians who worked in those hothouses would continue having jobs to support their families and to add to the Gazan economy. He must know that with seven universities and a ninety-two percent literacy rate, the Palestinians of Gaza have the facility to pursue beneficial occupations or to choose to use the multiple use construction materials for terror tunnels instead of for factories, roads, schools, and hospitals.

Stop blaming Israel! Look, instead, to the Palestinian leadership and to the brainwashed Palestinians, themselves!

"Peace will mean ending what amounts to the occupation of Palestinian territory," Mr. Sanders has said numerous times. But what does this expert on Israeli affairs based on having his having picked apples and pears half a century ago while living with American college students mean by "occupation"? Surely he is not referring to Gaza because we will assume that Mr. Sanders is astute enough to know that Israel pulled out of Gaza in 2005 in the "Land for Peace" deal. And what has Gaza done since then, work to improve its economy and the lives of its people or use whatever assets it receives from the United Nations and elsewhere to attack Israel?

Therefore, he must be speaking of Judea and Samaria, currently referred to as the West Bank. But "occupation" infers that an alien force invaded, captured, and is "occupying" the captured lands. That isn't what happened, as Mr. Sanders, unquestionably, knows. He knows, or as a person speaking on this subject he should know, that what happened was that Jordan invaded Israel and Israel repelled the invasion and pushed Jordan's army back, all the way back to across the Jordan River. The West Bank isn't "occupied" as Israel never invaded this territory. Because no settlement has been reached, the best one could call this region is "disputed territory," not "occupied territory." Shouldn't Mr. Sanders know this? And he, certainly, knows that all Israel has ever asked for to resolve this "disputed territory" enigma is for the Palestinians to acknowledge Israel's right to exist and stop their attacks on her. But don't ask Israel to commit suicide by, simply, allowing the Palestinians to do what they want to do which is to "kill the other side." This won't happen.

"Of course, I strongly condemn indiscriminate rocket fire by Hamas into Israeli territory, and Hamas's use of civilian neighborhoods to launch those attacks. I condemn the fact that Hamas diverted funds and materials for much-needed construction projects designed to improve the quality of life of the Palestinian people and instead used those funds to construct a network of tunnels for military purposes," Mr. Sanders, also, said in his "Middle East Policy" outline. Thank you, Mr. Sanders. At least a little recognition of the actuality of the problem although this awareness on your part has not stopped you from ranting against Israel on these very topics.

Then the *Times of Israel* on June 10, 2016, in an article written by Eric Cortellessa: Washington "Massively amplifying even Hamas's own figures, Democratic presidential hopeful Bernie Sanders suggested Israel had killed 'over ten thousand innocent' Palestinian civilians in Gaza during the war there in the summer of 2014, and said the high casualties were the result of an 'indiscriminate' Israeli military offensive. Hamas health authorities in Gaza put the civilian death toll at about *a seventh* of the figure cited by Sanders; Israel puts it lower still."

According to Palestinian figures cited by the UN Human Rights Council, one thousand four hundred and sixty-two civilians were killed out of a total of the two thousand two hundred and fifty-one Gaza fatalities during the fifty-one day conflict. Israel, for its part, has said that up to half of those killed on the Palestinian side were combatants, and has blamed the civilian death toll on Hamas for deliberating placing rocket launches, munitions, and military installations among civilians.

In an interview with the *New York Daily News* editorial board, the Vermont senator acknowledged that he did not have the exact figures memorized, but twice said he believed that the Palestinian civilian death count surpassed ten thousand and excoriated Israel for what he deemed its "disproportionate use of force."

Sanders's estimation far exceeds even that of official Palestinian sources. (It was clear from the context that Sanders was referring to the 2014 war; however, the Palestinian civilian death toll from all three rounds of Israeli-Hamas conflicts in the years since the terror group seized control of the Strip also falls far, far short of the figure he cited.)

When asked by the *New York Daily News* what he would have done in Israel's place, he said: "I think it is fair to say that the level of attacks against civilian areas…and I do know that the Palestinians, some of them, were using civilian areas to launch missiles…makes it very difficult…But I think most international observers would say that the attacks against Gaza were indiscriminate and that a lot of innocent people were killed who should not have been killed."

The height of prejudice, Mr. Sanders! Don't let the facts, even those you, yourself, articulate, stand in the way of what you choose to believe or, maybe, what it serves your political purpose to expound about.

Sanders spoke of "pulling back settlements in the West Bank, just as Israel did in Gaza," referring to then prime minister Ariel Sharon's decision to unilaterally remove all settlements from the Gaza Strip in 2005. That was the "Land for Peace Agreement," the agreement that, obviously, Mr. Sanders is unaware led to the thousand rockets a year bombarding Israel.

Sanders indicated that the US has an interest in improving the quality of life for Palestinians. So, how about the US making an effort to locate Yasser Arafat's missing billions that he stole from Palestinian Authority funds proclaiming that enriching himself helps the Palestinian people because he was the embodiment of the Palestinians so what benefits him, benefited them? Please, don't even suggest that my tax dollars be used to replace those stolen funds.

On the nature of how he would manage the US-Israel alliance if elected president, Sanders said: "To the degree that (the Israelis) want us to have a positive relationship, I think they're going to have to improve their relationship with the Palestinians." Does that mean that Israel will have to do the only thing that will satisfy the Palestinians? As Dennis Prager said, that "side wants the other side dead."

The *New York Times*, Mar. 10 2017, "Proposed Hamas Charter Would Designate 'Occupiers' Not 'Jews' as the Enemy" The article states, "Hamas, the Palestinian Islamist group that has governed the Gaza Strip for a decade, is drafting a new platform to present a more pragmatic and co-operative face to the world."

The original Charter written in 1988 declares Hamas's commitment to "obliterate" Israel and its struggle against "Jews." The new Hamas platform will state that its struggle is against "occupiers," and does not designate "Jews." A Hamas spokesman, Taher el- Nounou said that their struggle "is only against those who occupy our lands." Since Israel does not occupy Gaza, Mr. el-Nounou is, recognizably, referring to what the document states in its text about, "future claims to all of what Hamas considers Palestinian lands," an obvious reference to all of Israel.

This new document, just as the one it will replace, does not recognize Israel's right to exist nor does it state any change in Hamas's method, a policy of the use of terror and violence against Israeli citizens. The new document is designed using the sort of language that is more acceptable to the international community. "Ahmad Yousif, an expert on Islamic movements...said the new platform might help soften outside perceptions" of Hamas, What was that, Mr. Sanders, about treating these people "with respect"?

I repeat, because it's worth repeating, Bernie Sanders saying that he knows about Israel because he spent a few months on a kibbutz half a century ago is like one saying he knows about American foreign policy because he listened to jazz and smoked marijuana at Woodstock, also, about half a century ago.

Sunday, June 12, 2016 by Ben Sales "Kibbutz Shaar Haamakim, 1963 Bernie Sanders volunteered there for several months. Every morning, Bernie Sanders would wake up at 4:10 a.m. to pick apples and pears. Leaving the cabin he shared with a few other American college student volunteers, Sanders would have a quick bite of bread before heading out to the orchard. After two and a half hours of work, he and the other twenty or so volunteers would sit down for a traditional thirty minute Israeli breakfast of tomatoes, cucumbers, onions, bread and butter, and hard-boiled eggs. Then it was back to work."

What Bernie Sanders learned of Israel during his few months on a kibbutz living with American college students who were volunteering for the summer, as he was, is that Israelis who pick apples and pears in hot weather in Israel wake up at 4:10 a.m., have a quick bite of bread, and then work for two and a half hours before sitting down to a breakfast of vegetables and hard-boiled eggs.

Sanders reminds one of the young girls who go to ISIS to get married. They think they're going to be in an apartment and spend their time shopping, cooking, and cleaning. Instead, they're used as sex slaves for their "husbands" and traded off to another ISIS fighter when the husband wants a different "wife."

CHAPTER 16

A Beautiful, Affluent Gaza in the Sinai

On Monday, April 18, 2016, two years after the rash of bus bombings had diminished, a nineteen-year-old Arab, Adul-Hamid Abu Srour, detonated a bomb filled with nuts and bolts on a Jerusalem bus. In the burnt framework of the bus were more than a dozen wounded, a badly burned fifteen-year-old girl, and young Abdul who, two days later, died of his wounds in an Israeli hospital. Relatives declared him a hero and his mother, quoted in the April 22 *New York Times*, said of her dead son, "I'm proud that Aboud (using his nickname) did this…(and) videos uploaded to YouTube showed loud demonstrations of Palestinian youths in Bethlehem cheering" young Aboud.

Galilee Triangle Arabs demonstrate forcefully in opposition to talk of borders being repositioned to incorporate them into a Palestinian state; Jerusalem Arabs are likely to not to vote in Palestinian Authority elections worried about, conceivably, risking their Israeli residency, choosing to live under a Zionist rather than a Palestinian regime; but mothers embrace their dead sons with veneration for their deeds against an Israel that so many Israeli Arabs are grateful to be living in. What a conundrum! The answer, "The Hitler youth."

Those youngsters brought up under the Nazi regime were exposed to Nazi indoctrination, propaganda for Nazi purposes with no pretense of truth. The Palestinian people, today, generations after the creation of the State of Israel and having been subjected to their leaders have no resemblance to the Palestinians of Ari ben Canaan's (Paul Newman in "Exodus") friend, the young Sheik of the neighboring village of whose father Ari's father, Barak ben Canaan, said, "Speak that name only with respect." A people can change, depending on what it has been subjected to.

In the 1950s soon after the end of the Second World War, a large amount of the remainder of Europe's Jews immigrated to Israel. Due to the perilous state of affairs confronting them in the North African Arab countries, Jewish communities began to be transported to Israel. The Jewish Agency portrays "The Mass Migration of the 1950s" and the social problems this generated.

"There were considerable differences between the immigrants from European countries and those from Asia and Africa." The Jews from Africa had high fertility rates and were, as a rule, poorly educated, not nearly as well educated as the European immigrants. Complications surfaced in absorbing these new immigrants into Israeli society in the form of social stratification. Many of these new North African immigrants were sent to "development towns." These were new settlements established in out-of-the-way districts with the explicit aim of diffusing the Israeli population. Consequently, the process of disconnection and segregation of immigrants from developing countries became a factor in the growth of severe social difficulties.

"There was a strong culture shock for immigrants from North Africa." These more primitive people had come from "pre-industrial societies" in which the big, extended family was an influential societal unit. The women performed traditional tasks in managing the household and raising children and the father was likely to exert substantial patriarchal authority. Few, either men or women, had broad, overall education or contemporary vocational training. The immigrants brought with them their own communal and traditional standards which had been affected by the encompassing culture of their previous host societies.

"Israel, on the other hand, was a modern, industrial society." The dominant social unit tended to be the smaller, nuclear family and the father exercised less control over the members of the household. Israeli women usually worked outside the home and it was common for many to pursue their own professional careers. The more modern-day technologies and lifestyle in Israel necessitated a greater degree of skilled workers. Social, political, and cultural life in Israel was molded predominantly after European prototypes.

The North African immigrant father no longer possessed much of his past status in the family. The large family became an economic liability. Because of the absence of sought-after vocational skills and an enormous hurdle in acclimating to the new environs and because of their traditional role as housekeepers, women's roles in their new society were limited and they found themselves mostly unable to participate in the paid work force. The secular lifestyle of their new country appeared to refute many of their traditional principles. Israeli authorities frequently made no secret of their low esteem for what they considered as the "backward" or "primitive" society of the immigrants from developing countries.

These darker-skinned children of the North African immigrants went through the Israeli school system, obtained an education just like the children of the much more highly educated European-Israelis did. But they went home to their kindly, simple, North African-born and raised mothers. These new Israelis grew up, virtually, in two societies. It took another generation until the children of the next generation, also, went through the Israeli school system but they went home to their Israeli-educated mothers. They could still enjoy their grandmothers' love and fine cooking, but they are Israeli Sabras, born and reared in Israeli society not in the dual society that their mothers had grown up in.

The young Palestinian martyrs of today, the young Adul-Hamid Abu Srours, are a product of what their Azzam Pashas, Jamal Husseinis, and Dr. Hussein Khalidis did to their forbears and, of course, of Yasser Arafat who stole the Palestinian Authority's money proclaiming that he was the embodiment of the Palestinian people so what is good for him is good for them. And so are their mothers products of this propaganda that served the Palestinian rulers, but not the Palestinian people. These mothers grew up on the Arab versions of "Sesame Street" depicting fantasized atrocities by Jews against Arab children and they had parents and teachers who indoctrinated them to hate all Israelis. Is it any wonder that they aggrandize their sons and, in some cases, daughters, too, for sacrificing themselves in the murder of these abhorrent Jews? It will take at least two generations living in a beautiful, affluent Gaza in the Sinai to bring the Palestinian population back to where one can say, "Say that name, always, with respect."

An article in the *Canadian/Arab News* on the fortieth anniversary of the Six Day War proclaimed Abba Eban a liar for daring to suggest that the surrounding of Israel by an overwhelming force of troops, military hardware, and fighter planes "stood history on its head," regaling that this was no threat at all to Israel. Just recently on July 4, 2016, an Israeli Arab, Palestinian-Arab commentator Zuheir Andreus, published an article in the Israeli newspaper, *Haaretz*, "Israel Racism is Turning into Fascism," in which he speaks of "imperialism *under the leadership of global terror superpower the United States*...We were here before you and will remain after you," and "...the true owners of the soil—the Palestinian Arabs."

"We were here before you and we will remain after you...!" *He doesn't know! He doesn't know!* He is a Palestinian-Arab commentator. Can we assume that he is, at least to some extent, educated, and he doesn't know that Mohammed was born in the sixth century and the Jews have been inhabiting this land for thousands of years before that?

So how is Ari and Barak ben Canaan's respect to come about? Let's take another look at Stephen G. Rosenberg's description of what Gaza in the Sinai, what he deemed West Gaza, could become. Mr. Rosenberg's West Gaza would have "golden beaches and mountain resorts attracting tourists to the beautiful hotels that the American and European hotel chains would be vying to build in this new, thriving economy bringing tourists in through its new international airport and seaport." Mr. Rosenberg envisages that West Gaza's main domestic industry could be tourism, as is Israel's. He submits that West Gaza tourism might appeal to the same vacationers as Israel's tourism trade and could, conceivably, benefit from Israeli tourists filtering over into the delightful, new West Gaza and that West Gaza's agricultural sector could, once again, reap bounteous quantities of vegetables and flowers for its own consumption and for export; and West Gaza could, with a "literate, educated work force be fertile ground, also, for a future high tech industry."

Aboud Abu Srour, son of a mother indoctrinated to hate may have influence over his children born out of his own experiences. But if those children grow up in a vibrant Gaza in the Sinai with full employment, enjoying a good, middle class life, a comfortable lifestyle in place of the poverty imposed on them by their own fanatics and thieves, this is what they will be passing on to their children.

The solution to the Arab/Israeli problem: let Gaza in the Sinai Peninsula be Palestine.

The road to peace runs through the Sinai.

*****

On Mar. 24, 2018, the US Congress passed the Taylor Force Act to end American aid to the Palestinian Authority until the PA ceases to pay stipends to terrorists and their families, including the families of suicide bombers. The bill is designed to force the government of PA Pres. Mahmoud Abbas to end a policy of rewarding terrorism and describes the stipends as "lavish incentives to commit violence." Because a killer dies while committing an act of terrorism, the Palestinian Authority pays the killer's family a monthly pension *equal to several times the average monthly Palestinian wage*. The pension is paid as the Palestinian Authority's policy to pay a monthly cash stipend to the families of Palestinians killed, injured, or imprisoned for involvement in attacking, assisting in attacking, or planning to attack Israelis or Americans, or for other types of politically-inspired violence including riots, violent demonstrations, and throwing rocks.

Does the American school teacher in West Virginia who went on strike for a living wage or the factory worker in Ohio know that his hard earned tax dollars are going towards pensions for terrorists' families in amounts far in excess of what their Palestinian "martyrs" would have earned for killing American citizens? These payments are paid as a part of a Palestinian law in its slay-for-pay policy. In 2017, these funds amounted to $315 million, almost ten percent of the Palestinian Authority's total budget and approximately one hundred percent of American aid to the PA. Why is not the aid given to the Palestinians going to feed, clothe, educate, and contribute to the medical needs of the Palestinian people instead of giving the families of those who killed not only Israelis but Americans, also, a lifestyle far more affluent than their neighbors who the American taxpayers think they are supporting with their tax dollars?

Taylor Force, for whom the act is named, a native of a Lubbock, Texas, and a 2009 US Military Academy graduate was killed and at least ten other people including a pregnant woman were injured while taking an evening stroll along the Mediterranean seacoast in Jaffa when a Palestinian man went on a stabbing spree. Five of the injured were in critical condition. Force had served as a field artillery officer from 2009-2014 at Fort Hood and was a veteran of Iraq and Afghanistan. After completing his service, Taylor entered Vanderbilt University's Owen Graduate School of Management at to study for an MBA. At the time of the murder, he was visiting Israel as part of a study group examining global entrepreneurship.

The attack was the third of the day: two policemen were badly injured in a Jerusalem shooting, earlier, and a forty-year-old father of five was stabbed repeatedly before managing to wound his assailant with his own knife. The terrorist, later identified as twenty-one-year-old Palestinian Bashar Massalha from the West Bank Palestinian refugee camp in Qalqiliya, had stabbed his victims in at least three locations. The attacker was shot dead by police after a chase from the Jaffa Port along the Tel Aviv beach promenade. Because of the passage of the Taylor Force Act, his family will not be awarded a relatively lavish lifestyle paid for by the unknowing American taxpayer.

The Palestinian Authority is not the first to reward Palestinians for terrorist activity. Saddam Hussein used to issue grants to the families of suicide bombers in the amount of $25,000 as compared with $5,300 from Saudi Arabia.

Conclusion

By implementing Gaza in the Sinai, much of the turmoil in the Middle East will be eradicated. But, perhaps more important is the eminent additional catastrophe to not only the Middle East but to the world that will be avoided. By placing Palestinians or poverty stricken Egypt onto sound footing, the devastating civil war in Syria will not be resolved. However, the problems throughout the world, and especially in Europe, caused by the Syrian civil war will pale compared to these same problems multiplied many times that will occur should Egypt fail as a country, which it is, now, on the path to doing.

Syria, before the war, was a country of twenty-two million. A half million have been killed in the war, but a whopping thirteen million have become refugees, some held in close to uninhabitable conditions in refugee camps and the rest flooding those European countries that are willing to take them in and provide even minimal support for them.

Egypt is a country of ninety million. Short of a civil war, faced only with escalating costs for food and utilities and higher taxes, how long will it be before we see a mass emigration from Egypt to those same countries that have taken in their Muslim brothers and we witness the deaths that will, undoubtedly, occur amongst those looking to reach those countries? The emigrants may not equal fifty percent of the population, but if only around twenty percent flee from the poverty of their native Egypt, that will send an additional twenty million men, women, and children to the gates of Europe, and of the United States. They may have difficulty entering the United States with the new immigrant reforms, but how will Europe be able to cope?

And the West had best take heed and implement the stability that Gaza in the Sinai would bring to that part of the world as there could be an yet another, overwhelming problem to come: Jordan. In a Mar. 8, 2017 *Washington Post* article by Daniel Pipes of the *Middle East Forum*, Mr. Pipes points out the dangers to Jordan which are multifarious: ISIS lies in wait in Syria and Iraq just beyond Jordan's borders, enticing a segment of Jordanians; Jordan's trade with those two countries is, virtually, gone; in a region copious in oil and gas resources, Jordan, like Israel, has almost no petroleum; and potable water is in scarce supply, Jordanians who live in cities often allotted water one day a week and those in rural areas, at times, even less. Tourism, which was once a prime source of income, has waned precipitously due to the Middle East's instability. The king's recent assertion of authority grates on those demanding more democracy.

At least Jordan's water shortage may be, to some extent, soon alleviated. In Feb. 2015, Israeli and Jordanian officials signed a bilateral agreement for the construction of a sixty-five to eighty cubic meter water desalinization plant in Aqaba, Jordan. Israel and Jordan will share the production of this plant.

On Mar. 13, 2014, an article appeared in the *New York Times* stating that "Jordan had freed a soldier who had killed seven Israeli schoolgirls (7th and 8th graders) who were on a school trip to the 'Island of Peace'" south of the Sea of Galilee near the Israel/Jordan border. The soldier had served twenty years for killing the seven girls and wounding another five, plus their teacher. He was welcomed home as a hero (macho man for killing seven eleven and twelve-year-old little girls and a teacher) amidst celebrations honoring his release from prison. His first statement to the news media was, "There is no country named Israel."

Why wasn't he given twenty years for each schoolgirl he killed, to run successively instead of less than three years for each young girl he murdered?

With the purchase of the land in the Sinai from Egypt, feasibly by Saudi Arabia and the United Nations—which means, to a large extent, the United States—stability will be brought to this region of perpetual turmoil. Egypt will have the money to expand the Suez Canal to a workable second lane allowing for two way traffic and complete the rest of its Suez Canal Project utilizing its labor force, providing jobs with the compensation for those jobs flowing into the Egyptian economy and enjoy, approximately, thirty billion dollars left over to infuse into the expansion of her economy; the Palestinians will change their position of having the highest unemployment rate in the world to, no doubt, full or close to full employment building the new Gaza in the Sinai with its hotels, sea and air ports, farms, and beaches and keeping those jobs at the completion of the construction by manning and maintaining the new facilities; the millions of Arab refugees held for close to three quarters of a century in despicable, decrepit refugee camps in the neighboring Arab countries will have a home to return to as will the West Bank Palestinians, if they choose to migrate to the new, flourishing Gaza in the Sinai; the United Nations will be able to, virtually, eliminate the huge amounts of money flowing to the Palestinians nor will it have to prepare to expend in addition to these monies even larger amounts as similar support for a declining Egypt; and Israel will have the only thing she has ever sought, peace.

*****

On January 15, 2017, at the behest of French Pres. Francois Hollande, seventy nations including every European nation met in Paris in an attempt pressure the two opposing sides in the Middle East conflict to restart the Palestinian/Israeli peace process in an attempt to successfully implement the two-state solution that the international community has long agreed on, a Palestinian state existing next to Israel.

Restart the peace talks, *again!* “Insanity is doing the same thing over and over again and expecting different results."

Neither Israel nor the Palestinians sent representatives to this conference. Israel’s Deputy Foreign Minister Tzipi Hotovely likened the conference to a wedding without either the bride or the groom.

The *New York Times* on the following day stated, “No one has, yet, put forth an alternative that seems likely to gain international support and offer both Israelis and Palestinians more safety.”

The alternative is Gaza in the Sinai: the only viable two-state solution.

The road to peace runs through the Sinai.

Post Script

On February 1, 2017, newly elected Pres. Donald Trump sent a US army commando force into Yemen to weed out Al Queda operatives. His predecessor, Pres. Obama, had been reluctant to do this as his mantra was "No boots on the ground." But this reluctance to use human force to augment aerial attack—Obama relied on the use of drones—allowed Al Queda to grow virtually unimpeded as aerial attack alone, as the Israelis found out and which triggered the war of 2014, Operation Protective Edge, cannot do the job.

A Feb. 2, 2017, account of the commando raid in the *New York Times* reported that civilians were killed in the attack including an eight-year-old girl, the daughter of Anwar al-Awlaki, an American-born Al-Queda leader who was killed in a targeted drone strike in 2011. Al-Awlaki's daughter was an American citizen. In addition to this young girl, "grisly photographs of bloody children purportedly killed in the attack appeared on social media sites." These innocents had done nothing to harm America; however, when militants operate in the midst of their families, schools, and hospitals, innocents will die. This unacceptable and unpardonable action begs the question: is it the attacker or those who are using those innocents as human shields who are the blame for these needless deaths?

At this same time, the financial situation in Gaza due to the infighting between the PA, which was utilizing punitive sanctions against the people of Gaza in its struggle to wrest control of Gaza from Hamas, and Hamas was having a devastating effect on the Gazan people who, now, find their electricity cut to as little as four hours a day, hardly sufficient to meet their most meager needs. To compound this difficulty for the suffering Palestinian in Gaza, Pres. Donald Trump in January 2018 announced that his administration would withhold American dollars from UNRWA and called for a "fundamental reexamination" of the agency as the organization's staff had been, for years, caught promoting anti-Israel violence and its facilities used as storage depots by terror groups. Pres. Trump criticized the Palestinian Authority (PA) leader Mahmoud Abbas and his regime for receiving hundreds of millions of dollars each year from Washington without showing any appreciation or respect towards America. Some Middle East commentators have referred to Trump's business background and concluded that there will be no more free lunches for the Arabs.

The US froze a $125 million grant to the United Nations Relief and Works Agency (UNRWA), the UN agency for Palestinian refugees, Israel's *Channel 10 News* and the American *Axios* news site reported. Incitement to terror against Israel in UNRWA schools along with the documented use of its facilities as storage spaces for Hamas rockets and weapons have made the agency the target of vociferous criticism.

PA officials responded to the cuts with hyperbolic language, some of which was detailed in a *Washington Post* report on Jan. 17, 2018, headlined, "A Death Sentence: Palestinians Slam U.S. Decision to Cut Aid as U.N. Pleads for new Donors." Reuters *World News* reported on Jan. 16, 2018, that "UNRWA has proven time and again to be an agency that misuses the humanitarian aid of the international community and instead supports anti-Israel propaganda, perpetuates the plight of Palestinian refugees, and encourages hate." In a twitter post on Jan. 2, 2018, Trump said that Washington gives the Palestinians "HUNDREDS OF MILLIONS OF DOLLARS a year and gets no appreciation or respect." Trump added that "with the Palestinians no longer willing to talk peace, why should we make any of these massive future payments to them?" and stated that funds to the Palestinians are "on the table."

UNRWA was established in order to settle Arab refugees created from Israel's 1948 War of Independence in which Arab armies sought to destroy the nascent Jewish state. However, UNRWA uses a politicized, multi-generational definition of "refugee" as it considers all those Palestinians who lived in Gaza and the West Bank prior to the establishment of the State of Israel, Palestinians who never moved from their homes, and all the descendants of the seven hundred and fifty thousand Palestinians who fled there to escape the 1948 War all as refugees, totaling about five million. The United Nations has never considered not only the remnants of the European Jews who fled to Israel after the Second World War as they had nowhere else to go and their descendants nor the approximately one million Jews who were expelled from Arab countries and cannot return to those countries and their descendants refugees. Many in the US Congress have been saying since 2012 that the majority of Palestinians are permanently settled and should not be under the jurisdiction of any refugee agency.

Further commenting on Pres. Trump's "no appreciation or respect" tweet, a reason for his withholding US funds from the Palestinians, in addition to US Vice Pres. Pence being shunned by PA Pres. Abbas, on Jan. 30, 2018, a US delegation was forced to flee a Palestinian mob in the West Bank town of Bethlehem during a business conference. Violent Palestinian protesters stormed the workshop and kicked the delegation's vehicles as they left. Reuters reported that one of the cars was damaged.

Samir Hazboun, head of the Bethlehem Chamber of Commerce, said they had been holding a training session for local businesspeople about digital commerce with an American expert and a delegation from the US consulate in Jerusalem when the incident occurred. "This non-political program was one part of long-term US engagement to create economic opportunities for Palestinians," Hazboun said and added, "We were surprised when a number of angry protesters held an extraordinary protest which forced us to end the course and for the American trainer to leave immediately with the American consulate delegation."

The US Consulate in Jerusalem declined comment, Reuters reported.

A State Department spokesperson stated that "the United States opposes the use of violence and intimidation to express political views.

On Saturday, a crowd of Palestinians hanged and burned effigies of Trump and Vice President Pence in al-Aida, near Bethlehem, in response to what Pres. Trump had said, "We pay the Palestinians hundreds of millions of dollars a year and get no appreciation or respect. They don't even want to negotiate a long overdue peace treaty with Israel."

The magnitude of the failure of the program of supplying the Palestinians with massive amounts of aid, aid coming directly from the American taxpayer, can be evaluated from a document composed by the Congressional Research Service entitled, "U.S. Foreign Aid to the Palestinians" which states that since the establishment of limited Palestinian self-rule in the West Bank and the Gaza Strip in the mid-1990s, the U.S. government has committed *more than $5 billion in economic...aid* to the Palestinians who are among the world's largest per capita recipients of international foreign aid. The document went on to report that notwithstanding decades of generous aid given with goodwill, all the Palestinian leadership has managed to create is an unstable, divided entity crippled by corruption and cronyism with a dysfunctional polity and a feeble economy with a minuscule private sector and bloated public one utterly dependent on foreign aid."

The document states that humanitarian necessities have not been met in any meaningful way with the complete infrastructure hovering on the point of breakdown with constant power outages, undrinkable water, failing sanitation services, and overflowing with uncontrolled and untreated raw sewage. Without doubt, then, continuing with the same humanitarian aid will yield, in essence, similar results.

NE News Now, Feb. 23, 2018 reported PA Pres. Mahmoud Abbas's response to Trump's decision to cut aid to the Palestinians. "While addressing the United Nations Security Council Tuesday, Palestinian Authority (P.A.) President Mahmoud Abbas threatened the United States that the Palestinians would unleash a litany of Islamic terrorists if the Trump administration cuts tens of millions of dollars in funding."

During this fiscal crisis, it was reported that the President of the Palestinian Authority, Mahmoud Abbas, bought a private jet worth an estimated $50 million. The purchase came after the widely reported "major funding cuts from the U.S.," *The Times of Israel* detailed in a Jan. 24, 2018, dispatch. "Amid Funding Cuts, PA

Purchases $50 million Private Jet for Abbas." The jet will, reportedly, be delivered to Amman, Jordan within the coming weeks, where it will be kept for Abbas' use. *The Times of Israel* said that funding for the plane was "said to have been provided both from the PA budget ($20 million) and from the Palestinian National Fund ($30 million)."

During the writing of this book, Israel stepped up her building of homes in the disputed territories. (I do not use the misnomer "occupied territories" as Israel did not invade to conquer these territories so she does not "occupy" them; what Israel did was push the invading Jordanian army back and could, hardly, be expected to simply retreat to the pre-war boundaries leaving the area which she had liberated from the invading army, giving the Jordanians leisure to recoup, rearm, and attack, again. Perhaps, the correct term for these territories should be "liberated territories.") Presently, settlements are being built further into the disputed area, right up to the west bank of the Jordan River, not just additional neighborhoods adjacent to the already established West Bank settlements where new homes had, traditionally, been built. The world is reacting with condemnation as this would negate the possibility of restarting the futile "peace talks."

Again!

And what would an agreement forced by world pressure to *again* sit down at the negotiating table accomplish, some bottles of champagne uncorked, some backslapping and good cheer all around, and then more rockets bombarding Israeli cities, or another intifada? Shades of Arafat speaking peace in English and exactly the opposite in Arabic. Until the minds, the mentality, of the "Hitler youth" indoctrinated generations change, a change brought about by their prosperity in Gaza in the Sinai, all the agreements in the world will change nothing except for a very short period of celebration of a "peace" that will not last longer than the fizz in the champagne glasses. The Palestinian leadership will continue to abuse its people, Hamas will continue to steal what the United Nations supplies to these distressed unfortunates, and the Israelis will continue to be falsely blamed for the Palestinians' poor living conditions paving the way for more abuse and for labeling Israel an apartheid State, Israel whose Arab citizens currently live a lifestyle vastly above not only the Palestinians of the West Bank and Gaza but, also, vastly above their brethren in all the Arab nations.

The road to peace can, and should, be paved through the Sinai.

And, suddenly, some in the Israeli government have started using the word, "Annexation"!

Well, it's about time!!!

The Palestinians have had close to three quarters of a century since they first invaded the newly created State of Israel, established according to the United Nations division of the British Mandate, to stop their unending denial of reality: Israel is here to stay whether or not the Palestinians recognize this fact; and the Palestinians are, as has been shown for almost all these three quarters of a century, incapable of altering this fact no matter how many wars they start and rockets they fire. Acceptance of this undeniable fact by the Palestinian leadership is all it would have taken to avoid the epoch of depravity that the Palestinian general population has suffered both in Gaza and the West Bank, and to a much, much greater degree, in all the refugee camps in neighboring Arab countries.

Isn't it about time for Israel to build in the disputed lands, and to annex them? What could be gained by not building and annexing, another, repeat, three quarters of a century? Since things have not changed in this three quarters of a century, more and more appeasement will lead to what, the doubling of the time frame to a century and a half of Palestinian rejectionism?

Perhaps, it's time to change course.

Not only did Palestinians in the West Bank celebrate the release from prison of a soldier who fought his country's battles by murdering seven little girls in the "Island of Peace," three years later on Mar. 21, 2017 the *AP The Big Story* reported that the Turkish Islamic charity group IHH has been duped into funneling funds meant to help the needy of Gaza to Hamas for years in the guise of humanitarian aid.

Muhammad Faruq Sha'aban Murtaja, a Gazan building engineer, who was planted in the Turkish Cooperation and Coordination Agency (TIKA), revealed how he had hoodwinked the organization by shifting funds to the military wing of the Islamic militant group Hamas. He sidetracked the funds meant to feed the hungry into military training, the manufacturing of weapons, and the digging of terror tunnels into Israel. "One of Murtaja's schemes was to provide his superiors with lists of impoverished residents in the Gaza Strip who were candidates to receive financial aid. In practice, these lists were provided by Hamas and were actually militants."

Previously, the Gaza manager of the World Vision charity, a Christian humanitarian organization which helps children and families worldwide was charged with funneling millions to Hamas instead of helping the families the money was intended for.

NY Times Mar. 26, 2017 "Killing of Hamas Leader Could Open New Conflict" Mazan Fuqaha, commander of Hamas's military wing, the Qassam Brigade, was shot to death at close range. Presenting no evidence, Hamas blamed Israel even though this assassination could be the result of decimating rivalries among often fractious Palestinian factions, particularly Hamas's rival, the West Bank-based Palestinian Authority, or Egypt, or even Hamas itself. Fuqaha's widow described the killing of her husband as an "ugly crime." "Gaza's Interior Ministry has taken the extraordinary measure of closing border crossings with Egypt and Israel…except for patients needing medical treatment." (See the Miko Peled talk)

Fuqaha was convicted of planning a suicide bombing in 2002 that destroyed a bus killing nine and severely injuring others, some with limbs blown off, and was sentenced to nine life terms in prison. He was released in 2011 in the *thousand-prisoner exchange* for *one Israeli soldier*, Gilad Shalit, who had been held by Hamas for five years. While Mrs. Fuqaha, known as Nahed Assida, sat in mourning, dozens of children surrounded her dressed in Qassam suicide outfits and carrying toy guns (the making of terrorists!).

Mrs. Fuqaha said of her children, four-year-old Mohammed and eighteen-month-old Sama, "I will teach them resistance: Islam, jihad, power and expelling Jews from Jerusalem….I will be happy to sacrifice them to die for Palestine."

Note the difference in how life is valued: Israel traded a thousand prisoners to get back one young soldier!

How different the western mind is. We consider it a mother's obligation to protect her offspring, not to plan their demise. Mrs. Fuqaha is pledging to "sacrifice them to die," to sacrifice her four-year-old son and eight-month-old baby girl in jihad, but she doesn't consider her husband's involvement in killing nine people and mutilating others an "ugly crime."

Mrs. Faqaha, or Nahed Assida or whatever your name is, and you, too, Mrs. Srour, mother of Abdul, it is not only a mother's duty, it is her indebtedness to her children to raise them to the best of her ability to become happy, successful adults prepared to lead productive lives, not to sacrifice themselves in the killing of others.

So, what good would another attempt at bringing the two sides together, *again*, at the negotiating table do? Even if a much-heralded settlement is reached by, *again*, tweaking the present, unworkable two-state plan by moving a border slightly or by grudgingly giving in to some intensely negotiated concession that neither party, really, wants, the Faqaha children and those toy gun-wielding, suicide vest–clad children will grow up to be terrorists, jihadists.

A year later on Mar.14, 2018, the New York Times ran an article "Palestinian's Prime Minister's Convoy Hits Blast in Gaza Setting off Blame Game." The attack was thought to be an assassination attack on the Palestinian Prime Minister, Rami Hamdallah. Question were raised, immediately, about who was responsible, the Palestinian Authority, which had put financial pressures on the Hamas government last year including mass layoffs and crippling, daily power outages and exacerbating shortages of clean water, medicines, and other necessities blaming Hamas, the office of PA Authority Pres. Mahmoud Abbas saying it "holds Hamas fully responsible." A Hamas spokesman claimed that it had no role in the attack and blamed Israel.

Mr. Hamdallah had been *en route* to the opening of the long delayed wastewater treatment plant in Gaza. "A temporary arrangement between the Palestinian Authority and Israel is supplying power for the plant...officials are seeking a dedicated electrical line from Israel as a reliable power source." Power shortages, instigated in Gaza by the PA, have caused water treatment to be suspended allowing raw sewage to seep into groundwater polluting the local water supply.

On March 30, 2018, headlines in American newspaper including the *Washington Post* and the *Wall Street Journal* and others screamed that Israelis had killed seventeen Gazans during their "peaceful demonstration" at the Israel/Gaza border. One had to read deep into the articles to decipher what had, actually, occurred. On this day, Palestinians in Gaza initiated their "March of Return" by massing thirty thousand men, women, and children including hundreds of violent militants along the Israeli border. This was to be a peaceful protest (with a confrontational title exposing the basis for this mass gathering). Among those gathered were militants who had perpetrated violent acts against Israel, seventeen of whom were killed at the start of this "peaceful" demonstration, Hamas proudly proclaiming most as members of its military wing.

Although the majority of the demonstrators stayed the required three hundred feet back from the border fence (the IDF [the Israeli army] had fortified the border with elite ground forces and had warned demonstrators not to come within three hundred meters of the border fence), a few hundred advanced right up to the fence hurling stones from sling shots, throwing Molotov cocktails across the fence, burning rubber tires to attempt to ignite the fence and to provide a smoke screen to hide their actions at the fence, and firing assault rifles at the Israeli soldiers stationed at the border to prevent the mass infiltration, including the infiltration of armed terrorists, into Israel. Video footage shows Palestinian men with assault rifles attempting to break through the border fence. Not only was this an attempt to breach the fence and allow the mass infiltration of sworn terrorists into Israel but according to Hamas leaders Ismail Haniyeh and Yehya Sinwar, these violent protests ("peaceful protests"?) marked the beginning of a "new phase in the Palestinians' national struggle on the road to liberating all of Palestine, from the river to the sea," (a call for the destruction of Israel).

An Apr. 3, 2018, article in *Newsweek*, "...Gaza Has No Future..." stated that if the...riots had been about improving conditions in Gaza--calling for Israel (whom Hamas was attempting to destroy) to provide more water and electricity "spurred by poverty and a growing sense of hopelessness as Hamas uses resources meant for food, schools, and hospitals for tunnel construction and other military purposes,"--many could have been sympathetic to the mass infiltration into Israel over the border... It's because of Hamas's ceaseless activity to destroy Israel that Israel has a blockade against Gaza, as does Egypt.

"...the leader of Hamas, Yahya Sinwar—a man who has publicly committed to the destruction of Israel--stated at the start of the march, 'The March of Return' will continue...until we remove this...border." In other words, the goal of this "peaceful" march was to destroy the border fence and allow the tens of thousands of Palestinians gathered at the fence and, no doubt, the additional million plus Gazans to pour over into Israel. (This, when Pres. Trump, unable to build his wall, was signing a bill to station the National Guard at the US/Mexico border to prevent illegal immigration into the US as no one has the right to enter a country without that country's permission.) "The IDF and the Israeli government can be satisfied that the border was not breached, and no women or children were killed." Imagine how many Israeli women and children would be killed had the militants been successful in breaching the border fence!

The *Newsweek* article went on to say that "the Israeli army faced a dilemma regarding the Gaza protest. The Israeli Defense Forces feared that the true goal of the march was to get as many Palestinians killed as possible in order to gain the world's attention and depict Israel in the worst possible light" as missiles (from Gaza) were no longer as effective as previously and Israel was methodically demolishing the Hamas-constructed tunnels, financed with many millions of dollars from the aid it receives, and Hamas's attempts at reconciliation with the Palestinian Authority without agreeing to give up its weapons had failed.

In *The Next Palestinian Generation* by Gershon Baskin, Baskin states, "Palestine will not be freed by the stone, the knife, or the gun. Palestine will be freed when the young people understand that they need to take a direct role in building the state." That is not what they are being taught.

And it's not only children whose lives must be changed to a better life to halt the vicious cycle that more negotiations will not alter. On March 29, 2017, Haithan Faiz Nauri Muari, a former Palestinian policeman who had been sentenced to life in prison in 2004 for his involvement in the murder of Avrahami and Norzhich, IDF reservists who had strayed into downtown Ramallah in late 2000, was released from prison following a retrial that reduced the charges against him. Video footage showed a Palestinian man identified as Aziz Salha raising his blood-stained hands in celebration after dumping one of the bodies out of the second-story window.

This cycle must stop! The only way to change the thinking is to give these children and these indoctrinated adults, too, adults akin to Bashir Khairi, a good life, one they will not be so willing to give up in jihad based on the prejudices of their abused and indoctrinated parents and grandparents. They must be offered what they really want: a better life, the life they can have in Gaza in the Sinai in the shining light of a decent, good quality life, instead of the darkness they will, otherwise, subsist in.

With the change of course, with Israelis in control, the prosperity of Israel will extend to Judea and Samaria, the true names of the territory called the West Bank, a region drenched in ancestral and biblical significance dating thousands of years before the birth of Islam.

Those Palestinians who wish to remain and share in the region's new prosperity will be welcome as long as they put down their arms and contribute to the new society or, if they prefer, they can move to the newborn, fledgling Gaza in the Sinai where jobs would be waiting for them to boost them up into a middle class life.

Peace in the Middle East runs through the Sinai.

Acknowledgements

Many thanks to those publishers and authors who graciously gave permission for their works pertinent to the theme of *Gaza in the Sinai: The Only Viable Two-State Solution* to be reprinted here.

Bibliography: Works Cited

Ad Hoc Liaison Committee Report
Algemeiner Journal, The, Germany
Al Jazeera
Al-Monitor: The Pulse of the Middle East
Al-Umma
Arab-Israeli War: Origins and Consequences by William Roger Louis, Cambridge University Press
Arab News
Arabic Press
Arab research study conducted at Bir Zeit University
Associated Press
BBC News
BBC TV
Best Hoaxes and Pranks
Big Story, The
Bir Zeit University, Arab research study
Boston Globe, The
CAMRA, Committee for Accuracy in Middle East Reporting in America, The
Cambridge University Press
Canadian Arab News
"Catalyst for Change: Paths out of Poverty"
CBS
Chicago Sun Times, The
CIA, Central Intelligence Agency
City of Oranges
CNN
Columbia Electronic Encyclopedia
Columbia University Press
Commentator, The
Constantinople Convention of 1888
"Cult of the Suicide Bomber"
Daily Telegraph,
Dalia "Letter to a Deportee"
Daily Signal, The
Daily Star, The

Eban, Abba 1967 Speech to the United Nations Security Council
Elder of Ziyon
Electronic Intifada. The
Encyclopedia Britannica
"Exodus"
First World War.com
Fourth Geneva Convention of 1949, Article 78
Gatestone Institute
Global Cleantech Innovation Index 2014, The
Haaretz
Herald Tribune,
Heritage Foundation, The
History of Learning, The, UK
Holocaust Encyclopedia, The, United States Holocaust Museum, Washington, DC
Human Rights Watch
International Covenant on Civil and Political Rights, Article 9
Israel, a History, Martin Gilbert
Israel, Civil Administration Health Department
Israeli Aggression, publication of the Arab League
Japan Times
Jerusalem Post
Jerusalem Report, 1998
"Jewish Virtual Library, The"
Koran
Lemon Tree, The
Middle East, The: The Origins of Arab-Israeli Wars,
Middle East Media and Research Institute (MEMRI)
Miracles of the Six Day War
MK Media Watch
NBC News
NBM-200
New Middle East, The
New York Daily News
Newsweek
New York Times
"Awash in Turmoil Arab World Leaves Two-State Goal Adrift"
Odd Bull, War and Peace in the Middle East by Leo Cooper,

O Jerusalem, Larry Collins and Dominique Lapierr
Oslo Accords
Oxford Encyclopedia of the Modern World
Oxford University Press, The
Palestine Broadcasting Service's Arabic News
Palestinian Media Watch
PBS, Public Broadcasting Service
Redditor, The
Reuters *The*
Rockefeller Foundation, The
Slate Gist, The: A Cheat Sheet for the News,
"Soldier with the Arabs, A,"
Synopsis of the Israeli-Palestinian Conflict, A"
Tamr, Mustafa Effendian
Tazpit, Anav Silverman
Telegraph, The, Britian
This Day in History
Time magazine
Times of Israel
Times of London
Throwaway 874832749
Uncovering Israel
US Patriot Act
United Nations Partition Plan
United Press
Voice of Cairo
Voice of the Arabs radio
War and Peace in the Middle East
Washington Post, The
Wikipedia
Wildolive
World Heritage Encyclopedia The
Yahoo! tech
"60 Minutes," Lesley Stahl, 2003
1001 Facts Everyone Should Know About Israel by Michael Geoffrey Bard
1945 British Mandate Defense Emergency Regulations

1948: A History of the First Arab-Israeli War by Benny Morris, Yale University Press 2008
1949 Armistice Resolution

Index

CPSIA information can be obtained
at www.ICGtesting.com
Printed in the USA
BVHW051552271222
655051BV00008B/383

9 781719 370875